The Early Modern Englishwoman:
A Facsimile Library of Essential Works

Series I

Printed Writings, 1500–1640: Part 2

Volume 1

Anne Cooke Bacon

The Early Modern Englishwoman:
A Facsimile Library of Essential Works

Series I

Printed Writings, 1500–1640: Part 2

Volume 1

Anne Cooke Bacon

Selected and Introduced by
Valerie Wayne

General Editors
Betty S. Travitsky and Patrick Cullen

Ashgate

Aldershot • Burlington USA • Singapore • Sydney

Published by
Ashgate Publishing Ltd
Gower House
Croft Road
Aldershot
Hants GU11 3HR
England

BT
810.2
.A58
2000
v.1

Ashgate Publishing Company
131 Main Street
Burlington
Vermont 05401
USA

Ashgate website: http://www.ashgate.com

British Library Cataloguing-in-Publication Data
Bacon, Anne Cooke
  The early modern Englishwoman : a facsimile library of
  essential works.
  Part 2: Printed writings, 1500–1640: Vol. 1
  1. English literature – Early modern, 1500–1700   2. English
  literature – Women authors   3. Women – England – History –
  Renaissance, 1450–1600 – Sources   4. Women – England –
  History – Modern period, 1600– – Sources   5. Women – Literary
  collections
  I. Title   II. Travitsky, Betty S.   III. Cullen, Patrick Colborn,
  1940   IV. Wayne, Valerie   V. Jewel, John. Apologie or answere
  in defence of the Churche of Englande   VI. Fouretene sermons
  of Barnardine Ochyne   VII. Certayne sermons of the ryghte
  famous and excellente Clerk Master Barnardine Ochine
  820.8'09287

Library of Congress Cataloging-in-Publication Data
The early modern Englishwoman: a facsimile library of essential works. Part 2.
Printed writings, 1500–1640 / general editors, Betty S. Travitsky and Patrick Cullen.

See page vi for complete CIP Block 99–55930

The woodcut reproduced on the title page and on the case is from the title page of Margaret Roper's trans. of [Desiderius Erasmus] *A Devout Treatise upon the Pater Noster* (circa 1524).

ISBN 1 84014 214 6

Printed in Great Britain by Antony Rowe Ltd, Chippenham, Wiltshire

CONTENTS

Library of Congress Cataloging-in-Publication Data
Bacon, Anne Cooke / selected and introduced by Valerie Wayne.
      p.   cm. -- (The early modern Englishwoman. Printed writings, 1500–1640, Part 2 ; v. 1)
    Includes bibliographical references.
    Contents: Fouretene sermons of Barnardine Ochyne / translated by Anne Cooke Bacon
-- Sermons vii–xi, Certayne sermons of the ryghte famous and excellente clerk Master
Barnardine Ochine / translated by Anne Cooke Bacon -- An apologie or answere in
defence of the Churche of Englande / translated by Anne Cooke Bacon.
    ISBN 1–84014–214–6
    1. Predestination--Sermons.   2. Sermons, Italian--Translations into English.   3. Church
of England--Apologetic works.   I. Bacon, Anne Cooke, Lady, 1528?–1610.   II. Wayne,
Valerie.   III. Ochino, Bernardino, 1487–1564. Fouretene sermons of Barnardine Ochyne,
concerning the prestination and eleccion of God.   IV. Ochino, Bernadino, 1487–1564.
Certayne sermons of the ryghte famous and excellente clerk Master Barnardine Ochine.
V. Jewel, John, 1522–1571. Apologia Ecclesiae Anglicanae. English.   VI. Series.

BT810.2 .A58   2000
230'.3--dc21

                                       99–55930

PREFACE
BY THE GENERAL EDITORS

Until very recently, scholars of the early modern period have assumed that there were no Judith Shakespeares in early modern England. Much of the energy of the current generation of scholars has been devoted to constructing a history of early modern England that takes into account what women actually wrote, what women actually read, and what women actually did. In so doing the masculinist representation of early modern women, both in their own time and ours, is deconstructed. The study of early modern women has thus become one of the most important—indeed perhaps the most important—means for the rewriting of early modern history.

The Early Modern Englishwoman: A Facsimile Library of Essential Works is one of the developments of this energetic reappraisal of the period. As the names on our advisory board and our list of editors testify, it has been the beneficiary of scholarship in the field, and we hope it will also be an essential part of that scholarship's continuing momentum.

The Early Modern Englishwoman is designed to make available a comprehensive and focused collection of writings in English from 1500 to 1750, both by women and for and about them. The first series, *Printed Writings, 1500–1640*, provides a comprehensive if not entirely complete collection of the separately published writings by women. In reprinting these writings we intend to remedy one of the major obstacles to the advancement of feminist criticism of the early modern period, namely the unavailability of the very texts upon which the field is based. The volumes in the facsimile library reproduce carefully chosen copies of these texts, incorporating significant variants (usually in appendices). Each text is preceded by a short introduction providing an overview of the life and work of a writer along with a survey of important scholarship. These works, we strongly believe, deserve a large readership—of historians, literary critics, feminist critics, and non-specialist readers.

The Early Modern Englishwoman will also include separate facsimile series of *Essential Works for the Study of Early Modern Women* and of *Manuscript Writings*. It is complemented by *Women and Gender in Early Modern England, 1500–1750*, a series of original monographs on early modern gender studies, also under our general editorship.

New York City
2000

vii

INTRODUCTORY NOTE

Anne Cooke Bacon was actively involved in the religious controversies of her day, and her translations position her as a strong advocate for the Protestant cause. Born in 1528 as the second daughter of Sir Anthony Cooke and Lady Anne Fitzwilliam Cooke, she benefited from the new humanist learning provided to her and her sisters Mildred, Elizabeth, and Katherine. Her father was tutor to young Edward VI, and some sources say that she worked with her father as the king's governess (*DNB*). Muriel St Clare Byrne describes her as possessing 'an extremely shrewd and acutely critical intelligence, as highly educated as anyone in the kingdom, keenly interested in affairs': she was especially recognized for her ability to read Latin, Greek, Italian and French. Perhaps as early as February, 1553 (according to Robert Tittler), she married Sir Nicholas Bacon (1510– 1579), who became the Queen's Keeper of the Great Seal and a member of Elizabeth's Privy Council. The directions of the new Church of England were heavily influenced by this man and his two highly placed friends – Matthew Parker, who became Archbishop of Canterbury, and William Cecil, Secretary of State and the Queen's chief advisor, who was also the husband of Anne's sister Mildred. In addition to having responsibility for her six step-children from her husband's previous marriage, Lady Bacon also had two children with Sir Nicholas. Anthony, born in 1558, became a diplomat; Francis, born in 1560/1, was eventually promoted to Lord Chancellor and is known today for his contributions to philosophy through such works as the *Novum Organum*, which applied the inductive method to scientific investigation. Lady Bacon's energetic intelligence surely had its complex effects on her sons, for whom she showed an extreme solicitude in their adult years. She lived as an influential widow after 1579 and offered strong support for Puritans, to the point of illegally sheltering preachers who had lost their licences for refusing to wear clerical robes or preaching improvised sermons of their own rather than presenting prescribed homilies to their congregations. Lady Bacon died in 1610 at the age of eighty-two. When her well known son was nearing his own death, he requested in his will that he be buried next to his mother.

Translations of Ochino's Sermons

While she was in her early twenties, Anne Cooke translated the sermons of Bernardino Ochino, a popular Italian preacher who converted to Calvinism and was welcomed by the Italian 'foreigners' church in England. Her translations are printed in four different volumes of Ochino's sermons, one of which was issued at the same time as translations by R. Argentyne and two of which also included his translations. In 1548 two editions of Ochino's sermons were published: *Sermons of Barnardine Ochine of Sena* (*STC* 18764) printed five sermons translated by Anne but did not name her as the translator; *Sermons of the ryght famous and excellent clerke master B. Ochine* (*STC* 18765) printed six sermons translated by Argentyne and did identify him as translator. In 1551? *Certayne Sermons of the ryghte famous and excellente Clerk ...* (*STC* 18766) included twenty-five sermons. The first six sermons are Argentyne's translations published previously. The remaining nineteen are translated by Anne: numbers 7 through 11 from the 1548 publication, and numbers 12 through 25 appearing as new translations. Again Anne is not named as translator, but neither is Argentyne. Probably during the same year (according to the *STC*) another volume was issued from the same publisher with the title *Fouretene Sermons of Barnardine Ochyne, concerning the predestinacion and eleccion of god. ... Translated out of Italian in to oure natyue tounge by A.C.* (*STC* 18767). This edition included the last fourteen sermons from *Certayne Sermons* plus a dedication from Anne to her mother and a preface in praise of Anne's work, and it is reprinted in this volume. Still another edition was published in 1570? (*STC* 18768) that reprinted the same twenty-five sermons published in 1551?. Anne was the only translator named in this edition, although six of the translations were from Argentyne. Hence for whatever reasons, which may include the publishers' carelessness or desire to suppress the name of a female translator and their readiness to capitalize on her identity once it became known, these editions initially occluded the name of Anne Cooke in favor of Argentyne's and eventually occluded his name in favor of hers. The 1570? text, which also reprints Anne's dedication and the preface from *Fouretene Sermons*, appeared after Ochino had been denounced for heresy, had been exiled from Switzerland for questioning the doctrine of the Trinity, and had died in 1564.

The text that is reproduced here comes from the 1551? edition of *Fouretene Sermons*, because it includes the important dedication and preface and is the only edition of more than five sermons that does not also reprint translations by Argentyne. More than twelve copies of this edition are known to be extant, but at least three are imperfect and others have severely trimmed margins or have been bound so tightly that the text in the gutter is not visible. The copy reprinted here is from St John's College,

x

Cambridge, which is the most readable copy of this text I have seen. The annotations for the cropped marginalia, which appear on pages 1–2, are based on a comparison with the Newberry Library copy. Also included in the present volume are the five sermons by Anne Cooke first published in 1548 and reprinted in the 1551? gathering of twenty-five sermons but not included in her *Fouretene Sermons*. These are numbers seven through eleven in *Certayne Sermons of the ryghte famous and excellente Clerk Master Barnardine Ochine* (*STC* 18766), and they are reproduced here from a copy in good condition from the Bodleian Library. The preface to this edition, which provides some interesting information on Bernardino Ochino, is largely the preface signed by Argentyne in his 1548 edition. Yet it erroneously refers to only six sermons, because it reprints the earlier preface combined with the last three sentences, revised, of the publisher's address to the reader from that 1548 text. These five sermons plus the fourteen reprinted at the beginning of this book constitute all of the sermons that Anne Cooke is known to have translated and published.

The preface to *Fouretene Sermons* is signed by 'G.B', whose identity is unknown. It draws on the modesty topos to describe Anne Cooke as so 'shamefast' (restrained by shame, bashful or modest) that she 'would rather have supprest theym' (A2) had he not encouraged their publication, and it apologizes for any errors in the translation as arising from a gentlewoman who 'neuer gaddid farder then hir fathers house to learne the language' (A2v). It also praises Anne for her translation by way of opposing her to 'any pretty pryckemydantes' (those who are excessively finical about their dress, A2), who would claim that only doctors of divinity, rather than maidens, are fit to deal with such important religious matters. These fussy fellows (prickmydants or prickmedainties, *OED*) are condemned for wasting their time by giving too much 'womanly' attention to their apparel and 'vayne heathennyshe ostentacion', an allusion to the ornate vestments of Roman Catholic priests, or for parroting scripture and debating matters of importance 'wyth solemne countenaunces … as though the ordre of realmes appartained to them' (A2), a reference to those who used pretentious styles of preaching or constantly cited biblical verses without a sense of their larger meaning.

Anne Cooke dedicates these sermons to her mother, Lady Fitzwilliam Cooke, because they yield 'some parte of the fruite of your Motherly admonicions' (A4v). Those admonitions included her mother's discouragement of Anne's 'vaine studye in the Italyan tonge, accompting the sede thereof to have bene sowen in barayne, unfruitful grounde' (A3v). The association of Italy with Roman Catholicism and a more general decadence, in the eyes of many English Protestants, was enough to lead Lady Cooke to condemn the study of Italian. Anne's dedication presents the sermons as a justification for her own education in the language, returning to her own 'orygynal' (A3) the proof that 'your so many worthy sentences touching the same, haue not utterly bene without some note in my weake memory' (A4). Her accomplishments therefore at once confirm the overall effects of her mother's moral instruction and excuse her own transgression of her mother's prior injunction. The doctrines of predestination and election set forth in this translation have been helpfully examined by Louise Schleiner (34–43).

An Apologie or answere in defence of the Churche of Englande

In 1562 John Jewel's *Apologia ecclesiae anglicanae* was published in England (*STC* 14581). The book was designed to articulate the central tenets of the Church of England and its unity in the face of Roman Catholic accusations that it was divided within itself by disputes and schisms. John Jewel (1522–1571), who wrote the *Apologia* at the encouragement of William Cecil and others, eventually became the Bishop of Salisbury. In 1559, when he returned from the Continent along with other Protestant exiles after the death of Mary I, he was an active participant at the Westminster Conference in which old English bishops and returning Protestants debated the direction of the Church, and he co-authored the Declaration of 1559. When the *Apologia* was published three years later, it received high praise in England and came to be viewed as the authoritative defense of the English Church. The text was edited by Matthew Parker, the Archbishop of Canterbury. Parker also commissioned an English translation that was printed in the same year (*STC* 14590), but that translation was not adequate for such an important work, so Anne Bacon presented her own translation to Jewel and the Archbishop. The results are described by Parker in the preface to the edition reprinted here: 'it hath passed iudgement without reproche. And whereas bothe the chiefe author of the Latine worke and I, seuerallye perusinge and conferringe youre whole translation, haue without alteration allowed of it'.

An Apologie or answere in defence of the Churche of Englande was printed in 1564 with an Epistle from M. C., M[atthew Parker]. C[antuariensis]., recording Jewel and Parker's appreciation for Anne's fine work (*STC* 14591). It was important that such a text be available in a language understood by the people as well as the clergy. Parker praises the translation not only as an 'acceptable dutye to the glorye of GOD' but as having 'honourablie defended the good fame and estimate of your own natiue tongue, shewing it so able to contend with a worke originally written in the most praised speache'. He also assures readers that he and Jewel were unwilling to 'winke at faultes' in the work in order to please Lady Bacon, explaining that her discernment and dislike of flattery together with 'the layenge open of oure opinion to the world, the truth of our friendiship [*sic*] towardes you, the unwillingnesse of vs bothe (in respecte of our vocations) to haue this publike worke not truely and well translated, are good causes to perswade, that our allowance is of sincere truth and understanding'. Anne's work has done honour to 'the kinde of women' (i.e. womankind) and 'to the degree of Ladies' as well as 'to the Author of the Latine boke, in deliueringe him by your cleare translation from the perrils of ambiguous and doubtful constructions: and in making his good woorke more publikely beneficiall'. That benefit was broadly based, for Lady Bacon's translation of *An Apologie* became the official English version: it was used by Jewel himself in his later theological disputes and 'was placed in parish churches for the edification of clergy and people' (Booty, xlii).

The text of this translation also appeared in John Jewel's *A defence of the Apologie of the Churche of Englande, an answeare to a certaine booke by M. Hardinge*, which was published twice in 1567 and again in 1570 and 1571 (*STC* 14600–2). There are minor variations from Lady Bacon's version in these texts, but John Booty sensibly finds a fair portion of them to be a product of printers' errors rather than Jewel's corrections of the Bacon text. In the twentieth century C. S. Lewis commended this translation highly:

> Anne Lady Bacon … deserves more praise than I have space to give her. Latin prose has a flavour very hard to disguise in translation, but nearly every sentence in Lady Bacon's work sounds like an original. Again and again she finds the phrase which, once she has found it, we feel to be inevitable. … If quality without bulk were enough, Lady Bacon might be put forward as the best of all sixteenth-century translators (307).

The text reprinted here is an unusually clear copy from Williams College, which also has the advantage of including an engraving of Lady Bacon that serves as its frontispiece. This engraving was not published in the 1564 edition. The engraver was Henry R. Cook, who flourished from 1800 to 1845 and copied a painting by Sylvester Harding (1745–1809). The portrait is mounted on a stub of this copy, opposite the title page. In all complete copies, such as this one, a tract appears at the end called 'The manner how the Churche of Englande is administered and gouerned'. This is most likely by Parker himself, as John Booty observes in his 1963 modern-spelling edition of the text, which was prepared for the Folger Shakespeare Library and based on that library's copy of the 1564 Bacon translation.

(I am very grateful to Elizabeth McCutcheon for providing information that improved this introduction and to Patrick Cullen and Betty Travitsky for posing challenging questions to which it serves as only an imperfect answer.)

References

STC 18767 (*Fouretene Sermons*), *STC* 18766 (*Certayne Sermons*), *STC* 14591 (*Apologie*)

Ayre, John (ed.) (1850), *John Jewel's Works, Vol. IV*, Cambridge: Parker Society

Beilin, Elaine V. (1987), *Redeeming Eve: Women Writers of the English Renaissance*, Princeton, N.J.: Princeton University Press

Booty, J. E. (ed.) (1963), *An Apology of the Church of England*, Ithaca, New York: Cornell University Press for The Folger Shakespeare Library

Byrne, Muriel St. Clare (1934), 'The Mother of Francis Bacon', *Blackwood's Magazine*, 236, July-December

Hogrefe, Pearl (1977), *Women of Action in Tudor England*, Ames, Iowa: Iowa State University Press

Jardine, Lisa and Alan Stewart (1998), *Hostage to Fortune: the Troubled Life of Francis Bacon*, London: Victor Gollancz

Lamb, Mary Ellen (1985), 'The Cooke Sisters: Attitudes toward Learned Women' in Hannay, Margaret Patterson (ed.), *Silent But For the Word: Tudor Women as Patrons, Translators, and Writers of Religious Works*, Kent, Ohio: Kent State University Press

Lamb, Mary Ellen (1990), *Gender and Authorship in the Sidney Circle*, Madison, Wisconsin: University of Wisconsin Press

Lewis, C. S. (1954), *English Literature in the Sixteenth Century*, Oxford: Clarendon Press

Schleiner, Louise (1994), *Tudor and Stuart Women Writers*, Bloomington, Indiana: Indiana University Press

Spedding, James; Ellis, Robert Leslie; and Heath, Douglas Denon (eds) (1862, repr. 1968), *The Works of Francis Bacon: Vol. VIII., The Letters and the Life*, New York: Garrett Press

Tittler, Robert (1976), *Nicholas Bacon: The Making of a Tudor Statesman*, Ohio: Ohio University Press

Travitsky, Betty (ed.) (1981), *The Paradise of Women: Writings by Englishwomen of the Renaissance*, Westport, Connecticut: Greenwood Press

Whiting, M. B. (1931), 'The Learned and Virtuous Lady Bacon', *Hibbert Journal*, 29

VALERIE WAYNE

Anne Cooke Bacon, trans.: *Fouretene Sermons of Barnardine Ochyne* ... (*STC* 18767) is reproduced by permission of St John's College, Cambridge. The textblock of the original is 11.5 x 6cm (without running titles), 12 x 7.5cm with running titles (octavo).

The cropped marginalia in *Fouretene Sermons of Barnardine Ochyne* should read as follows on the lines noted below:

B3v	l.1:	Rom. iiii.
	l.3:	ii Cor. iii.
	l.4:	Joh. iii,
	l.14:	Ephe. i.
B5v	l.9:	i Cor. ii.
	l.15:	Ephe. i.
	l.16:	Jhon. x.
	l.24:	Luke. x.
B6	l.17:	siue not as doc
B6v	l.18:	i Cor. ii.
	l.19:	Luke. xvi.
B8	ll.19–27	This is not spoken to de- clare that it is possible for gods elect to be wholy geuē to synne. but if it were possi- ble, yet should they recouer that pestilence.
C1v	l.6:	Luke. xvii.
	l.11:	i Tessa. i
	l.12:	i Timo. iiii
	l.13:	Rom. viii
	l.14:	Gala. ii.
	l.15:	i Cor. iii.
	l.26:	Gala. ii.

	1.27:	Joh. xiiii.
	1.28:	i Cor. ii.
C7v	1.18:	Rom. iiii.
	1.25:	Luke. x.
	1.26:	Math. xv.
	1.27:	Math. xvi
E2v	1.13:	Ephe. i.
	1.25:	i Cor. i.
	1.27	ii. Cor. i. [?]
E4v	1.4:	Proue. xix.
	1.7:	Rom. vi.
ff. 3v	1.6:	Ephe. i.
G2v	1.11:	Hebre. i.
	1.12:	i Cor. i.
	1.13:	Rom. viii
	1.17:	Prou. xxiiii.
	1.28:	Psal. xxxi.
	1.29:	Jhon. x.
G4v	1.16:	Math. xiii.
	1.17:	Ephe. ii.
	1.18:	ii Tessa. ii
H1v	1.3:	i Timo. i
	1.4:	Rom. iiii.
	1.5:	Luke. viii.
	1.13:	Gala. v.
H7v:	1.6:	i Joh. iiii.

¶ Fourtene

Sermons of Barnardine Ochyne, concernyng the predestinacion and eleccion of god: very expediente to the settynge forth of hys glorye among hys creatures. Translated out of Italian in to oure natyue tounge by. A.C.

☞ It is good to hyde the kinges secretes, but to decleare and prayse the workes of god, it is an honorable thing. To. xij.

☞ I wyl saye to the north, let go and to the southe, kepe not backe: but brynge my Sonnes and my Daughters from the endes of the world, namely all those that be called after my name. For the haue I created, fashyoned, and made for mine honor.

Esa. xliii.

The titles of
the Chaptres,

❧ To the Chꝛiſten.
Reader.

WHEn theſe tranſlated Ser mons of the famous Bar nardine were come to mpne hand, Jentpll Reader, J th= ought it mete to publyſh thē to the ende ſo Godly Apoſtolyke doctryne ſhould not be pꝛiuate to thoſe onely whych vnder= ſtande the Italian toung, ſynce thoꝛow the honeſt trauel of a wel occupied Jen telwoman, and verteouſe meyden they ſpeake in Englyſhe: whoſe ſhamfaſtnes would rather haue ſuppꝛeſt theym, had not J to whoſe handes they were com= mptted halfe agaynſt hyꝛ wyll put them ſourth, biddyng them bluſh that deſerue blame: foꝛ thys of her parte J dare ſafe= ly affyꝛme craueth perpetual pꝛaiſe and if any pꝛety pꝛyckemydantes ſhal hap= pen to ſpy amote in thys godly labour (as J doughte not but the nyſytes wyl) ſeynge it is meeter foꝛ Docters of dȳui= nitye to me ddle wyth ſuch matters thē Meydens, let thē remēber howe womā= ly they waſt their tyme the one part iu

A.ii.   pꝛickes

prickeynge and trymmynge to vayne
hethennyshe ostentatiō, and in deuisyng
newe fashyons of apparel, to whome if
in their glasse appered the sowle fautes
of their fylthy cōdiciens as playnely as
the defautes of theyr forsayde faces, I
doubt much whether thei wold delight
to toote therin so often as thei do: the o-
ther part speakyng in pypnt lyke para-
tes wyth solemne countenaūces, debate
matters of impoꝛtaūce, & graue weight,
as though the oꝛdꝛe of realmes appartained to them, oꝛ els warbling woꝛdes
of scripture in all their doynges, deface
the thyng they most bable of. But I require the (Chꝛistiā Reader) wyth iudgement to reade, & in the equal balaunce of
Scripture to way these learned & godly sermons, whych thou shalt fynde (I
dout not) of iust weyght with the sacred
woꝛd of God: I foꝛbare to pꝛayse them,
lest I should say to lytle, defend them I
nede not the authour lyuinge and here
amongest vs: a man whose lyfe wythout woꝛdes were a suffyciente pꝛotecci-
on to hys woꝛcke. If oughte be erred in
the translacion, remēber it is a womās
pea, a Ientyl womās, who cōmenly are
wonted to lyue Idelly, a maidens þ neuer gaddid farder thē hir fathers house
to learne the language. Fare wel & vse
hyꝛ laboꝛ to the amendement of thy lif.
                    B.B.

¶ To the right

worſhypful and worthyly
beloued Mother, the Lady. F. hyr
humble Daughter wyſheth encreaſe of
ſpirituall knowledge, with ful frui-
cion of the fruites
thereof.

Ince the
Oryginal
of what ſo
euer is, or
may be cō=
uerted to a
ni goodvſe
in me, hath
frelye proceded (thoughe as the
miniſter of GOD) of youre La=
dyſhyppes mere carefull, and Mo=
therly goodnes, as well in procu=
rynge all thynges thereunto be=
longeynge, as in youre many, and
moſt Godly exhortacyons, where=
in amonge the reſt it hath plea=
ſed

sed you, ofte, to reproue my vaine
studye in the Italyan tonge, ac=
compting the sede thereof, to haue
bene sowen in barayne, vnfruitful
grounde(syns God thereby is no
whytte magnifyed)I haue at the
last, perceiued it my duty to proue
howe muche the vnderstandynge
of youre wyll, could worcke in me
towardes the accomplyshynge of
the same. And for that I haue wel
knowen your chyfe delight, to rest
in the destroynge of man hys glo=
rye, and exaltynge wholy the glo=
ry of God: whych may not be vn=
les we acknowledge that he, doth
fore se and determyne from wyth=
out begynnynge, al thynges, and
cannot alter or rewarde after our
deserued worckes, but remayne
stedefaste, accordynge to hys im=
mutable wyll, I hane taken in
hande to dedicate vnto youre La=
dyship this smale number of Ser
mons

mōns (foʒ the excelēt fruit sake iñ
thē conteined, pʒoceding from the
happy spirit of the santified Bar=
nardyne, which treat of ẏ election
and pʒedeſtinaciō of God, wyth
the reſt (although not of the selfe
title) a perteynig to the same effect
to the end it might appere, ẏ your
so many woʒthy sentences touch=
ing the same, haue not vtterly ben
wout some note in my weake me=
moʒy, Ꝫ al be it, they be not done in
such perfectiō, as ꞇhe dignitie of ẏ
matter doth requyʒe: yet J truſt Ꝫ
know, ye wil accept ẏ hūble wil of
the pʒesēter, not weghing so much
the excelnecy of the tranſlacion, al
thoughe of rygh te it oughte to be
ſuch as ſhould not by the groſnes
therof depʒiue the aucthoʒ of his
woʒthynes. But not meanynge to
take vpō me ẏ reache, to his hygh
ſtyle of thealogie, and fearyng al=
ſo, leaſt in enterpʒiſynge to ſette
foʒth

forth the bryghtnes of hys elo=
quence, I shuld manyfest my selfe
vnapte, to attaine vnto the lowest
degre therof. I descend therefore,
to the vnderstāding of myne own
debilitye. Only requiring, that it
may please youre Ladyshippe to
vouchsafe that thys my smal la=
bor may be alowed at your hādes
vnder whose proteccion only it
is committed wyth humble re
uerence, as yeldyng some
parte of the fruite of
your Motherly ad=
monicions, in this
my wyllinge
seruyce.

☞Your Ladyshyppes Daugh=
ter most boundenly obedient,
I.C.

ℭ Whether predestina-
cion oughte to be wrytten, spoken, oꝛ thought: the fyꝛste
Sermō.

Here are ma
ny that wold
not here pꝛede
ſtinacion ſpo-
kē of, noꝛ once
named, and if
they might let
it, it ſhuld ne-
uer be pꝛea-
ched, and that
is becauſe it ſemeth them to gyue offence,
and ingender cōfuſion amonge the people.
ℭ J cannot denye, that many curiouſe per
ſons wyth thepꝛ darcke natural lyght (willing to ſe thinges ſupernatural that cannot
be ſene but by fayth) do fal into thouſandes
of errours, and cauſe other to fall into the
lyke. Al that they maye imagine by foꝛce of
wyt, pleaſynge to thepꝛ owne coꝛrupt reaſon (of that hyghe ſecrete) they thyncke it to
be true, wythout other teſtimonye of holye
ſcriptnre. And thereby haue intangled their
bꝛaynes, darkened thepꝛ myndes, and offen
ded thepꝛ conſciences. Curpoſytye is an vn
ſacy-

ſatiable beaſt, it would pearce thozowe all
thynges, and yet cãnot get out of his darke
and intricate labozinthes, noz once lyſt vp
the heade to diuyne ſecrettes. And if we ſuf
fer our ſelues to be guyded of it (in thinges
ſpeciallye ſupernaturall, neyther wyll it at
any tyme be ſatiſfied, noz we ſhall neuer
percepue the trueth. ffoz immedialye after
it paſſeth the bozders of the natural lyghte,
it goeth alwayes blynded and at aduentur.
Therefoze it muſt be put a ſyde and (bzyng
pnge hys vnſaciable wyl to an ende) walke
by fayth to deuyne ſecrettes honozyng thẽ
wythout further dyſcuſſion. And if we be
pzouoked to ſerch them out by the wanton
nes of humayne wyt: we oughte to remem

Pzou. xxb. ber that, which is wzittẽ: He that ſearcheth
the maieſtie of God, ſhalbe ouercome with
the glozye thereof. It is our offyce, to be cõ
tẽt, with as much as God hath vouchaſed
to open vnto vs in the ſacred Scripture, in
the whych, he hath gpuen vs lyght ſufficy
entlp. But note, that as it is euel to be curi
ouſe in wyllynge to knowe moze then that
whych in the ſcripture is contepned, and to
vs reueled, ſo is it alſo euell, to be ignozant
and not to ſeke to vnderſtaude as much as
therin is: foz that in them ſpeaketh the holy
goſt who gyueth none offence but edifyeth

In

In them is wꝛiten nothyng pernicious, vn-
pꝛofitable, oꝛ hapne, but onlp commodious
and neceſſarp. Nepther ought it to offende
anp man, when it is ipoken of, in the maner
that Paulle ſpeaketh of it. And we nepther
mape noꝛ ought to be moꝛe circumſpecte in   Gala.ii.
ſpeakyng therof then Paule, pe then God,
that ſpeake in hpm. Thpnckeſt thou haplpe
that Paule (pea rather Chꝛiſte that lpued in
hpm, and moued hpm to wꝛpte) dpd erre in
ꝑ he wꝛote of it in ſuche ſoꝛt, as he dpd? The
holp goſt would neuer haue gpuen vnder-
ſtandpnge thereof in the holp ſcripture, if it
had bene euell. Thou wplt ſape, the pꝛea-
chpnge of it in ſuch maner as Paule wꝛpt-
teth: gpueth offence, as it is euidente. J anſwere that Chꝛiſt crucified, was an offence   i.Coꝛ.i.
to the Hebꝛues: therfoꝛe the apoſtles dpd e-
uell to pꝛeache it. The goſpel ſemed folpſh-
nes to the wpſe of the woꝛld: And therefoꝛe
it ſhoulde not be taughte. The trueth is diſpleaſaunt to the falſe chꝛiſtians, thep ſpnde
offence of the goſpell, and Juſtificacion bp
Chꝛiſte, ſhoulde it then be kepte in ſilence?
Wherfoꝛe wilt ꝑ that we holde oure peace
of that thpng whpch Paule wꝛitteth? How
can the woꝛdes of the holp goſt offend, that
haue bene pꝛonounced and wꝛptten onelpe
foꝛ oure ſaluacion? Jf thou be offended ther
wpth

wyth, it is not becauſe it gꝛueth the occaciõ
but foꝛ that thou takeſt it without anp gift.
Nepther oughte the thereof to ceaſſe, moꝛe
then the Apoſtles left pꝛeachynge, thoughe
manp were offendpd therwyth. Thou wilt
ſape, to pꝛeache the Goſpell is neceſſarpe,
Wherfoꝛe that oughte noꝛ to be lefte foꝛ offence: and J ſape that pꝛedeſtinacion is a
great parte of the Goſpell. Wouldeſt thou
not thpnke thps a goodlpe Goſpell oꝛ glad
tpdpnges, that God from wpthout begpn-
npng, had by his mere grace, and by Chꝛiſt
crucified, elected vs to be hps childꝛen, and
that we be ſuer in hps handes? Jt is a thing
moſte neceſſarpe, to pꝛeache thoſe good ne-
wes, in the whpche ther is dpſcouered vnto
hs the exceadpnge goodnes of God, that
aboue all other thpnges doeth moue vs to
be ennamored of hpm, And he that is offended wpth pꝛedeſtinacion, pꝛeached in the
maner it ought to be, is alſo offended wpth
the Goſpell, Knoweſt thou (that whpche in
dede doth hurt, althoughe it appeare not to
the blpnde and frantpke woꝛlde) that anpe
man pꝛeacheth it after ẙ humaine docꝛrine?
But it mape be thou wpltſape, let vs come
therefoꝛe to the particulars. Doeth it not
ſeme to the, offence, to pꝛeach that god hath
electe ſome and not other ſome? He that he-
reth

reth theſe wordes, wyll thyncke God to be
parciall. I anſwere and fyrſt I ſaye, that
god cannot erre: nor wyll otherwyſe then
iuſtly: yea hys wyll is ſo ryghte, that as he
alway wylleth any thyng, it is euen by that
wyllynge moſt iuſt. Therefore none ſhould
be offended wyth hys workes, for as much
as he maye dyſpoſe vs after his owne way,
and ſhewe hys pleaſure vpon vs more then y
potter vpon hys pottes: and al wyth iuſtice
& equite. ffor what bond hath god with vs?
Moreouer, by the ſynnes of Adam we are   Rom.ix.
al loſt, and he myghte iuſtlye damne vs al,
but he ſaueth as manye as hym pleaſeth:
and yet we complayne, where we are not
woorthy by ſufferyng al puniſhmente to ſet
furthe the bryghtnes of hys gloꝛye. Yea it
oughte to be preached that God hath elected ſome, and not other ſome: for to ſmite to
the earth the wiſdome of man, and to make
him al humble and ſubiecte to God. Now   Rom.iii.
is it not neceſſary to be knowẽ that we ſhal
not all be ſaued, and that many ſhalbe dam
ned? And conſequently God hath manye e-
lecte and manye reiected. Thou wouldeſt
ſaye, thys ſhoulde gyue no occacion of offence, if it were preached, that thoſe that
he hath choſen, are choſen for ther merites,
and thoſe he hath forſaken, are forſaken for
theyr

theyꝛ wickednes but thei ſay ẏ thoſe he hath
elect, are elected by hys mere grace, wythout woꝛkes, and that oure election and ſal-
uacyon dependeth hollye vpon God. And
thys gyueth the offence to the woꝛlde. J anſwere. Jf this be offence, Paule hath gyuen
it him ſelfe, becauſe it is the doctrine of him
ye rather of the holy goſt. Wylt thou be o-
ffendyd, if Paule magnifie ẏ fre mercy, ſe-
yng God hath elected vs to the laud of hys
gloꝛy, as he wꝛytteth? We cannot magnify
it ſufficiently. But thou feareſt it ſhould be
lauded and exalted to much. Jf it were told
the thou were elected by they woꝛkes, then
would J thou ſhuldeſt be offended, foꝛ that
it would make the beleue thy ſaluacion, to
depend vpon thy ſelfe, wherby thou ſhoul-
deſt be begiled. ffoꝛ of thy ſelfe cōmeth thy
damnacion, and of God thy ſaluacion. Yea
as often as thou thyncke ſt thy ſaluacion in
anye part eto depende vpon thy ſelf, it dꝛy-
ueth the, eyther to dyſpare oꝛ to be exallted
in preſumpcyou. And in ſuch caſe thou can-
neſt neuer put in God all thy hope, noꝛ all
thy loue, neyther haue perfect quyetnes of
mynde, noꝛ of conſcyence. Thou wouldeſt
ſay, that who ſo knoweth that God aboue
is reſolued vpon all thynges : waxeth colde
in well doyng, and ſayth, what nede J moꝛe
to

Margin:
Ephe.i.

Rom.ix.

Rom.viii.
Ephe.i.

Ofe.xiii.

to trauayle, God hath immutably determi
ned and resolued all that is to be, I maye
passe my tyme in pleasure, for if I be elect
I shall euery way be saued, And if I be reprobate, I cannot saue my selfe, thoughe I
neuer ceased to axe it, on my bare knees.
Thou percepuest not, that he which sayeth
so, doth dyscouer hym selfe shewynge that
he neuer dyd good workes, & yet he would
hys saluacion should depend vpon hym
selfe. Thys sort of men, if they do any good
(as they call it) it is to wyn heauen, and not
for the glory of God . Therefore if they
should beleue that theyr saluacion and elec
tyon dyd not come of them selues (as men
that were not moupd wyth the zeale of the
hanor of God) they would dwell in Idlenes, yea, gyue thepm selues to lyue lycenci-
ously, and vngodly, wythout respecte of
the dyshonour of God, they are fearefull
Seruauntes and hirelynges, and not sonnes of God, they serue thepm selues and
not God, and thepm selues they worshpp.
The electe do neuer become could, but are
the more feruent, by hearynge that their e-
lection and saluacion is onely in the hand-
des of God, they know by fayeth, that the
lorde louyth theim so much (specially synce
Chryste hath dyed for thepm on the crosse)
that

that they are ſuer of theyꝛ ſaluacion. Yea
they feale ſomuch the goodnes of God in
Chꝛiſte, and by Chꝛiſt, that if it weare poſ
ſyble(whyle that ſpirituall felyng dyd remayne in them)that they cold beleue them
ſelues to be repꝛobate (foꝛ as muche as by
thys,god is no leſſe good)they would not a
ny thyng the leſſe loue hym, oꝛ trauayle to
honoꝛ hym, euen as Saule ceſſed not moſt
coꝛagyouſly to fyght foꝛ ẙ gloꝛy of God, al
though it was foꝛetould him of hys death.
The elect vnderſtand in ſpirit ẙ they are the
childꝛen of God. Wherfoꝛe they are foꝛced
by ſtrength of loue & learne to haue condici
ons couenient to theyꝛ ſo hye eſtate:& are al
ſo aſhamed to do a wycked woꝛke,not ſeme
li oꝛ ſetting to ẙ bewty of their dignitie. And
ſo much moꝛe thẽ the other,do they feare to
ſinne, by how much moꝛe they know ẙ god
doeth in thys pꝛeſent lyfe, punyſhe hys le-
gitimate childꝛẽ, moꝛe thẽ the baſterdes. If
and aſtrologyer ſhould tell an ambycious
man that he ſhoulde be pope, althoughe he
dyd put vndouted truſt there in, yet foꝛ all
that he woulde not be Idell, but would ſet
furth hym ſelfe by all meanes poſ ſible to
come to ẙ dignitie. Euen ſo ẙ ſones of god,
the ſurer thei are of their eleccio̅ ſo much ẙ
moꝛe they vnderſtande the greate goodnes
of

i. Re. xviii.

Iobꝛn. xii.

of God.They are alwaies forced therfore,
more & more by good workes, to make certeine to them selues the knowledge of their
eleccion . Euery one wyll trauaple for the **ii. Pet.i.**
thinges of the world.There is none that sai
eth J wyl be Jdle, or J wyll not eate, for alwayes J shall lyue, and be ryth and happy
in the thinges of the world, if God haue for
sene and determined it. Only in those thinges perteining to the soule, predestinacion
hindreth them by making it aschylde to their
wicked life.But know thou that those whiche of such a benefit take occasiō to become
worse, (though alreody with their hart they
dyd the same thinges and wolde haue done
it in worke if they had thought them sure of
their saluacion) shew thē selues to be repro- **ii. Cor.xi.**
bate, & not to feele in Christ the great good-
nes of God. Sathan is he that being trans-
formed into the similitude of an Aungel of
lyght, trauapleth to perswade that our eleccion dependeth vpon vs. This was the opinion of Pelagius : and the Pelagians are
they that be offended with this great mercy
of God: they thinke that God neither may,
can, or wyll do other then reason . Then of
force muste it be good to be preached, to the
end it may be knowen, y the time is alreody **Esa.lv.**
come of the couenaunt and promised peace

B.i.   that

Math.xiii.

that he which hath eares to vnderſtãd, may
vnderſtãd, as haue ẏ ſhepe of chꝛiſt ẏ heare
their paſtour. It is alſo good to be ſpokẽ of,
to the ende ẏ that be not hyd but declared,

Ihon.x.

which (by ẏ wyll of God ¿ foꝛ oure pꝛofite)
is wꝛitten therof in holpe ſcripture: ¿, ẏ the
ſpecial cure ẏ god hath of vs, may be know
en, ¿ how we ſhuld ſerue him frely as childꝛen, ¿ not as timerous ſeruauntes ¿ hire-
lingcs. Yea ¿ that it may be vnderſtãd, that
God (being abſolutelie the Loꝛd) may do al
that he wil, ¿ what he willeth is iuſt, ¿ to the
end alſo, ẏ in our electiõ may be diſcouered
to vs, in ſuperabũdãt maner, his fre mercy,
¿ that it may be ſene how we are pꝛeuented
by innumerable benitites, ¿ alſo ẏ mã maye

Pſal.xxviii.

know ẏ he is only vanitie, ¿ euer an vnpꝛofi
table ſeruaunt. Paradiſe we litle woꝛth if
with our woꝛkes wee could wyn it but it is
the inheritaunce of ſonnes, ¿ not a reward
foꝛ ſeruauntes. I wolde knowe what men
wold ſaye, if God ſhuld ſaye to them: chuſe
whether ye wyl ſtand to my election and ẏ
which I haue determined of you, oꝛ ẏ I diſ
anulling (if this wer poſſible) al that I haue
purpoſed to do with you, ſhuld reſolue me
holi to put it in you. And to ſaue you if ye do
good woꝛkes and perſeuer in them, ¿ if you
do ẏ contrary to dãne you. I am ſure then
men

men should know their owne frailtye, igno=
raunce & malice. And on ye other partie ye exce=
ding bountye of God, & remit it holp to him a=
gain, & much more if thei loue him, for ye gre
ter glory to god, pea & also for their own pro
per commoditie, for it shuld neuer be done, if
it depeded vpon them selues. And therfore for
euery respect, euery one shuld stade to gods
determinacio, if it were for nothinge but to
do honour to him. It is a thing more magni
ficet, & to god more conuenient, to geue para=
dice by fre mercie, the if he shuld sel it: his li
beralitie is therby most discouered. Then,
for his greater glory I would alwaies say,
god hath geue me this. And also for mi own
commoditie, ye wheras now I hold my salua=
cio sure (for that I know it hageth only vpo
god) I wold thinke me daued, or at the least
presuming on my self, stand in dout. if in the
least point it did deped vpo me, because god
incoparably doth loue me more the I can do
my self. Pea, I am ye greatest enemy & trai=
tor to my self ye may be. Therfore me ought
bi euer cosideracio to cotent the ye their sal=
uacion doth stande in the haude of god: pea
in taking ye whole cure of vs, he hath shew=
to vs most dere loue, he hath willed vs to be
sure of it . And therfore he woulde not
truste to vs, knowinge wee are so vnper=
fect, that if we had paradise in our handes,

we should let it fal to therth where now we
are sure knowinge that al our sinnes cā not
let the diuine eleccion, neither quench or diminishe the diuine charitie. Pea, hereof our
sinnes toke occasion to be shewed with excesse of moze loue. We are not by this inuited to moze Idlenes, noz to watche when
we shall haue Manna from heauē, neither
to be wickedly occupped, but we are drawē
and moued so much moze to loue him, as he
is discouered to hs by moze bountie and charitie. But those that are not by Christe regenerate, are of so base & byle a mind through
sinne, that they can not thinke God to be so
liberall as to geue heauē without our wozkes. But they ought at the leaste to thinke,
that to bye it the bloud of Christ is sufficiēt
without adioyninge therto their wozkes to
boote: which surely are rych iuels to be min-
gled with his. God is so frāke, that he hath
geuen vs Christ, and in him al thinges, and
canst not thou thinke he hath geuen the heauen? It is also our greater glozie, that God
hath loued vs somuche, that his owne selfe
hath wylled to take the care & charge of our
saluacion. And so to that ende hath wylled
his only sonne to die vpon the crosse, so that
if with all our trauaile we might enter into
heauen by our selues: the glozie only of the
                                     crosse

Roma, b.

Roma, biii.

crosse is a far greater glory then any other
which by our selues we could attaine. Yea,
there is no other trew glory, then to glorie
to be so much loued of God, that he hath to
saue vs, put his sonne vpon the crosse. He
may not dwel in his owne loue, that willeth
to be happy, and only glory in God. If we
myght glorye of our selues, we should haue
whereof to waxe proude and prefer our selues afore oure brethern, where otherwyse
we should haue occasion to be humble, and
geue to God all honoure and glorye as to *1. Timo. i.*
him it apperteineth. And further such as beleue the selues to be by grace elected, saued
sonnes of God, heyres and sure therof, not
only because ther remaineth no more to get
(God in Christ hauing geuen them all) but
also by the great vnderstanding they haue
of the goodnes of the Lord: they are costra-i
ned to worke as children for the glori of their
father, and not for their owne gaine, and so
also sure of their saluacion, with Christ they
turne them with al their force, to seke the sal
uacion of their brother: they demaund also
grace with a bolder spirite and confideuce,
sence they axe it not for their owne lucre,
but for the honor of God, and to his laude *Ephesi. i.*
and glory: so y in the worldes to come, may *Rom. vi.*
be sene y aboundant riches of his fre mercy. *Psal. xxxii.*

B.iii.   More-

Rom.tiii.
Gala.iii.
1.Cor.iii.
Joh.iii.

Moreouer such hope to be hard for that thei
thinke not to deserue grace, neither put their
trust in their owne workes, but in the goodnes of God, being inspired and moued ther
to by the holy gost. Suche also as feele that
our saluacion dependeth not hpon hs, but
oure damnacion, and that it standeth whole-
lpe in the hande of God: are forced to turne
their backes to them selues, and theyr faces
to God. Where as the cotrary belefe, wold
make the contrary operacion, they would
withdraw them from God, and seke to rest
with hope in them selues; also if God had e-
lected hs with this condicion: If we wolde
do well, we should be hnder the lawe contrary to Paul, neither we should be saued,
for the law saueth not but worketh wrathe,
aud is the minister of cursing and damnacion. Let him therfore that lusteth haue Christ
for his iudge, for I wyl none of him, but as
a sauiour. If our eleccion by fre mercy dyd
haerme hs, he wold not the haue elected hs
so. But note them that thinke to haue theyr
eleccion in their owne handes, & thou shalt
se that thei are in their owne loue and trust,
presumtuous, and full of vyce: and yet for
all thys they be so hlprd and arrogant, that
they wyll haue heauen by iustice.

    But let hs praye to the Lorde that he
                          gyue

gyue them knowledge to the ende they may
render to God all laude, hono r, and
glozye, throughe oure Loꝛde
Jeſus Chriſte. Amen.

🙶 (∴) 🙷
(∴)

Howe excellent oure election is, the seconde Sermon.

Aul magnifieth our
election, firſte in his behalfe that hath elected vs,
ſayinge : Wee are elected
neyther by man noꝛ Aun-
gell, but by God: Hyer
can not he go. Then concer-
nynge hym that elected vs, oure election
is muſte excellente. And lykewyſe concer-
nynge the circumſtaunce of tyme, although
aboue there is pꝛoperlye no courſe of tyme.
He elected vs (as Paull wryteth) before the
conſtitucion of the woꝛlde: meanynge from
wythoute begynnynge, ſooner coulde he
not electe vs.

Ephe. i.

B.iiii.   And

And moreouer he sapthe, that he elected vs
which are most base, most vile, most abiect,
wormes in comparison of him. Bi the sinne
of Adam we were all despled, infected, in
firme, frapl., blpnd, malingnaunte, full of
venim, contrari to god, enemies and rebels:
so that a thinge more miserable coulde not
haue binne chosen. Paule doth also magni
fy oure election, in respect of the dignittie,
to the whiche we are elected, and sapth, he
hath not chosen vs to be hps seruauntes or
frendes, but to be hps children, nothpng to
god can be more npghe, entire and dere, the
his children, nether is it possible to imagine
a greater dignitie. It doth include al other
vertues and goodnes, it is so hpghe and excellent. Being then elected from so miserable an estate, to be the sones of god, he hath
Rom. vlil. also chosen vs to be the brethren of Christe
& therbp with him coheires of god: pea the
worlde is oures. Christ with al his gpstes,
al that is the fathers is the sonnes, therfore
al is ours p is gods, whose goodes we mai
dpspose as children their fathers. And bpcause we should shame to be the sonnes of
god, not hauing the maners, graces, and
vertues conue ient to suche a dpgnitie, therfore not onlpe oure heauenlpe father, hath
cholen vs to be his sonnes, but hath blessed
vs

vs, not wyth wordes onlye, but wyth effectes, not as Isaac blessed Iacob or Esau,
but wyth all spirituall blessinge in thinges
celestiall. And so accordyng to Paule, hath
made vs mete to be partakers of ye felowe-
ship of lyght, & delyueringe vs from the power of darkenes, hath ledde vs into the kingedome of his beloued sonne: God then withoute beginninge did determyne to iustifye,
glorifye, and magnifie those that he hadde
elect, and euen so he hath done: as Paule
wryteth, who also exaltyth our election for
that cause, sainge: that it was not our good
worckes, which God forsawe wythout beginning, that were the cause of our electiõ,
but he chose vs by mere mercie, accordynge
to the decreed purpose of his owne wyll, to
the laud and glorie of his mercie, we were
not then chosen bycause we were holye,
but bycause we shoulde be holly bi his election, and to shewe in the worldes to come,
the abundante riches of his grace. Paule
also shewyth the worthines of our electiõ,
by respecte of the dignitie of the person by
whose meanes we are chosen, and saithe, he
hath willed, that betwene vs and him there
shuld be one mediator, neither he wold it to
be an angel, but Christ the sone of God. He
meaneth not onlie a mediator with wordes,
but

(marginal notes) Colo.i / Colo.i / Rom.viii / Ephe.i & ii / i.Timo.ii. / Ephe.i.

but with his owne bloud ,and death. Paul
doth exalt our electiō as concerning ẏ end,
ffor bicause he hathe elected vs for his sonnes, to the end we may taste (not only in the
life to come, but also in this present)things
so highe, happpe, riche, and pure, that the
eie hath not sene, nor the eare hath not hard,
nor into the hart of man(being carnal) hath

Cor.ii.

at any tyme entred, he hath then elected vs,
to the ende (that regenerate bi Christe Jesu)

ephe.ii.

we shuld walke to God by good workes, ẏ
we may be hollie and inreprehēsible, before
his presence. Our election is also excellente
by the suertye therof, for that the elect are in

ephe i.
Jon.x.

the handes of God. Therefore shal not thei
perishe as Christ sayth, yea they can not pe-
rpshe, euen as they can not bee pluckte oute
of his handes . Therfore oure election is
moste happpe , so that nothynge oughte so
muche to bee reiopsed in , as to bee the elected and chosen of God. Therfore it is read,
the disciples returning to Christ , and reioi-
singe with greate gladnes, that euen the be-
ray deuelles were subiecte to them , Chryst

Luc.x.

amonge the reste of wordes, bade them thei
shulde not reiopse of the subiection of the de
uels, but that their names were written in
heauen:by which wordes, he did shew ,that
we ought to make a singuler Jope of our e-
lecciō

lecciõ, for that includeth, and bringeth with
it the some of all our wealth, since then that
our eleccion is so excellent, rpche, sure, and
happ. Let vs pray to God to geue vs lighte
and grace, to percepue it, to thende, that
tastinge in it (with the spirite) the
mpghtie goodnes of God, we
may rēder him al laude. ho
nor: and glorye, by Jesu
Christe our Lorde.

¶ If wee maie knowe in
this present lyfe, whether we be
in the grace of God, ¶ one of his
electe or not, and in what maner the thyrd Sermon.

¶ It is not to be dou=
ted ꝑ God seeth all thin-
ges, specially his legittimate childrē, sēce he him
self hath chosen them to
that dignitie. Christ also

This hole ser
mon must be
warily red, ¶
wel vnderstā
ded, or els it
must be taken
but as persua
siue not as of
trine,

ii. Timo. ii
Ephe. i.

knoweth, ¶ knew thē alwaies, ꝑ which was
very conueniēt. sence his father had geuē thē
to him for that he shulde b theyr gouernor,
shepherd, ¶ brother, and ꝑ he shuld saue thē
tõ his own death: he knew thē, ¶ doth know
his shepe euen as himselfe sayd, yea frõ the
beginning he knew who shoulo beleue.

Jhon. vii.
Jo hn. vi.

But

Math.xlii.
But it is not now conuenient, that we may
oꝛ can deserue distinctlye, the elect from the
repꝛobate, to the ende we may be moꝛe feruent in exercisinge charite, with all men, as
if they were bꝛethern with vs in Chꝛist, the
which we would not do towarde the repꝛobate if we knewe thē distinctly: But in the
ende, the tares shalbe seperate frō the good
wheat:none then beinge in this pꝛesent lyfe
knoweth certenly of his neighbour, if he be
of the elect oꝛ not, noꝛ also whether he be in
the fauour of God:we may only haue therof an obscure, confused, vncertein, and say-
lyng knowledge by cōiecture of ꝑ outward
lyfe and woꝛkes, of whom Chꝛist speaking,
sayd.Ye shall knowe them by their fruites.

Math.vii.
But foꝛasmuch as we see not the hertes of
men, which oftentimes (although within

Coꝛ.ii.
Mat.xvi. ꝫ
they are vngodly and abhominacion it selfe
in the spght of God, neuertheles coueringe
them with the veyle of hipocrisie maskinge
therin)they apeare to be sainctes. Therfoꝛe
without speciall oꝛacle, we can haue no certeine knowledge therof.But J saye ꝑ euery
elect, whyle he is in th,is pꝛesent lyfe, beinge
come to the yeres of discression, maye, and
ought to know it of himself, not by natural
lyght(by meanes wherof thinges superna-
ural can not be perceiued, as the excellent
diuine

diuine wyl toward vs) but by faithe, without other speciall priuilege. And this not to
hauing respect to them selues, where is nothing sene but worthy damnacion, neither
with considering or beholding the selues in
God without Christe, for in y case he must
shew himself to vs a iust iudge ful of wrath:
then we neither se our selues his sonnes, nor
in fauour. But with liuely faith beholding
both our selues, & God in Christ, we se our
selues to be in the fauour of god, & his elect
sonnes, & god to be pacified with vs in loue
and our only father. Such then as liuely be
leue, y Christ for the hath died vpō y crosse,
haue the holy gost within them, & are in the
fauour of God, bicause that faith doth puri
fie the hert.* And further J say, that al they
which in this present lyfe to beleue liuely
in Christ (pea were it for a moment of time)
shalbe sauid. Thei are electe and sonnes of
God, and may be suer and certeine, of their
saluation. And that this is true, the wordes
of sainte Jhon ought to suffise, which saith,
that he is the sonne of God, therfore electe
and sauid, who so beleueth Jesu Christe to
be the sonne of God. And also Christ sayde
who so beleueth in me hath lyfe euerlasting
neuerthelesse it may clearlye be prouid that
none beleueth liuelye in Christe, but he that
beleueth

This muste be
warly red and
well vnderstā-
ded or it is not
true. But if y
vnderstande
what it is to
beleue in christ
with a liuely
faith thē there
is no daunger
at al.
i.J.40.b.

but he that beleueth Chrpst to be wholy his
rightwisenes and that he is saued thozow-
lpe bp him, and he that seethe this wpth supernatural vnderstãding hauing no respect
to him selfe noz his wozkes, but oulp to the
goodnes of God discouered in Christ vpõ
the Crosse, can not by anp meanes be disce-
ued, bicause ꝑ light which he hath to be in ꝑ
fauoz of God, elect to saluaciõ, cã not grow
but onlpe of the bountp of God, considered
in Christ, wherof can spring no false noz de-
ceitfull knowledge. ffull well map he be begiled and shalbe, that doth behold his wozkes, and bp them thinketh that he is in the
fauour of God and his sonr. But seing him
selfe in Chzpst saued, chosen & in the fauour
of God, it muste nedes be said, that he seeth
the truthe, and that which is once trewe although it were but foz the twincke of an eie
must be saide to be euer true, he then whiche
beleueth in Christe, were it but a minute
of an houre, in percepuing of him selfe elect
bp Christ, seeth that which is true, therfore
shall it euer be true, that he is one of the legitimat sonnes of God, sohat the same his
faythe, be not in anpe maner founded vpon
him self, noz his own wozckes, but in christ,
and the diuine excellence, and that it be not
a certeine trifleinge, lighte, baren and deade
                                    opinion

opinion, but a liuely faithe. It must be said then that Judas had neuer perfect faith, nether was elect to saluaciō, although he was chosen to the apostelshippe. and the like say I of al ÿ reprobate: al such then as haue had at anie time liuely belefe to be saued in christ may be suer of their saluation. And so also they, whiche haue once at the least bene perfectely geuen to God, and committed to his gouernaunce, vpon the couenaunte, tha[t] he shall serue himselfe of them accordynge to his owne purpose, and with truste that by Christ and his mere goodnes he hath accepted them for his owne, they maye also beleue that they are saued, bycause that he shal be no lesse God to them, then thei shal be promised of him.

Therfore hauing had in that couenaunte liuely faythe, that God wyll forgeue them as his Chyldren, in suche sorte, that he wyl conducte them to saluacion, although they (as muche as lyeth in them) were continuallie prompte to all euyll: yet is it necessary to saye, that sence God hathe taken them for his (as they knowe by the lyuely faythe that they haue hadde thereof) that they shall ouercome that wycked one and haue honoure therby.

This is not spoken to declare that it is possible for gods elect to be wholy geue to synne. but if it were possible, yet shoulld they recouer that pestilence

foe

For hys goodnes passithe theyr euelnes he wold not haue inspired them to gyue them selfes, if from withoute beginning, he had not elected them and takē thē for his owne. Some peraduenture will saye, if we were onlye ones suer to haue beue for a litle time in the fauour of God, to haue had his spirit in vs, and liuely faith in him, that we did beleue suerlye to be his elect: yet we knowe not if it haue bene a perfect fayth or not, we feare it to haue bene a certeine cold opinion and leste we were begiled in beleuing to be in gods fouor and elected of him. J answer that this is an euidente signe, that ye haue neuer had hitherto liuelye faith and know-ledge of christe. For as it is vnpossible to haue fyre within the brest and not fele it, so is it impossible to haue in the hart christ, the holye ghoste, ardent charitie and the fierye lighte of faythe, and not to perceiue it, and this is, for that his lighte is so clere and ef-fectuous, that not only it maketh thē to se, and liuelie to fele with the spirit, that christ is deade for them vpon the crosse, that they are elect and sauid, but also it dothe make them knowe, that it whiche they see, is by diuine inspiracion, that it is the holye spirit whiche testifieth vnto the pr spirite, that thei are the sonnes of God, Whose testimonie

Rom. viii.

is

ſo moꝛe clere, open, firme, and certeine, then
al the outward oꝛacles and miracles of the
woꝛld, which without the inward teſtimonie of the ſpirit, can leaue vs none other then
doubtful. Now, ẏ he that hath in him Chꝛiſt
and the ſpirit of God, doth fele, know, and
pꝛeceiue it: it is clere by Chꝛiſt which ſayde
that the woꝛld knew not the holy goſt, but
that he was knowen of them in whom he
was. And by ſaynct John, which ſayd alſo
In this we know that Chꝛiſt is in vs, euen   i. Jho. iii.
by the holy goſt which he hath geuen vs.
Therfoꝛe ſayd Paul, trie your ſelues, make   ii. Coꝛ. xiii.
ſome pꝛofe of your ſelues, is it poſſible that
ye ſhould not knowe Chꝛiſt in you, if ye be
not repꝛobate? And in an other place, know
ye not how ye are the temple of God, ⁊ that
the holy goſt dwelleth in you? The holy ſpi-
rite goth ſearching throughout, and iudgeth   i. Coꝛ. ii.
euery thing, ⁊ fayth is ſo clere, ꝑ it ſheweth   Eſa xxiii.
vs the pꝛofunditie of god: ⁊ thou wilt that it   Roma. xv.
be blynde of it ſelfe. Yea Paul ſayth, that   Luke. i.
the holy goſt is geuen to vs, to the ende we
myght know thoſe thinges that haue ben ge-   i. Teſa. i.
uen vs of Chꝛiſt. The kyngdom of God is
peace (as wꝛiteth Eſai and Paul) withoute
ſeruile feare, in much certentie. Therefoꝛe
as Chꝛyſt ſawe, that he was in the fauoure
of his father, and his beloued ſonne, ſo alſo

do the electe se them selues, all thoughe not
with so cleare lighte and certentpe, but that
thep goo somtpme doubtpnge, stumbling,
and wauering. But thep oughte wpth the A
postles to prap Christ to augmēt their faith.

pke.xvii.

And seke with their good workes continuall
ly to make knowē to thē selfes more perfect
their saluation and vocation, that therbp as
bp the effectes or fruites thep shuld come in
to the ful riches of certeine perswacion, and
vnderstandinge of their election and salua-

Tessa.i
Timo.iiii
om.viii
ala.ii.
Cor.iii.

tion. Paule also knew he was in the fauour
of God, in faith, hope and charitpe, elected
the sōne of God, saufe and suer, and that he
had the holp gooste and Christ within him,
when he said that he was one of them that
Christ was come to saue, and that he knewe
in whome he beleued, that he loked for the
Crowne, that nothpnge colde seperate hpm
frō the loue of God, whiche had elected him
before the constitution of the worlde, that he
had the spirite of adopcion of the sonnes of
God, and that Christe was he, who lyued
and spake in him. Saint John also said: we
are suer we know God, and that we liue in
him, worldlie and carnall beastes are thep,

Iala.ii.
oh.xiiii.
Cor.ii.

which know not God in the holpe gost, nor
thosethpnges which be his, euen as men vnt
regenerate, thep are rustical papsasstes of so

a.v.

abiecte and hase a spirite, that they can not
beleue that God hath loued them so much,
that by the death of his only begotten and
most intierly beloued sonne, he would saue
them, take them for his chyldren, and make
them his heyres: But astonied of theyr sinnes, they are euer afrayed of hell. Where
the regenerate fele in such sorte the charitie
of God in Christ, that they knowe them selues to be saued. Neyther canne they once
thynke that Christe (who hathe all his fathers power and shall be theyr iudge) wyll
refuse, lose, or dampn e them, and geue sentence agaynste his brethern and members, Math.xxviii
for whom he dyed on the crosse, and would
dye agayne if it were necessarie. They haue Ephe.t
in them also the holye goste for an earneste
of theyr saluation. But if God had geuen
vs nothyng but our beynge, should not we
forthat onlye benefite, feele so muche the
greate goodnes of God, that we myght be
sure and certayne of our saluacion? And
nowe he in euery creature dothe sparkle towardes vs loue, with innumerable benefites, yea in Christe vpon the Crosse, casteth
be the flame of perfecte charitye, and shall
not wee feele so muche the goodnes of God
that wee should beleue to be his electe?

L.ii.   If

If one onlye shulde be saued I wold truste
suerly to be he, if al the men & angells wold
tel me that I were dampned, I cold not beleue them, although thei did alledge al the
reasonnes possible, but I wolde euer giue,
more truste to Christe alone, who vpon the
crosse, with his bloude and deathe, doeth
tel me I am saued, thē I wold to al the rest,
for he alone, hath more power in me, thē al
the reasons & authorities without him. Pro
uided only ȳ I se him w liuely fayth, dead
for my saluacion. Yea in that case seing my
selfe, by Christ, to be ȳ sone of God, I wold
with. Paule excomunicate the very angels
as superior to them, if thei wold saie the cōtrary, or gainesaie the gospel, and the great
loue and benefit, which in that case I shuld
fele by Christ. Paraduenture thou wilt say
it semeth me not, that I cā be suer of mi saluacion, because I am fre to do euell, so mai
I sinne & be dāpned. Our life is in such sort
variable, that to giue a certeine iudgement,
we must tarye the end, for euery one wolde
haue thoughte, that Iudas shuld haue bene
saued when he was called of Christ, & yet it
is sene, that it is contrarye. I answere, thou
begilest thy selfe, in thinkinge thy saluacion
dependeth vpon the likelyhod of thy workes. Paule affirmeth, that God hath elected

vs

vs by his mere mercy in Christ, not bicause
we were holp, or for that he foresawe oure
good workes, but because we should be holp, and should do good workes, and perse-
ueryng in thē, we should dye in his fauour
and grace: Inwardly doth God cal his e-
electe, geueth them knowledge of him, and   **Roma.viij.**
doth iustifie & glorifie them. Therfore doth
Paul adde and say, if God be with vs, who
cā be against vs? And he ment if we be once
electe, we can no more lose our selues: meanyng, there is nothing that can let the eleccion of God. Yea euery thing serueth to sal
uacion, euen sinne. Therfore where thou sai
ests, thou mayst sinne, it is true, and perad-
uēture thou shalt sinne. Neuertheles if thou
be the electe, thou shalt algates ryse againe
and be saued: wherof thou mayst be certein
and sure, so that once at the least thou haue
percepued thy selfe in Christ, and by Christ
saued, neither thou oughtest so much to dis-
payre in thy selfe, as that thou shuldest not
much more trust in ẙ goodnes of god, know
yng that the Gospel is not the law, but mer
cie, and know thou that when the electe fall
in any sinne (whiche God doth not permitte
but for the benefite of them, and the other e-
lecte) whilest they are in that erroure, they
fele in them selues, a certeine hydde vertue,
       C.iii.   which

whiche withholdeth and refrayneth them,
from doyng worsse, it biteth, nippeth, and re
prehedeth them of the euel fact, and doth en
duce and spurre them to conuert. There remaineth euer a certeine hate of sin, although
they be sometime ouercome of frailtye. So
that they neuer turne frō God with al their
power, nor run wholy to vice with a lose bri
dell. God hath them euer for his owne, and
gouerneth them as his lawefull Childrene.
And speaking ofte in their herts he saith that
which he said to his Apostles: feare not litle
flocke, for it hath pleased youre father, to
giue you his kingdom of his mere goodnes
although you be vnworthy. And if thou wol
dest bring in Salomō, who sayth, none knoweth whether he be worthy of hate or loue,
I answere. It is clere (chysflie by the wordes
whych folow) that he ment, that man were
he neuer so iust & wise, was so blinde in this
world, that he cannot know by the workes
of God, y is by prosperity or aduersity, whe
ther of him self, he be worthi of hate or loue.
And this is bicause God giueth his giftes so
indifferently, to the good and euell, to the e-
lecte and reprobat. Thou wilt say yet, Paul
said: my cōscience doth not reproue me yet am
I not therby iustified before God, therfore
it cannot be knowen. But I answere, that
thentē

Luke.xii.

Cor.iiii.

thentent of Paul was to saye, that thoughe
by grace of the Lorde he had ministred the
Gospel,in suche sorte, that his conscience
dyd not rebuke him of any erronre(whiche
was imputed vnto hym for a sclaunder of
false chziltians)neuer heles he held not him
selfe iulte for this, neither was he iulte, he
iudged him selfe iulte by Chzilte, and not by
preaching the Gospel irrepzehensibly in the
syght of man, but yet not in the presence of
God, for that he hath not preached it wi the
whole force of spirit, fayth, & loue. So that
here Paul did condene the opiniõ of them,
which iudge thē selues iulte by theyr owne
workes,but he doth not reproue the iudgemēt of those, which iudge thē selues righte-
ous & saued by the bountie of God, & death
of his only begotten sõne: but doth approue
it. With Paule also agreeth Job, when he   **Job.ſ.**
sayde,that although he were iulte,he durste
not iudge him selfe so, that is, he durste not
holde hym for ryghteous, by his owne proper ryghteousnes and workes, but by the
iustice of Chzilte.

Sence then that it maye and oughte to
bee knowen of vs, that wee are in the fauoure of God, and hys electe, lette vs
force vs continuallye to encrease in more
knowledge of the Goodnesse of God:

            C.iiii.   ſo

So that firmelp establpshed in the lpuelpe
fapthe of oure saluacion, we maye as
chpldzen render hpm all honoure,
laude, and glozpe : bp Jesus
Christ oure Lozde. Amen

(،ؘ) 🙰 (.·.) 🙰 (:؛:)

¶Wbhether it be good
oz euel to beleue that we are
electe : the fourthe Sermon.

Sme saye that it is
euel to beleue that we are
electe, bpcause, that as the
beliefe io be reprobate,
bzingeth men in dispepze:
so the beliefe of eleccion,
is caule of presumpcion. But the iuste and
the holp flpe bothe the oue and the other ex‑
tremitie. Thep are not exalted in presump‑
cion, beleuing to be electe; noz fallen in the
botomles ppite of dispepze, wpth beliefe of
damptiacion, but kepe the meane wape, e‑
uer standing betwene both. And J sap that
it is true, that none ought to dispepze, oz pet
to presume, but assuredlpe to hope and be‑
leue to be saued and elected; Marp bp oure
owne

owne workes, this is an euyll vyce, and
ought to be fled. But to beleue to be elected
and saued by the liberalitie of God, by the
deathe of Chrifte vpon the croffe, and hys
workes: thys is no prefumprion, but a hope
whych hath regard (as diuine & theological
bertue) not to oure merites, but onlye to
God by Chrifte. And as we cã not loue him
so muche, but that we euer lacke of the perfection, so can we not to muche hope & truft
in him. Pea we lacke euer bycaufe we do
not promife of God fo muche as we fhulde
do, he that beleueth to be fauid, becommeth
not proud, nether magnifieth him felfe, nor
his workes, but the goodnes of God, and
the grace that we haue by Chrift. Therfore
is it not euell. Peraduenture thou wylt faie
one oughte to ftande in feare. J agre therto,
in the reuerend and fonuelike feare, the whi
che importeth obferuaunce of reuerence to
God, but now not fo bile: for we ar no more Rom. viii.
feruauntes but fonnes, not Hebreues but
Chriftians, we are not vnder the lawe but
grace, we haue God for our father, and not
onlye for a Lorde. Therefore our office is Rom. vi.
to loue him like childrene, and not to feare
him, as feruauntes, fence that we haue the Rom. viii
fpirite not of feruitude but of adoption, of ye
fonnes of God. Jf our faluacion did depẽ

iu

in any parte vpon our selfes : J wolde saye
we ought to fear our dānaciō yea to be sure
therof: but sence it is al in y hādes of God,
therfore beholding not oure selues, but hys
goodnes discouered in Chrilt vpō the crolle
we may be suer and certeine of our saluari-
on. Perfect charitie chaleth away al seruile
feare, & faith neuer douteth, if it be perfect:
the feare then of our damnaciō groweth of
imperfectiō of our charitie, faith and hope.
We ought neuer to feare the mercyfulnes
of God, but our owne wyckednes. Thou
woldelt saye, if we were wholie confirmed
in grace, we shuld not nede to feare, but we
synne daylie, therfore it is necessary to stād
in doubte. J answere that yet thou goelt a-
boute, to builde my hope vpon my worckes
the whiche shuld be no hope but a presumpcion. Jf we shulde hope wyth condition if
we do well, and perseuer therin, my hope
shulde stande wyth desperacion, for of my
selfe J knowe J ought to despaire. Jf J had
the synnes of the whole worlde, yet wold J
molte stedfastly beleue to be saued without
anye feare of dampnacion, nether may this
be sayde to be euell, for that J woulde not
builde my hope but vpon Chrilte. Jf thou
woldelt saie, y feare of dampnaciō cauleth
men to abltein frō sinne, therfore it is good.

J

L. Jhe. iiii.

I aunſwere, that it cauſeth men to refrayne
in their owne loue, as doth the feat of death
wherby they become dayly more ſenſuall in
them ſelues, and therfore truely, worſe inwardly. Feare worketh wrathe in God, e-
uen as the lawe both: and although it cauſe
the abſtaine frō ſome euill outward worke,
neuertheleſſe the venime remaineth within,
the which is ſo much the worſe, as it is more
vnited to the inwarde partes, yea that feare
geuen to the vngodly, is the ſcorge of God.
The electe (knowinge that God in this preſent lyfe doth punyſhe more the legittimate
chyldre then the baſtardes) abſtaine alſo by
this feare more then the other. But truly the
loue of God , the quicke feelynge of hys
greate goodnes, to beleue firmely by Chriſt
and his grace to be the ſonnes of God, elect
and ſure in deede, are thoſe thinges whyche
mortifie hus to the worlde and to our ſelues,
and maketh ſynne diſpleaſaunt to vs , euen
frō the botome of the hert. Therfore where
the ſeruile feare maketh Ipocrites, the ſon-
lyke loue maketh true chriſtians. If y woldeſt ſai, to beleue ſo, is a thing veri perilous
becauſe y herof thei take occaſiō to liue idle,
yea to geue them ſelf to al vice, ſaiyng I wil
make my paradiſe in this world , for euerye
wai I ſhal be ſauid, ſéce y alredi I am elect.

3

I answere that whē one beleueth to be elect
and perceiueth in spirite the mercifulnes of
God in Christe, then God tasted in Christe
hath in the herte such efficacie and strength,
that he can not offende, but is forced to dyspraise the worlde, & is rapt to so highe estate
that he falleth to obliuion of the world, him
selfe and his paradise, setting only God before his eies. Therfore sayeth sainte John,
Who so hathe this faithe, sanctifieth hym
self. So as thē of chariti springeth but goodnes, euen so is it, of this faith & hope. Knowest thou where in is the parille? In beleuing
to be elected, by theire workes, and by beleuinge in Christ not stedfastlye, but to haue
only a certaine barraine, idle and a dead o-
pinion therof, the which stādeth in ye worste
life, in suche sorte that of that colde and vn-
frutefull faythe, they may take occasion to
geue thē to Idelnes, and all vyce. But now
not of that perfecte faith, the which is effectuous in doinge workes by loue, beinge an
enflamed lyghte, the whiche is neuer withoute burninge. If also thou wouldest say in
beleuinge to be electe thou shouldest perad-
aduenture be begiled, therfore it is euell. I
wold yet answere, that I wolde soner geue
faithe to the holy gost, whiche testifieth in ye
hartes of the electe, that thei are the sonnes
of

Joh. 1ʒ.

Gala. ꝺ

The fourth Sermon.

of God (as Paule wꝛiteth)then to the that woldeſt put me in doubt of it . The electe to heare inwardlye in their hertes a ſpirituall boyce , quicke and deuine , whiche biddeth them not doubte, and that they are ſuer of theire ſaluacion , & that God loueth them, and hathe taken them foꝛ his childꝛen, and that thei can not periſhe:the teſtimonie of God is greater the mans.

Rom.viij

Jhon.x.

Therfoꝛe not onlie he is to be beleued afoꝛe man , but he deſerueth to haue giuen vnto him vndoubted credite. Jf thou woldeſt ſai, it might be ,not the ſpirite of God but their imaginacions . J ſaye , that what ſo euer it is they knowe better then thou ,foꝛ that (as Paule ſaithe) none knoweth what is in ma but the ſpirite of man,that is within hym.

i.Coꝛ.ij.

ffarder J am ſuer,that the ſame ſpirit whiche ſaith to me, J am elected is the ſpirite of God bicauſe the faithe J haue of my electi-on,ſpꝛingeth not of my woꝛckes , but onlye of the goodnes of god,vnderſtand in Chꝛiſt and foꝛ that of his goodnes can growe ne-ther gyle noꝛ falſhod ,therfoꝛe am J ſuer to be in the trueth.Deceites & falſhedes ,mai, & do come,of the belefe to be ſaued,by woꝛ-kes, and elected:Moꝛeouer the lyght whi-che the electe haue of their ſaluacion , is ſo cleare,that they do not onlye ſe them ſelfes sure

The fourth Sermon.

suere therof, but they knowe also, that the lyghte and knowledge they haue, is supernaturall & diuine. But we suppose as thou sayst, that in beleuinge to be electe onlye by Christe and the goodnes of God, I myghte be begiled (whiche is false and impossible) yet wolde I still saye, let me be deceiued for it is good to be so begiled, sence I can finde no thinge, that so much doth kindel me into a sincere and pure loue of God, as to beleue to be elected bi his mere goodnes. Therfore vsinge it to make me inamored of God, I oughte not to be withdrawen, chifelie for y I am happpe, onlie bi that faythe, of y whiche whosoeuer is voide, is not yet entred in to the kingdome of God, where is nothinge but ryghtuousnes peace and Ioie.

Finalli Paule beleued to be elected as in many places he saythe, yea he gloried therin (neuertheleffe in God) and so to beleue he induced others, the which, if it had bene euel, he wolde not haue done. Therfore if it be not euel, let vs also with Paule, glori vs by God in Christe, who likewyse induced the Apostles, to beleue y theyr names were write in heauen, that theyr heauenli reward was plentuous, & that they shulde iudge the xii. tribes, & therby brought them to beleue thei were electe, and that is also suer, that if

that

The fourth Sermon.

that belefe had bene euell, he wold not haue
caused it. Thou wilt saie, thou oughtest not
to compare thy selfe, equall wyth the sainctes, I saie it is true that I oughte not to presume to be like them, or help by myne owne
worckes, for while I presume of my selfe, I
muste of force become a deuell, but it is not
euell to compare with the saintes in veritie,
for they were humble, and in beleuing that
they were elect, they gaue to God all laude
and glorye but ause they did not beleue to be
of the electe for their merites, but for Christes. And wold to God, I mighte beleue y
firmelye and with stedfast fayth, the sacred
scriptures are ful, that we ought not to des-
peire of our saluacion, but that we oughtto
hope and beleue to be all readye saued, and
dayly to certifie oure selues therof bi doing
good worckes, which are a testimonie to vs   l. Pet.i.
of oure election, and that we shulde also in-   i. John.iiii.
crease in charitye, to take from vs all feare
of oure dampnació tó the end we may serue
God without feare, in rightuousnes and ho
linesse as Zacharie sayde. And likewise wee   Luke.i.
ought to demaund perseueraunce in the good
w faith to obtein it. Therfore to trust to be
saued, y of the elected y to hope y beleue to
be saued y of the electe, is not euel. Paul also saithe: oure hope was neuer confoundeb
nor dyd shame to them that had it.

The fyfte Sermon.

And lykewyse that fayth, was neuer beguiled. Wherfore then is it euyll that I beleue
stedfastly to be saued by Christ? Let vs beholde then wyth open eyes of liuely fayth,
Christe vpon the crosse, in whome we se
presentlye the goodnes of God in the
face in suche sorte, as we maye beyng pilgrimes, to thende wee
may render to him al laud,
honor & glory through
Jesus Christe oure
Lorde. Amen

¶ Whether it be necessa-rye to saluacion to beleue that we are elected or not: the fyst Sermon

ped. xx.
Mar. xvi
Iohn. iii.

FAyth is very necessarye, because that withoute it, not onlye God cã not bee pleased, but he that beleueth not shall be condempned, and is already iudged. But it is also impossible, that one that doth not beleue to be elected should beleue as he ought to do any of the articles necessa

nceſſarie to ſaluaciõ. And to proue þ this is
true, if þ beleueſt not þ thou art one of the e-
lect, thou beleueſt not in God, in the maner
that thou arte bounde; bicauſe that it ſuffiſeth not to haue a certeine dead opinion that
God is, but thou muſte effectuouſly beleue
that he is thy God, þ he loueth the, that he
is propiciatory to the, þ he is cõtinually beneficial to the, that he hath moſt ſpecial cure
of the & cauſeth euery thinge to ſerue the to
ſaluacion, & therfore that þ arte electe. Yea
who ſo beleueth not that he is electe, doeth
not fele in ſpirite, the benefite of Chriſte.
Therfore beinge without Chriſt, he is withoute God, and knoweth him not as Paule
wryteth. Then howe is it poſſible that thou
mayſte beleue perfectli that he is thy father
ſf thou do not beleue that thou arte his ſon,
and therfore his heire & ſaued. Thou canſt
alſo neuer earneſtlie beleue that God is omnipotente, if thou vnderſtande not, that continually he vſeth his omnipotecie towards
the, in doinge the good. Whiche when with
the ſpirite thou dideſt proue, thou ſhuldeſt
of force beleue thy ſelfe to bee his heyre, if
thou beleue not thou arte elect, howe canſte
thou beleue that God hathe created the
heauens, and the earthe, & that he ſuſteineth
& gouerneth all to thy behofe hauing of the

Ephe.i.
Gala.iiii.

Gala.iiii.

D.i.   moſt

moste singuler cure:it is nedefull,that with
liuely fayth,imbrasinge al the worlb for thy
owne , thou perceiue effectuallye the goodnes of God , in euerye creature.And when
that is,thou shalt be inforced to beleue ,that
thou arte the sonne of God . Thou canste
not also beleue in Jesu , that is that he is to
the Jesus and sauioure , if thou beleue not
that thou arte saued , nether canste thou beleue that he is thy Christe , that is to saye a
Prophete kinge and prieste ,if thou fele not
in spirite,that he doth illuminate and ligh-
ten the,as a prophet;rule the as a king,and
as an onlye prieste is offered for the vpon ye
crosse.The which if thou didest beleue thou
shuldest also beleue to be elected.How shalt
thou beleue that Jesus is the only begotten
sonne of God,thi Lord come into the world
to saue the,and geuen to the,with al his deuine treasures and graces , if thou dost not
beleue,thy selfe to be one of his lambes , ye
canste not beleue (as thou arte bounde to
do)that he died for the,nor perceine his ex-
cessiue charitie, so that with Paule ye maist
Rom. viii. saye,nothing can seperate me from the charitie of God. It is necessarye to beleue,that
Christ vpon the crosse hath satisfied for thy
sinnes , and that he hath reconciled the ,sa-
tiffied to his father and saued the,and therfore

fore that þ art the ſone of God: he that bele=
neth (as he ought) þ Chriſt is ryſe to iuſtifie
vs, doth alſo know him ſelfe ſaued, ꝓ ſo he þ
perfectly doth vnderſtand that Chriſte our
head is aſceded into heaue ꝓ entred for vs in
poſſeſſiõ of paradiſe, perceiueth him ſelf ri= **Philli.iii**
ſen with Chriſt, ꝓ alredy bi hope being aſcen
ded into heaue, practiſeth with þ minde in   **Ephe.ii.**
paradiſe, where Chriſt is ſitting iu peacea=
ble poſſeſſiõ of thinges celeſtial: he ſaieth to
Paul, we are made ſafe by hope, it ſuffiſeth   **Rom.viii**
not to beſeue þ he ſhal iudge the quicke ꝓ the
dead þ which alſo the deuils beleue, but that
the ſetence ſhalbe al in thi fauour, hauing to
thi iudge, him þ died vpõ the croſſe for thee.
We cã not liuely beleue the ſeding of þ holy
ghoſte, if we fele it not in oure ſelues: and if
we do feale it, we ſhalbe forced with Paule
to ſaye, the ſpirite of God rendreth teſti=
mony to oure ſpirite that we are the ſonnes
of God, therfore heires and ſaued. Nepther   **Roma.viii**
is it inoughe that there is a church of God,
but thou muſte beleue to be a porcion ther=
of, ꝓ one of the lyuely ſtones, ꝓ therfore one
of the electe. And to beleue the cõmunion of
ſainctes, thou muſt feele, that as a meber of
Chriſt, he doth perticipate his grace to the,
and þ thou art therby ſaued, þ muſt alſo be=
true þ remiſſiõ of ſinnes, þ is not only that

he dothe pardon sinnes , but that he hathe
pardoned the thine, and so elected the. Euen
so thou must beleue, that thou shalt rise glo=
rious, and haue life euerlasting . Then ther
is no article of our faith, that can be beleued
in suche sorte as it ought to be , of those whi=
che do not beleue they are elected . To the
Christian it is then necessary to beleue that
God is his God , and father: that he worc=
keth all for his benefite , and that Chryste is
come, was borne , hath liued, died and risen
againe for his saluacion , so that with liuely
faith he imbraceth Christ wholi for his own
with al his treasur and grace. And likewise
al his life, death, resurrection, assention and
glorye, and perceiueth the charitie of God
in Christe, as if there hadde bene no mo but
onlye him selfe in the world, and that Christ
for him onlye, wold haue wrought and suffered, no les then he hath done. The which
when thou dost beleue , thou shalt perceiue
thou arte elect . Yea he that beleueth not he
is electe, can not praye as he oughte, beinge
withoute faithe, withoute the whiche (after
Paul) we can not effecteously recommende
vs to god, bicause y we must aske in faith, if
we wil aske in veriti & be hard, now if y beleue not to be his sone & heire, how cast y (as
Christ taughte) say our father, & as a sonne
                                            wil

Roma.r.
Jaco.i.

with cōfidence aske him grace. Praier may
wel be made, of infidels and Ipocrites, but
lyke folishe scoffers and mockers. When ye
saiest, halowed be thy name, thy kingdome
come, thou must haue in the, the spirit of adoption of the sonne of God. And as the sōne
is moued of vehemente loue, pure and sincere, to desire the kingdome and glory of the
father: so must thou (seinge the, the sonne of
God) with a deuine spirite, by the force of
loue, aske and desyre that thy heauenlie father be honored, and reigne in his elect with
oute rebellion. Likewyse shalte thou neuer
thancke God with all thy herte, if thou beleue not to be one of ye elect: yea if thou shalt
doubte therin, or thinke to be dampned in
thy harte, and in thy lyfe, and paraduenture
also with thy wordes, thou wilte dispraise
him, that he hath giuen the a beinge, that he
hath create the world, sente Chryste, and so
the rest his benefites, and wilt saie. If I am
not saued, what do these thinges profit me?
it had ben better for me, ye I had neuer ben,
as Christ said of Judas. If I shalbe damp- **Mar. xiiij**
ned, the death of Christ serueth me not, but
doth inflame & burne, w al ye rest of his benefites: ye canst not in perfection the thācke
god, if ye feare dampnaciō. But who so bele- **Rom. viij**
ueth he is one of ye elect & therby ye al things
          D.iii.   serue

ſerue him to ſaluacion, euen the verpe trou-
bles, he holdeth for a ſpeciall grace and benefite, in them perceiuinge the goodnes of
God, he giueth him thanckes with all his
herte. Who ſhal he be that committeth him
ſelfe holp to the gouernaunce of God (as e-
uerp one oughte to do) if he beleue not that
God is his father, that he pardoneth him, ₹
doth take of him moſt ſinguler cure? Other
wiſe they ſhal neuer truſt in God, but with
Adam ſhall feare him, and flpe, ſekinge to
hide him ſelfe from the face of God, nether
is it poſſible, to loue God in veritie, honor
him as he ought to be honorð and approue
for iuſte and hollpe all his worckes, and ſo
delite wholpe in him, if he fele not in Chriſte

Gala.iiii.

ſo much the goodnes of God, that he ſe him
ſelfe hps ſonne ₹ alſo heire. If he know not
him ſelfe to be a ſonne, he ſhal feare as a ſeruaunt, and in all his worckes haue reſpecte
to him ſelfe, his paines, diſpleaſures, incom
modites, diſhonoures, and hel, or els to this
paradice, and nut to the glorpe of God. As
he that ſeeth him ſelfe a ſoune, lord of al and
heire and ſuer therof: ſuch a one worketh on
lp bp ſtrength of ſpiirt, ₹ vehemēcie of loue
to the glorp of God, to whome he hath turned his whole intent, ₹ to that ende ordreth
his whole lpfe. Alſo it can not be poſſible, to
                                          loue

loue thy neighbour as thi selfe, as a brother
in Chrilt, and member to the of ꝑ same bodie,
if thou do not beleue to be in the nomber of
the sonnes of God. And finalli ther can not
one good worcke be done, but of them that
are regenerate, sonnes of God, members
of Chrille, and haue in them the holy spirite
which teltifieth in their hertes, that they be
the sonnes of God. And mai parteli be sene
howe false and vngodlye, is the doctrine of
the antechriltians, that where as it is cheif-
lye necessarie to beleue that we are elected,
& also aboue all thinges molt commodious
thei force the selues to withdraw euery one
frō this fayth, perswading them to stand in
doubte, as thoughe they had wherin to mi-
strulte the goodnes of God, vpon whome
onlie depeudeth oure saluation, as our damnacion doth of our selues. But let vs praye

Ơ Cor. iiil.

to God to open our eyes, to the ende
.they maye no longer blaspheme,
but render to God all honor,
laude, and glorie, by Je-
su Chrilte our Lorde.
☞ Amen. ☜
☞ (∴) ☜
D.iiii.

¶ If it be good to seeke
to know wherfore God hath some
electe and some reprobate: the spxt
Sermon.

Hy desyre maye be wycked, as it is in many, to whõ it apeareth that it should haue ben better, if God (who being of power as he is) had elected all men, and semeth thẽ, that in this God hath lacked of charitie, yea in theyr language, they say in their herrte secretly. If we had bene God, we would haue elected all, and would haue had more charitie thẽ he. Now behold, whether this be vngodly, folyshe, proude blasphemy, or not. They Imagine to haue more loue to the soules, then he, that for to saue them gaue his onely begotten and dearly beloued sonne vpon the crosse. There are some other, to whom it semeth on the one syde, that god can not erre: and on the other parti, hearinge that he hath reproued many, they thinke the cõtrary. They are not certeine by fayth, that God can not erre, and that al that he willeth, must nedes be iuste. Therfore to make it clere, they go
searching

John. III.

searchyng, wherfore he hath not electeb all
men, and they would fynd a cause where is
none. If such were godly, they shuld quiete
and satiffie the selues, & shuld haue their felicitie in the deuine pleasure, without searching
to asked any hyer. It is euyl then to seke wher
fore god hath elected some, & other some not
if this grow of the suspicion that God may,
or haue erred. The godly knoweth certeinly
by faith y he can not erre, & hereupon resteth.
There are some that aske after it of arroga-
cie and presumpcion.   They woulde be answered, that god had elected them for they
good workes, to haue wherein they myght
glory of them selues. And when they heardsay
that God hath elected them by grace, it displeaseth them, they gainsaie it, seming them
there resteth nothinge to glory in. And they
perceiue not that thys is the whole glory of
the humble and true christiane , to be saued
by the mere grace of God, and Christ cruci
fied, and to glorie only in God by Christe,
and in them selues not to ie , but thynges
worthy to be ashamed of, to thend y to God
only be honour and glory. It groweth also
to many of vnreuerence , for if they coulde
se howe inaccessible the maieftie of God is,
howe irreprehensible is his wyll, and howe
incomprehensible is his wisedome, they wold

i. Timo. iii

not

Roma. ŧ.

not set them selues to dispute with God, spe
cially if they knewe howe blynd, darke, frã
ticke and folyshe they be. And who art thou
sayd Paul, that wilt dispute with God, answer and contend with God? Paul was re
turned from the thyrd heauen, where he had
heard secrets, so hygh that it was not lawfull to speake to man. Neuerthelesse doynge
reuerence to the diuine secret indgementes
he sayd: O profound riches of the wisedome
and science of God, how incõprehẽsible are
his iudgementes? And man, blynd, folyshe,
and vngodly, is so high minded, that he wil
do wronge to God, condẽpning him, and re
proue his holy, iust, & irreprehensible indgementes. And how many are thei that seke to
knowe, speake & wryte of it, and be commẽ-
ded therfore? And al that they can Imagine
by force of their owne wytte, and naturall
knowledge (which can not perce so hygh secretes) they put in writyng. And they are as
arrogant, as if they were in goodnes and sa
pience superior to God: to be adored of the
worlde, they condemne the workes of God.
Ther are mani which are not cõtẽt to know
asmuch as God hath vouchsaued to opẽ to
vs, but they wold knowe also a great deale
more. But it is not the office of a good seruaunt, to wyl to know al the secretes of his
Lorde: yea the sonne ought to contente hym

with the fecretes of his father, and to knowe
of it only, as much as is reueled to him and
to be fuer and certeine, that he wil not faile,
to manifeſt al that ſhal be expediēt for him,
euen ſo we ougʒt to contente vs, to knowe
that which God hath, and dothe reuele vs,
knowing that he doth loue vs in ſuch ſorte,
that we haue not wherin to doubte, that he
wyll faple to manifeſt vnto vs, all thoſe ſecretes, the knowledge wherof ſhalbe profi-
table and neceſſari. Yea chriſt him ſelfe ſaid **Jhon.xv.**
that he had made knowne all that he hadde
heard of the father. oure office is to ſeke, to
taſte and fele with the ſpirite, that which he
hth opened to vs, and we map alſo deſire
to know all that pleaſeth God to reuele vs,
for the benefite of oure ſoule, and his glory,
nowe for that God (to beate downe carnall
man, to the ende that to him, be geuen al honoure, laude and glorye) hath vouchefated,
to open in the holy ſcriptures, wherfore he
hath elected ſome, & other ſome he hath not:
Therfore we mai & ought to ſeke to know it
that we map ſo much ȳ more honour God:
but we ought to beleue it to be ſo, as God
hath declared, & to cōtent vs with that way,
God hath taken, in electing & reprobating,
neither to thinke nor ſuſpect, that God hath
erred, nor ought to deſpre any other wape,
                                        but

but to be satisfied and pleased, with so much
as pleaseth the Lorde, without beinge curi-
ous, in wyllynge to knowe more, then
that which pleaseth God to reuele
vnto vs, and all that to thende
that by Jesus Christe we
may render him al ho
nor, laude, & glo-
rie. Amen.

(∴)

¶ Of the diuerse effectes
that it worketh in man to beleue
that our eleccion is al in the handes of
God, and that of him only it depē
deth : the seuenth Sermon.

 T is scene by expe-
rience, that of one selfe
cause, doth growe some
times contrary effectes.
And is euidēt bi the sun,
whiche hardeneth mire,
and melteth waxe : and this is by theyr diuerse disposicions. Euen so of the belief that
our elecciō is wholy in the handes of God,
dothe springe in men contrary effectes, by
theyr contrary disposicions. The vngodlye
perceiuing

perceiuing that in the deuine minde is resol
ued theire beinge, to be saued or damnned,
they are wroth to God, thei blaspheme him
with their hearte, they cal him parciall and
bniulte, they giue them selues to do euell I
noughe . sayinge euerye wape : that shalbe
which God hath infallible foresene, & im-
mutabli determined, yea their faltes thei cast
in the face of god, thinking y he is the cause
therof, many also despaire of their saluacion & presume more of them selues, then they
hope in God, they beleue that they shuld be
saued , if their saluacion dyd depende vpon
them selues, & therfore if thei could disturbe
the deuine counsaples , and make that 'their
saluacion shuld not be in the handes of god,
they wolde do it. And this is for that they
knowe not their owne greate mysery howe
blynd, infirme, frail, and vnprofitable, thei
are to God impotēt of them selues to good
nes, and full of all wickednes, and that thei
dyd neuer worke (if it were put in the balāce
of deuine iustice) that merited not to be punished, and so likewise they fele not y great
goodnes of God, nor the benefits of Christ
but thincke him to be Irefull, reuengable,
disdaineful, proude, parpetuall, vniust and
malignaunt, as them selfes are. There are
some whiche haue not perfecte fayth, but
　　　　　　　　　　　　　　　　　　thei

they are not so vngodly as the fyrste. Nowe
these when they heare say, oz thincke ẏ their
saluacion is all in the handes of God, they
remaine confused and euell contented. And
this is also foz wante of knowledge of the
goodnes of God, they truste partly in God
and partly in thē selues, they loue not God,
noz truste noz hope perfectly in him they remaine doubtfull, and knowe not whether it
be best to depend all vpon God oz not, ant
it semeth them that it shulde haue bene beste
that in some parte it shuld depend vpō them
selues : ꝭ yet thei thincke it wel beinge al in
the handes of God, troubled in suche sozte,
that thei cā not tel which to chuse: Therfoze
they liue in a great perplexiti. They consult
some times with the holpe scripture oz with
thē that haue, the knowledge of the truth, ꝭ
they find that it is al in the handes of God,
ꝭ they iudge (whē their eies are somewhat
opened to the goodnes of God ꝭ their own
miseries) that it stādeth wel, and that so it is
beste, but then harkeninge to humane pzu-
dence, the whiche not beinge wholpe moz-
tified, wolde haue parte of the glozye to it
selfe (so pzoude it is.) And as that, that is
blynd, and seeth not the impotencie and ma
lignitie of man, it perswadeth him that mā
might in som part be saued bi him self, wher
els

elles he mai despaire, if it stand al in ꝑ hand
of God. Therfore it cōcludeth, that it were
better if it dyd depend vpon vs, and chieflye
for that men become negligent, in thinkinge
that it depēdeth wholi vpō God: where thei
wold stpꝛre them selues to be feruēt, if they
dyd beleue that in any parte it rested in thē.
And although such finde the contrary in the
sacred scriptures, neuertheles they force thē
with the obscure lighte of their blynde pꝛu-
dēce, to draw it out of the texte, expounding
it as may beste serue to their purpose. But ꝑ
godly perceiue on the one side, iu such sorte
their owne proper ignorance, frailtie, impo
tencie, & malice: And on the other partie the
great bōūtie of god in Chꝛist crucified, that
it cōtenteth them to be so, all in the haude of
God. not only for ꝑ it hath so pleased god,
but also for their owne cōmoditie: becaufe
that whereas if in the leaste iote it depēded
vpon them, they should holde thē selues dā-
ned. Now they fele so muche the excellencie
of god, that certified of their saluacion, thei
knowe thē selues elected, & hold it to be sure
sꝑyng vp faith that it is al in the hāde of one
their so mightie, sapient, excellēt & louing fa
ther. Wherfore by this benefite, thei are sti-
red to loue hiin singulerly, to thāke, laude,
and serue hym as childrē for his mere glory
with-

wpthout respecte at all to them selues, theit
hel or heaue. And if God would set in their
handes, although he would be bounde that
they should be able to do al thinges to ease
toward thepr saluacion, yet they wold not
accept the bargaine; and that is because thei
knowe that they are contrary enemies and
traytours to them selues; so that if they had
paradise iu thepr handes, then they should
let it fal to the ground. And also for that, thei
do make experiment and proue so great cha
ritie of God in Christ, that it certifieth them
of thepr eleccion. They can not thinke that
Christe bepng thepr iudge, and dipng vpon
the crosse for them, should geue sentence a
gapnst them: yea they know, that who so be

Ioh.iii.
leueth in hpm shall not be iudged. but shall
be so certeine of his saluacion, that he shall
not nede to make discussion of his lyfe, for
there shal not be any to accuse hpm, neither
should it be conuenet that those which haue
the spirit of God, and are his sonnes, the
brethern and members of Christ, should be

Iohn.viii.
examined and iudged. But with Christ thei
shal be iudges of the other. Therfore the e
lect, sure of their saluacio, wold not chafige
Christ thepr iudge wpth any in thps world,

Math.xij.
although it were thepr deare frynde or nere
parent. Yea if God did put in thepr arbitre-
ment

ment to haue Chꝛiste. foꝛ theire iudge oꝛ els
to be their owne iudges of the selues, with
full power to geue sentence in their fauour
althoughe it were not iuste, yet to be appꝛo
ued, they wold foꝛ all this, chuse Chꝛiste to
be theyre iudge, foꝛ that they truste moꝛe in
him then in them selues. Also thei loue God
so much, that they wold not gloꝛy, but only
in him by Chꝛiste. And this is al there true
gloꝛye. Yea if they colde let oꝛ disturbe the
deuine counsaple, oꝛ if it were necessarye to
be dampned they wold chuse, rather to be
in paine foꝛ the will of God, then in all the
pleasures. disagreingr to the deuine wyl (if
it were possible) they counte them selues vn
woꝛthy to suffer foꝛ the wyll of God. They
holde them selues happye to honoure him
with sufferinge, and wyth beinge where it
pleaseth to their loꝛd, they lamente onlye of
the iniuries they haue done to God, but of
that whiche God wyll do of them with the
spirite, they are contente, although the flesh
be repugnaunte and wold not suffer. This
shuld be a hel to them, when God (if it were
possible) wold not dispose them to his gloꝛi
but to vse them to his honoure they wolde
satisfy them selues with all, and content the̅
to know it so to be the deuine pleasure: now
these are in a continuall paradise by faithe

F.i.   as

allreadye they haue had the sentence geuen
in their fauour, by hope they are ascended
into heaue, sayinge with Paul: we are made
safe by hope, and by loue they enioye God.

tom.viii

In the then of the belief, that their electiō is
all in the handes of God, groweth firme
fayth, and hope to be saued, the loue of God
sincere and pure, and chrystiane vertues, tō
the frutes of good worckes. I wolde haue
pitie on the firste sorte, but their desperaciō
groweth of an vngodlye minde, yea it is
moste impietie, to despayre of the goodnes
of God, moste perfect, shewed in Chryste
crucified, as in one his liueli Image. I haue
compassion of the second, and enuye at the
thirde. The seconde maye easelye be cured
with shewinge them theire frailtie, igno-
rauncie, and malice, and on the other partie
the omnipotencie, infinite sapience, perfecte
goodnes, pitie, mercy and chariti of God,
shewed in Christe vpon the crosse. Of the
firste, I do not despaire vtterli, but I knowe

Math iii

well it is verie difficile to cure thē, but God
is of power, of the stones to rayse vp chil-
dern to Abrahā, they haue nede to be prayed
for, and that the Lorde take frō before their
eies, suche veiles of ignorauncye, & make
them see their owne great miseries, and the
incomprehensible goodnes of God, to the
ende

ende that reknowledging al their wealth to
come of God, they maye render him al honor, laude, and glorie, by Jesu Christe oure
Lorde. Amen.

Howe it ought to be an
swered to the ꝑ lamente that God
hath created them foreseyng theyr
dampnacio: the eight Sermō.

Here are manye, the
which althoughe of God
thei haue had their being,
& manye other benefites,
neuertheleſſe they thanke
him not, but are vngrate-
full. They are ſorye, and lament of all the
wealth they haue had of him, ſaying : Lord,
if the being where thou haſt geuen vs, with
the reſt of thy gyftes, dyd ſerue vs to ſalua-
ciō, we ſhuld thāke thē therfore: But bicauſe
they ſerue vs not, but to dāpnacion, therfore
we cā not but cōplaine vs of the. Nowe to
theſe ought to be anſwered thus: Either pou
beleue to be of the electe or not . If they ſaye
pea: it ought to be ſayd to thē, ye ſhuld thāke
God of ſo much grace, that he hath ſhewed
to pou alreadp, in choſinge pou frō ſo baſe a
being, to ſo high an eſtate, & pou lamēt pour
ſelues: beholo if pour ingratitude be greate.

L.ii.   And

And if they wolde saye we are not sorye for
oure selues,for we beleue to be elect,but for
compassió on those poore ones ƴ reprobate.
Then J wold to be sayed , it is no true pitie
to haue compassion vpon them,that are vngodlye,againste the deuine goodnes, shewed cheifly in Christe crucified. Thincke you
happelye ,to haue more charitye then God?
take heede that poure demaunoe, wherfore
God hath create the reprobate,grow not of
the doubte ,that God can do them ani iniu-
stice.Do pe feare ƴ God,being verye righ-
tiousnes,pea charitie it selfe,can do thẽ ani
wrong? But if you liueli and verilie did beleue to be electe by Christe,by mere grace ƴ
mercye of God,ye shulde feale in suche sort
the deuine goodnes , that there cold not enter into poure minde so vngodlie conceptes.
They are in good custodie,beinge in the hã-
des of God . They are in the power of one
which neuer did,n or mai do,one of ƴ leaste
cruelties,pea he neuer doth iustice,but it is
with great mercie. Will ye knowe more of
the deuine secretes then Paule ?which rapt
to the thirde heauen,heard thinges so highe
and so secrete , that to man it is not lawfull
to be spokẽ of? It suffised him onlie to know
Chrift crucified. Js it not thincke pe inough
to pou to knowe Chrift crucified , in whom
are

The.i.

Cor.i.

Cor.i.

are hidden all the treasures of the wisdome
and science of God. And if that suffice you,
in Christe is sene non but the electe, the re-
reprobate are withoute Christe, & in Christe
only ought we to contemplate and beholde
our election, your office shuld be to attende
to your selues, to encrease dailye bi Christe,
in greater knowledge of the bounti of God,
and to make certeine to ye worlo with good
worckes, youre vocation and election, and
not to be so curiousse of other, forgettinge
your selues. And if thei wold saie, we doubt
and feare also leaste we be reprobate, & ther
fore we complaine vs, and wold know whi
he hath created vs, forseing our dampnacion: nowe these muste be exhorted not to despaire, but to contemplate & loke in Christe,
in whome they shall se them selues elected.
And so thei shal not haue wherof to take occasion to lament, after it must be sayd to the
for as muche as ye do not beleue yerelyet
be of the electe, it is a signe, that ye haue not
liuely lyghte of Christ, nor of his greate benefite, & not knowinge Christe, it behoueth
to saye with Paule that ye know not God
in veritie, and that ye are without him. And
howe is it possible the, that you beyng with
out God, and without the true knowledge
of him, shulde vnderstande and knowe hys

i. Timo. iiii.

ii. Pet. i.

Gala. iiii.
Ephe. ii.

E.iii.　　highe

high secretes. It is not possible to know soner the deuine iudgements then God. Ye be
therfore without faith, and I proue that it
is true, because that if ye had faith, ye shuld
se so clerelye that God doth eueri thing wel
and can not erre, that you wold aske non o-
ther reason. And for that who so is without
faith, is franticke concerninge the deuine
thinges, it must nedes be saide that you are
euen so, and now is it a fransi, your demaũ
ding a reason of the creacion of the reprobate, neither shulde it be possible to satisfie
you, till suche time your reason were healed
bi faithe. Yea while that ye are so withoute
lighte supernaturall, beinge therof not able
to conceiue, he that shuld serch to quiet you
with resones, shulde also enter into a fransi
with you. Humble then your selues to God
and aske him faith and not resones, because
that thinges supernaturall, can not be sene
but by faith. Insatiable is the golfe of folish
and frantike curiositi, the godlye adore the
high & incõprehensible iudgemẽtes of God
and with humilitie, thei are contente to tast
in them bi faithe, some drop, of the deuine
sapience & goodnes: where the vngodly pre
suming without faieth, haue a wil to perce,
to the inaccessible counsaile of God, and remaining in darckenes, become madde and
folyshe: ye perceiue not that ye want ȳ true

cōceiuyng of God. If ye thinke ÿ God may
erre, oʒ do any thing vniuſtly: you wyl perhappes adde light to that perfect light, rule
the diuine ſapiéce, coʒrect that infinite good
nes, iudge that inōgeles iuſtice, ꝗ ondēpne
that ſupʒeme mercy ꝗ charitie. If thou didſt
ſe the hyghnes ꝗ magnificēce of God, ꝗ on
the other ſyde, the baſenes ꝗ vanitie of man,
and how in al thinges he depēdeth vpō him
ye ſhuld ſe ÿ he neuer puniſhed thē ía ſuche
ſoʒte, that they deſerue not to haue a greater
punyſhemēt, being ſo franticke ꝗ pʒoud, ye
are not capeable noʒ woʒthy to haue ſyghte
of the hygh iudgemēt of God, yea you deſerue to remayne ſo cōfuſed. And foʒ that, it
is the iuſt iudgemēt of God, that foʒ the ear-
neſt peine of your hel, ye ſhuld go euer with
your troubleſome thoughtes, cōpaſſinge by
ſuch darke ꝗ inextricable mates. Therfoʒe
although I could geue you a reaſō of al the
woʒkes of God, I wold not do it. Humble
you thē to God, ꝗ aſke him fayth, foʒ with ÿ
only ladder, we aſcēd to ÿ intelligēce of the
ſecretes of God. And thē whē ye ſhall haue
faith, ſeinge ſo clere ꝗ ſupernatural light, ÿ
god doth all thinges well, ye ſhall nomoʒe
care foʒ a further reaſō. And if alſo ÿ ſhuldeſt ſeke it, it ſhuld be with a godly mynd to
be ſo muche the moʒe able the better to beholde God, in his iuſt ꝗ holy iudgementes.

And then I wold saie to you, y̆ God might haue saued al, but he hath not willed it, yea forseing the dampnacion of the vngodly, he created them, not for to saue them, or to the end thei shuld be saued, but to serue him self of thē, so much y̆ more to be shewed brighte and glorious, to the world. The which is a more beutyful, more riche, more happy, and more wonderfull ordinaunce, then if synne had neuer bē in y̆ world. And this is bicause Christe and his electe (of synne) haue taken occasion, to honoure God more then if the world had euerben innocent, and God with greateste sapience, dyd reduce all the disordres, into a more meruelous order, then if the world had neuer ben disordred by synne. If synne had not bene, the saintes had neuer bene persecuted, inprisoned, and slayne, no more Christe crucified. Where then shulde haue bene their victorye, their Palme, triumphes and crownes? And if the reprobate wold say: we are forced to confesse y̆ God hath done well to permit the sinnes of the electe, that after as the prodigall sonne, of his erruur & miseries, toke occasion to open his eies & know him self, yea, & to returne to his father, to humble him selfe to repēt with hart, & axe him pardō and therbi to taste the fatyerly charitie, when he pardoned him, in

more

moze perfecte maner, then he had done be¬
foze: so the electe, of theire sinnes take occa¬
sion the better to know them selues, and the
bountie of God, and it is no small benefite
of God, that he suffer him selfe to be woun¬
ded of his children, and beare with it, to the
end that some daye, opening theire eies, thei
may se their greate ingratitude, and the ex¬
cessiue loue that he beareth them. God also
of these, may be afterwarde suerlye serued,
at euerye noble and great enterpryse, as of
them that are altogether his, not onlp for y
he hath created and preserued thē, but much
moze because that by sinne being loste, with
the bloud of his only begottē sonne, he hath
recouered them. And so was Christe serued
of Paul, & of his other mighti chāpions, we
muste of force confesse also, that God doeth
well to permitte the sinnes of the reprobate
to exercise the elect in vertues, for the grea¬
ter triumphe of Christe and his glorie. But
it semeth that it shulde haue bene better, y
after that God had serued his tourne with
them, he shoulde touche theire herte, and
geue them his knowledge, and his grace, so
that they also of theire sinnes should take
occasion, to reknowledge theire vice, and
the goodnes of God, so that they might be
saued, to them ye ought to say: sence ye con¬
fesse

fesse, that God hath done well, to permitte
the sinnes of the reprobate, ye can not deny,
but that for thē thei deserue to be dampned.
Ye are also forced to sai, that god dampneth
them iustli, sence that thei haue sinned: God
then doth wel to permitte them to sigue, and
when they haue sinned, he may iustli damne
thē because that boluntarilie thei did sinne,
and the falte was theires and not Goddes.
Ye can not then complaine you of God, if
he dampne you, but are constrained to saie
he doeth well. And if they saie it is true, but
yet it shulde seme vs to be better, and with
his greater glorye, if after he were serued of
thē, he wold saue them. To these J answere
firste that is beste, whiche pleaseth God, +
because it pleaseth him to dampne thē, therfore that is beste. Then if God in the end of
the life, shuld geue light to all, And so at last
euery one shuld conuerte, thei wold do ma-
nie more enormions sinnes thē they do. ffor
the bngodlye wolde saye, we maye do eueri
euell, let vs take oure pleasure and liue frelie, without any feare, for euery waye in the
end we shalbe saued. And for that one onlye
sinne is worse thē al the peines of the dampned, therfore it is beste, that they be dampned. Theire dampnation serueth also to the
electe, in as much as that seruaunte whiche
wheu

when he seeth iustice done to his felowe seruaunte that before woulde haue strangled hym, knoweth the goodnes of his Lorde, and the malignitie of the man: so the electe, by seyng in the dampned the iustice of god, do come to more knowledge of his mercye and iustice, and also of theyr owne miserie. God is serued then of the reprobate, to illustrate and setforth his glory, and vseth the for instrumentes, not only whyle they are in this lyfe, but in death and in hell. His glorie also is more discouered (as Paul wryteth) by hauinge in his great house vessels of golde, of syluer, of wodde, and earth, of mercy, & of wrath. But let vs thanke God that he hath elected vs, and praye hym that he geue vs so muche lyght of his goodnes, and so muche feruencie, that althoughe he wold euer be angry wyth vs, not onely we should be content, but that we holde it for a singuler priuiledge, that he wyl vouch safe in such maner to serue him self of vs, to thende that in euery state, & for euer, we may render him al laude, honour, and glorie, by Jesu Christe oure Lorde. Amen.

❧Wherfore God hathe
elected vs : the nynthe Sermon.

T ſhuld be no leſſe
then a verp folyſheues,
when one entendinge to
ſpeake of coloies, ſhuld
bzynge in the opinion of
one that is boine blynd.
and not illuminate by miracle. So is it mad
neſſe in the thinge ſupernaturall, to alledge
the iudgement of them that are not inſpired
but with naturall vnderſtandinge. And by
aduenture haue talked ,of high, hydde & de·
uine ſecretes ,euen as it hath ſemed well ,in
their owne blind and darcke vnderſtāding,
hauinge therby their eies euer open, to mag
niſie man. Now bicauſe that of the ſuperna
tural matters , ther is ſo much knowē as is
reueled and opened to vs. Therfoie lokinge

Ephe.i.

in the holy ſcriptures, J find that God hath
elected vs by Chzyſte, that is , that God lo·
kinge in the progeny of Adam, ſaw nothing
there that was woizthy of our election : but
tourninge the regarde to his own goodnes

Math.iii.
Ephe.i.

and Chzſtes, in whom he was ſo wel plea·
ſed, that bi him he did electe vs , he therfoie
choſe vs not becauſe we were holie ,but be·
cauſe

cause we shulde be, so that the deuine grace
founde no saintes but made saintes. There
fore did Paule geue thanckes to God, that
had made vs mete to the enheritaunce of
saintes. He chose vs then because it pleased
him so, for he loued vs frelie without seinge
in vs any thinge, worthy therof. He elected
vs (as wryteth Paule) after the decreed pur   Eph.i.
pose of his owne will, to the laud and glory
of his fre mercie and not for our worckes.
So that not bicause we were iuste and worthi in his sighte, he did electe and cal vs, but
(as Paule saieth) bicause he hath elected,   Roma.viii.
therfore he doeth call, iustifie and glorifie
vs. In suche sorte, that he willed not the end
for the beginninge sake, but the beginninge
for ye end sake. He hath saued vs, after Paul
not by the worckes that we haue done, but
by his mercy. In another place he saieth, y
he hath deliuered and called vs with his ho
lye vocation not after oure worckes but ac-   ii. Timo.i
cordinge to his pourposed mercie, giuen all
readie to vs before the creatiō of the world:
so then, as of the secretes reueled to the litel
ones and hidden from the wise and prudent
Christe did giue none other cause, but for ye
so it pleased the father, so of our electiō there Math.xi.
may no nother cause be alleged, but only be
cause it is the pleasure of God. Paule wil-
            leth

leth that the purpose that God hath made
us, mape not depende vpon our workes, because it shulde not be firme as it is, nor we
sure, as Christ sayth we are, and Paul also.
If thou woldest say, that Paul to the Rom.
spake of the eleccion of Jacob & Esau, concerning the spzst byzth, & not concernínge the
heauenly inheritaűce J wold answere that
Paule with that trope, dothe declare the ma
ner of the eternal eleccion to paradise, oiher
wyse the eleccio of Jacob, shuld be in vaine,
in the which is sene (touching the thinges of
the pzesent life) nothing but calamitie & trou
ble. But the pzincipall intente of Paul is to
pzoue that although the carnall Hebzues be
not saued, it resteth not therfoze, that Jesus
is not the Messias, foz ý the pzomises were
made to ý spiritual hebzues, ý which in faith
do ímitate & folow Abzaham, & they are the
elect. When God also in Mala. sheweth to
the Jues that he hath loued thē, because he
loued Jacob of whom they descended, and
hated Esau: His reason had ben vnuailable
if God dyd loue and chose hy wozkes.
foz ý Jewes might haue answered: if thou
didest loue Jacob & the Hebzues, it was because thou didest foztee their good wozkes:
and in lyke case thou wouldest hane done to
Esau and the Gentils, if thou haddest foze-
sene

Roma.iꝛ.
John.x.
Rom.wíllj
Roma.ir_

Mala.l.

Roma.iꝛ.

ſeue any good workes in them. But Paule
ſheweth that the Meſſias is come alſo to the
gétils, becauſe God geueth his gyftes with
out hauinge reſpecte to workes. Jf thou demaund wherfore he hath elected thé? Paul
anſwereth, becauſe it is written: J wyl ſhew
mercy on whom it pleeſeth me . Therfore
Paule doth inferre and bringe in, that para **Roma.ir.**
diſe is not his that wyl, nor that runneth or
laboreth. by hymſelfe to get it : but his that
God wyl ſhewe mercy vnto. He myght alſo
haue anſwered, that although God hated
Eſau, before he was borne, & before he dyd
ſinne, he is not therfore wycked, for he had
hym not in hate or he did foreſe his wickednes. But he ſaith that he doth indurate whó
he wyl, to ſet forth the brightnes of his glorie. And to his purpoſe he doth alledge the
example of Pharao. Now tel me howe it is
poſſible that God can force in vs any good,
if he determine not to geue it vs? Thou wilt
ſay, he ſaw that ſome could vſe well frewil,
and ſome not, therfore he choſe the fyrſt, and
refuſed the ſeconde, they coulde nct vſe it
well wythout hys grace.

Wherefore then dyd he determine to
geue that grace of well vſynge to the one
and not to the other?

　　　　　　　　　Jt

It behoueth to returne to the deuine wyll, and saie, because it pleased him not: for the blinge wel of fre wil is the effecte and frute and not the cause of election. Peraduenture thou wylte saye, he did determine to geue grace to all, but he sawe that some wold vse it wel and those he chose, and some euel, and those he forsoke. But tell me, the vse of that grace is also the gyfte of God, wherfore did he not determine to geue that grace to all, a also to vse it? Thou muste nedes saie at laste also, because it pleased him not. If thou wilt saie, those that vsed it not well, was not because thei lacked the grace to vse it, no more then the other, but they did not occuppe it when they had it, the defaute was theires a not of God, nor of the grace. If it were so, we shuld haue wherin to glorye in our selues. But Paul is in the contrarie, a willeth that to God ought to be rendred all honour and glorye, so as fro him commeth al goodnes. We might also of our selues, seperate vs fro the reprobate, and so our hope shuld not be al wholy in God, our saluaciō could not be certeine and sure, as Chryst said: nor the cause of oure election so hid, as Paule saieth it is, yea fre mercie shulde be no more fre merci, if we might be saued by woorckes and paradise shuld be a rewarde, and not a

gifte

i. Cor. iiii.
Romm. iiii.
i. Timo. i.
Iaco. i.

Ihon. r.
Rom. iiii. vi.
ii. and ri.

gyfte cleane agaynst Paule . The Hebrues
dyd mo warckes then the gentils, and neuertheles he did chose the gentils, and reproued
the Jewes , that sought to be iustified by
theyr workes. God from the beginning for
sawe in vs nothing but repugnancie and re
belliõ agaynst his grace, being by the sinne
of Adam, the children of ire, proue , and en-
clined to all euyl. Paule calleth our eleccio,
the eleccion of fre mercye. Dauid sayth: he
saued me, because he loued me, and because
it pleased him. He saueth then his electe because he delitethe in them , and distributeth
his mercy, after his owne wyl. Thē he hath
begotten vs voluntarily by mere mercye,
and not by our workes: so that the .rij. Apostels dyd not chose Christe, but he chose thē
to the Apostleship . So we be not they that
haue cholen God to saue vs, but God is he
that hathe chosen vs to saluacion . Euen as
Paul was called withoute workes by free
mercy , because it pleased God ; so he was
elected to shewe his mercie, and the aboun-
daunt ryches of his glorie. It is humilitie it
selfe, to beleue that we are chosen by grace.
Thys opinion geueth al glory to God, and
to vs only confusion . And because we can
not erre in glorifyng to much the fre mercie and bountie of God, and abatinge the

Ephe.ii.
Gene.viii.
Rom.ri.
Psal.rvii.
ii.Reg rxi.
Psalm xliii
j Cor ii.
Jaco.i.
Jhon.rv.

Acte.ir.
Gala.i.
i. Timo.i.
Ephe.u.

f.i.   price

pryde of man. Therfore it is most sure, yea,
although it stode not wyth the holye scriptures, as it doth. And the more it displeaseth
the carnal man, because it cōfoundeth al hys
glorye, so much the more it is pleasing to the
spirituall, because it magnifieth God, Christ,
his fre mercy, & the gospel. And to say my o-
pinion, it pleaseth me best, to be all wholy in
the hande of God. Yea if mine electiō were
in my custodie, I wolde (if I myght) render
it vnto God, in whose hand, it must of force
be better, and more sure. Yea woe to vs if in
the least point it did depend vpō our selues.
Se then what becommeth of them that ima
gine (although falsely) that it dependith only vpon the goodly workes that they do, to
make thē selues elected again, wher on ꝥ o-
ther partie, ye shall se, that those which with
lyuely faith, beleue to be by the mere mercy
of God, and by the death of Christe, in the
number of the electe, and sonnes of God
(for that they fele in Christe, and by Christ,
the greate charitie of God,) are by strength
of the spirite and loue, forced to do workes
to bee wondered at: not seruile, for they see
them selues heyres, but the workes of a
sonne, sincere and pure to the glorie of their
lyuely father, beynge preuented by loue.

　　If thou wouldeste beleue, we are not
　　　　　　　　　　　　　　　worthy

woꝛthpe to be so elected by free mercye, J
woulde aunswere, neyther that Chꝛyꝛste
shoulde suffer foꝛ vs vpon the Crosse, but
dyd he not therfoꝛe die? Chꝛiste hathe not
elected vs, because we were woꝛthy therof,
but foꝛ the gloꝛie of hꝭs goodnes: The cause **Ephe.6**
of oure eleccion is not then to bee soughte,
but at the diuine wyll.

Of the repꝛobate, J entende not to dispute, wherefoꝛe God hath cast them of, because it is neyther nedefull to vs, noꝛ pꝛofitable to knowe. Jt serueth to humble vs,
and to knowe better the greate goodnesse of
God, that wee are elected by his grace, and
not by our workes.

The chꝛistiane ought to beleue to be one **Ephe.1.**
of the chosen, and it ought to suffise hym to **i. Coꝛ.ii.v.**
haue Chꝛiste foꝛ his booke, in the which he
seeth hym selfe electe, and to knowe that
that apperteineth to hym. And although
Paule to the Romanes spake a woꝛde therof, it was but incidently oꝛ by the way, foꝛ
it doth apeare it was not his pꝛincipal intēt
to seke the cause wherfoꝛe God doꝛhe repꝛo
bate and caste them of. Jt is inoughe foꝛ vs
to thynke ꝑ the omnipotencie of God, beyng infinite, hath neither limites noꝛ bōdes,
ther-

therfore may he do with his creatures with
out contradiccion: and the deuine wyl may
do of them, determine and wyll all that, that
with hys whole power he maye do, beynge
the whole ruler, and necessarily most ryght
in all hys wyll, yea the her pxyghteousnes
it selfe. Wherfore honorynge the byight and
lyghte iudgementes of God, let vs beleue
that God dothe not condempne, but wyth
iust and irreprehensible counsayle, albe it the
iustice of his iudgementes be to vs incomprehensible, and that none is in hell, but by
hys owne wyckednes: Our office is then to
humble vs, and content vs in the diuine wil,
reknowledgyng that we be not worthy, althoughe we suffer all punishment, to set
forth the brightnes of the glori of god,
to whom, for al his workes, is due
all honoure, laude and glorye
by Jesus Christe oure
Lorde. Amen.

Romm.xi.

S it is wꝛittē, god
leeth frõ the beginninge
and foꝛ euer al thynges,
and hath of all, certepne
and infallible ſcience, ⁊
particularlye knoweth
hys electe,theyꝛ lyfe and their end. So then
as God, by the neceſſitie of his bꝛinge can
not be coꝛrupted,neither diminiſhe noꝛ aug-
ment,beyng infinite and wythout ende,noꝛ
be altered,beyng moſt ſimple and pure,noꝛ
chaunge place, beynge hnmeaſurable, fyl-
lyng al places:ſo alſo maye not his determi
nacions be chaunged:neither by ignoꝛaunce
foꝛ lacke of foꝛeſight and conſideꝛacion,nei-
ther foꝛ defaulte of power, ſince he can not
be letted oꝛ weakened, noꝛ his wyl reſiſted.
Neyther may he chaunge by malyce, oꝛ foꝛ
want of plētiful goodnes, foꝛ his purpoſes
are moſte good and ſyme. God then is
immutable in all his doyngꝛs, chaungeth
not as chyldꝛen, noꝛ lyke olde men, but as
Danid ſaith:The counſayl of the Loꝛd ſhal
ſtande foꝛ euer:that muſt nedes be that god
hath determined, neither is it in our power
to chaunge his purpoſe, diſturbe the diuine

ff.iii.   coun-

Baru.iii.
i.Joh.iii.
ii.Ceſſa.ii.

Roma.r.

Mala.iii.

counſaples , deſtroye diuine ordinaunces,
nor lette hys wyll, whych is Empreſſe, and
owres of the hand mayden. Therfore what
God wylleth, muſte bee, and not ẏ he muſt
wyl after our phantaſie. Nowe becauſe we
are not to be elected, but (as Paul wryteth)
God hath elected vs , before the conſtitucion of the worlde, and is in his determinaci-
ons immutable, it is of force therefore to be
as he hath determined. So likewyſe he ſeeth and knoweth all thynges frome the be-
gynnyng, wyth certeine ꝗ infallible knowledge: it is therefore neceſſitie that, that bee,
whyche he hath foreſeene, or elles it muſte
nedes be that God may chaunge , and that
of oure lyfe and ende he hathe no perfecte
knowcledge, but a doubtful opinion, wherin alſo he may be beguiled , and that ſaying
were a moſt wyckednes. Thou wylte ſaye
to me , thou arte deceyued in imaginynge
that aboue is tyme, and ſucceſſion of tyme,
and that God hathe foreſeene and determined all that is yet to be, ſo that hys determi
nacion and knoweledge is alreadẏ paſſed,
in ſuche ſorte, that he can not otherwayes
knowe, nor wyl, without his chaunge whiche is impoſſible. And therfore thou indae-
eſte it neceſſitie , that all that come to paſſe,
whiche he hathe foreſeene and determined.

But

phe.i.

The tenth Sermon.

But it is not so, for aboue there is no ende
or succession of tyme, nyght nor daye, ney∙
ther was nor shall be, as there is here vn∙
derneth the heauens, ther is onlie all the pre
sente tyme, and onlye one moste clere daye
of one inseperable instaunte, the whyche by
hys eternitie extendeth to the succession and
processe of all tyme. And J answere, that J
knowe ryght well, that to God euery thing
is presente, although beyng vnder thys ce∙
lestial Sphere, where is folowynge of time
to make vs better vnderstand, we vse with
Paule to saye he hathe elected vs : but tell
me, doest thou beleue that the eleccion of
those that are in thys presente yere, and lyke
wyse those that shall be, is nowe in beynge
in effecte and present before God, or not.
Jf thou sayest no, then shal it neuer be, for to
him is no time to come. Jf thou sai yea, then
maye it not be wythoute mutacion in God,
sence thou grauntest it once to be.

Jf thou wouldest saye it myght be nobe∙
ynge, yet it coulde not be no beynge, but in
the instaunt of the Godhead, in whych thou
grauntest all thynges to bee, for as muche
as aboue is no succession or course of tyme,
and so in that selfe instaunt indiuisible, thou
woldest haue it possible, not to be any being
and yet a beyng : for asmuch as it is not so.

ff.iiii.   There∙

Therfore if thou consent that God (I saye
not hath sene) but doth se and determine all
thynges, sence that God is immutable, and
his science infallible, ⁊ that ther is no course
of tyme, by all meanes, lykewyse it is to bee
sayde, that, that must nedes be, which God
wyth perfect infallible knowledge doth for
see, and stedfastly determine. Because that
(if wyth God there were any time past) eue
as that coulde not, not be whiche God had
foresene by his infallible prescience, and immutably determined: no more can that thing
not be, which he doth presently se and determine. Thou wylte say, I graunt that al that
shal be, which God doth forese and ordeine,
and so God shall not be beguiled, nor yet
chaunge, but yet neuertheles it myghte be y
cotrary, although it shal neuer be. But thou
seest not howe thou art deceiued, thou grau
test that al the electe shal be saued, neuerthelesse thou sayest they may be dampned: And
wherto serueth this, may be, if in effect they
shall not be dampned. Therfore this argueth but in wordes, it is curiouse and vnprofitable. Nowe, as if thou woldest graunte
that an elect could be damned, thou shuldest
be forced to saye that God maye chaunge.
Therfore thou sayest, that all may be saued,
which argueth yet that the electe may be dā
ned,

ned, and so thou muste nedes confesse, that
God may also be beguiled, ꝯ varie in his ordi
naunce, which is impossible. That the elect
then may be dampned, it is a thynge false,
hereticall, and vnpossible: it can not be verefied by no sentence compound nor deriued,
sence that in God can be no muracion nor successio Therfore if he be elect, he must nedes
be saued, and it must nedes be sayd, that the
eleccion of them that shall be saued (I wyll
not say hath ben but standyng in that eterni
tie) is in beynge because that if it were not
nowe, it shulde not be hereafter, sence there
neither is, nor can be with God, but alway
the present tyme. Then God hauinge in his
diuine mynde geuen vs paradise frome the
beginninge, and when he geueth neuer repe
teth (as Paule wryteth) it is of necessitie to
saye that the electe be saued. Paule wryteth
that the eleccion of God is firme, and the di
uine purposes stedfaste, and that the Lorde
knoweth his wyth perfect infallible knoweledge, which ought to be to vs a sure foundacion, whereupon we maye stablyshe vndoubted fayth of our saluacio. To this purpose Paule sayd, that those that God hathe
knowen for his, and therfore elected ꝯ purposed to saue them, those he hathe predestinate to be conformiable to the Image of his
sonne

Rom. ri.

Roma. iiii
Roma. ix.

sonne, and those, hauynge them after created, he doth call wyth an inwarde callynge,
in suche sorte, that they answere agayne, for
because they are the sones of God, therfore
they heare hys vopee, and beleue hp beynge
ordeyned to eternall lyfe. Yea he draweth
them, and geueth them a newe herte, and
these that he calleth he iustifieth, he geueth
them Christe, and the spghte of hi.n, faythe,
hope, and charitie, and all other christiane
vertues apparelynge them, he dothe enrich
them wyth many gyftes, treasures, and graces, & afterward doth happely glorifie the.
Therefore from the fyrste to the laste it foloweth, that the electe must nedes be saued.
Paule added and sapd: if God be wyth vs,
who can be agaynste vs: meanyng, if God
hath elected vs, and determined to saue vs,
he beynge omnipotente, and hath taken vpon hym thys enterprise to saue vs, who shal
let hym? Yea he would haue sayde, no man,

Joha.x.
because that Christe sayde, none can take
them out of the handes of my father: it happeneth not to God as to man, whyche many tymes dothe wyll a thynge, seketh and
Roma.xi.
canne not fynde, as the Hebrewes, whyche sought theyr saluacion, and coulde not
atchieue it, and that because they soughte it
not vp Christe, by fre mercy, nor by faythe,

                        bus

The tenth Sermon.

but bp woꝛkes. Jt is not so wpth God, be=
cause that he, when he wplleth anp thynge,
it commeth to passe, and his eleccion (as wꝛi
teth Paule) commeth to effecte. Moꝛeouer
God hath geuen his electe to Chꝛpste, and **Iho.rd.r.rbii**
dꝛaweth them to hpm, and those that go to
hpm dꝛawen of the father, he chaseth not a=
wape, as hpm selfe sapde: he loseth them
not, but knoweth them foꝛ hps shepe, he cal
leth them to hpm, thep heare hps vopce, he
pꝛapeth foꝛ them muste effectuouslp, and is
euer hearde. Foꝛ them he shed hps bloude, **Math.rh.**
and gaue his lpfe, euen as foꝛ them onelp he
was sente, and came into the woꝛld, to them
he dothe manifeste God, geueth them lpfe,
and maketh them happp. Thep are then in
good handes, beynge in Chꝛistes, out of the
whpche none shall take them, as hpm selfe
hath sapde. Thep map perplshe that are the **Iho.rl.r.rbii.**
sonnes of perdicion, as Judas, but not the
chpldꝛen of eleccion. The elect are sure, foꝛ
ther was neuer none of them that perplshed
noꝛ neuer shal, pea it is vnpossible, foꝛ chꝛist **Math.rlii**
speakpng of the false pꝛophets which shuld
be in the kpngdome of Antichꝛist, sapde thep
shoulde seduce the verpe electe, if it were
possible, foꝛ to shewe that it was not possi=
ble, pea foꝛ thepꝛe sakes, those dapes shall
be shoꝛtened,

ⅩⅡ

Al that God hath wrought and shall worke
is for his electe, for whome he dyd create
the world, & preserue the same, sente Christe
into the worlde, and wylled that for them he
shulde dye vpon the crosse, for them he hath
most speciall care.   If God made suche
accompt of the Hebrues, that to thend their
name shoulde not be forgotten on the earth,
he dyd ordeine that if the fyrste brother died
wythout chylde, the second was bounde to
rayse vp sede to his brother :thinkest thou y
he wil not make rekening of his elect whose
names are written in heauen? Yea, I wyll
thou know, that although Christe be he, by
whose meanes al y elect are saued, neuerthe
lesse not by his impotencie, beyng geuen to
hym all power, but because the thynge of it
selfe is impossible; Christ can not saue a reprobate, nor damne an electe. Nowe muche
lesse is it in our power, if we be electe, to
dampne our selues, or if we be reprobate to
saue our selues, yet ought we not to cease to
worke wel, because that if we are sure to be
dampned, we are yet bound euery way, for
his infinite goodnes, moste hyghly to honour hym. Let vs then geue thankes to god
that hath not only by mere mercy elected
vs for hys, but to thende we myght be sure
of oure saluacion, hath ordeined that oure
dampnad

Deut.xv.

Luke.x.

Mar.x.
Math.xxviii.

dampnacion ſhal not lye in our owne pow=
er(beynge his electe) and with thys geueth
bs ſuche grace, that we may in this preſent
lyfe, render hym all laude, honour, and glo
rye, by Jeſus Chriſt our Lorde. Amen.

Whether God do agra=
uate, harden and blynd the h ertes
of men or not, and in what maner:
the eleuenth Sermon.

T is read in the
holye ſcriptures , that
God put in Saul a wic=
ked ſpirite to vere hym
and a lyng ſpirite in the
mouth of the Prophets

to begyl Achab, ꝫ that by Sathã he moued
ꝑ hert of Dauid to nũber the people againſt
his precept. And moreouer he doth harden,
blynde , and make groſſe the hertes of per=
ſons, and geueth them ouer in to a peruerſe
mynd. And Paul wryteth,that he hath ſhut
by al men in vnbelief ꝫ ſinne. And although
many helde for vngodlines thys maner of
ſpeaking, ꝫ therfore thei do not onli abſtain
frõ pronoũcinge ſuch lyke wordes, but alſo
go about to expoũd ꝫ make thẽ better; emẽ=
dinge

dinge them, forcinge them selues to brynge
them after their phātasie , to suche a way, ÿ
theyhaue a kynde of godlines therin. And J
thinke they are moued to do this, to thende
that of these thinges men should not take
occasion to thynke that God were the cause
of spnne, or els to imagine wyth the Mani-
ches to be, ii.first beginnings, the one good,
cause of the good, the other euel, cause of the
euell. Neuertheles J wyll not , ought not,
may not wyll to be more holpe then God,
that speaketh in holpe scriptures. And it is
more wickednes to wyl to correct the tonge
of the holy gost, because that none speaketh
nor can speake more circūspectlye then he,
nor with greater thyrst of our saluacion, to
the zeale aud honour of God. Wyth al this
euery one ought to knowe that we are the
cause of spnne and not God : yea it cau not
be thought, that God is a God , if it be not
thought that he is wythout faulte, wythout
euell, infinitely good and iust . Therfore as
to vs is due all confusion, ignominie, dishonor, reproche and euel, so to God all honor,
laude, and glorye. Jt is not euel then to pronouce these wordes , in the maner that they
are wrytt̄, saiyng that God doth agrauate,
harden, and blynde, but it is good.

Thou wylte saye, tell me how these wordes

des are to be vnderstande , that God dothe
harden, blynde, and suche lyke: so that therby J may not take any occasion of offēce. J
aunswere , that after the opinion of some,
God doth harden , and so blynde the herte
of a person, in as muche as he foreseeth and
forepreacheth his hardenes, as he did forese
and foresaye the obstinacie of Pharao. But
knowe thou, that when he sayde to Moses,
J wyll harden the hert of Pharao, he wolb
not onelie say, J foresee that he wyll be hard
herted, and J tell it the before , for then the
wordes whiche he spake after , shoulde not
haue agreed therwith, whyche were : for to
shewe my power, that my name maye be de
clared throwghout the whole worlde.

But wyth those wordes he threatened to
punyshe hym, as it is read that he punished
mo people for theyr sinnes , wyth blynding
them, hardenynge them, with lettyng them
do after theyr desyres of theyr owne hertes,
geuinge them ouer into a frowarde mynde,
in passions and shamefull effectes.

Therfore there are some whyche saye,
that God manye tymes dothe harden and
blynde sinners, when sufferyng, yea geuing
them prosperitie, and distributinge his mercy and benefites, when they oughte to open

theyr

Deut ii.
Esai. vi
Jhon xii.
Psalm lxxr.
Roma i.

theyꝛ eyes to ſo greate benignities of hym,
and be inuited therby to repent and chaūge
theyꝛ lyfe, they, of this bountie of God take
occaſion to become woꝛſe, euery daye moꝛe
blynde and indurate.   But I ſaye that the
hertue and alſo the bice ſtandeth not in pꝛoſperitie noꝛ yet in aduerſitie, but in the men
them ſelues. So that as to the electe euerye
thing woꝛketh to ſaluacion, and by the ſpeci
all grace that they haue of God ſerue hym
in aduerſitie as in pꝛoſperitie: ſo to the repꝛo
bate, euery thyng ſerueth contrarye, & hurt-
eth, yet by theyꝛ defaltes as not only pꝛoſperitie & aduerſitie, but alſo the pꝛeachinge
of the Goſpel, and the miracles do hurt and
hynder them. Therfoꝛe Paule ſayd, that as
to the electe, Chꝛiſt was the odour of lyfe,
ſo to the repꝛobat, he was ẏ odour of death.
It is nedeful then to ſay that God doth har
den and blynde the hertes of the repꝛobate,
not becauſe he geneth thē aduerſitie oꝛ pꝛoſperitie, noꝛ becauſe he ſuffereth them, and
ſheweth them many benefites, but foꝛ that
he geueth them not grace to vſe them, and
the commoditie therof, to the gloꝛy of God:
It may be truly ſaide that he dothe harden
and blynde the hertes of the ſinners, when
he taketh from them, oꝛ geueth them not his
grace, noꝛ the vnderſtandynge of his wyll,
because

Rom. viii.

ii. Coꝛ. ii.

wpl, because that in such case, it is force that
man remayne blynd and indurate, and that
euery thynge serue them , to the dishonor of
god, wher as if they had that inward grace
euen of theyr sinnes, they should take occa
sion to honour hym. God doth blynd men,
whē withdrawyng his lyght, he hydeth his
face, and as Moses was vailed, so spredeth
he the vaile of ignoraunce ouer the herte of   Deute.xxxi
the reprobate: so that god in withdrawinge
the lyght of his grace, blindeth the hertes of
infidels, in such sorte , that not only the gos- i'. Cor.iii.
pel is hyd from them (as Paul wryteth) and
they erre, but standyng in that darckenes,
they can not beleue. And so also doth he har ii Tessa.ii.
den, not for that he geueth prosperitie or ad- Jhon.xii.
uersitie (of the which the electe also are partakers) nor because he withdraweth not the
grace, but the sweetenes and the sensuall fe
lyng therof, of the which many saintes wer
voyde: nor yet for that he moueth their hertes to euell, or cause in them any obstinacie
or euell qualitie : but only in wythdrawyng Ezechi.xi.
hys grace, which molifieth a herte of stone
and maketh it fleshe , it is of necessitie ỹ the
hert remain hardened . And so lykewyse he
chaseth awai the sinner, whē he doth not cal
hym, ꝗ draw him to him before . Yet for all
this god sinneth not , for he is not holde nor
bõde to geue us this grace, he may hardē ꝗ

            G.i   moli-

molifie after his owne pleasure, yea the sin
ner meriteth not onlye to be punished with
payne and priuacion of paradise, but also
wyth priuacion of his grace: and that this
is true, iudge, if God had kylled Pharao,
when he caused all the Hebrues chyldren to
be caste into the floude: woldest thou haue
sayd that god had bene vniuste? Surely no.
And yet if then he had died, he had ben dam
ned, and remained obstinat for euer. Wher
fore myght not god execute iustlye, the same
sentence, as concerning blyndyng and har
dening, vpon others, wyth wythdrawinge
hys grace? And on the other partie (as they
are preserued) that thal be not amisse to pre
serue him in life for a few mo daies to be ser
ued of hym, as of an instrument of wrathe,
prepared frome the beginninge, to exercise
his people in vertue, to thende that deliue
ryng them so diuinely, they myght knowe
the great goodnes, power, & iustice of god.
And so beynge his name celebrate through
out the world, he might be feared & loued.
And finally all to hys owne glory, as wry
teth Paul & Moses. The iudgementes that
we geue vpon the secretes of god, are verie
madnes, if by faith we do not enter into his
sanctuary. God dothe inwardlye call the e
lecte, as Paul wryteth, and they beleue that
god, as theyr only father, wyl neuer forsake
them,

Roma.ir.

Exo.rrriii
Psalm.lrri.

Rom.viii.

them, but shall endue thē wyth suche grace, that al thynges shal serue them to saluaciō, euen synne, in the which god wyll neuer let them fall, but for theyr benefite. They are not offended to heare saye, that god, by ab- staynyng his grace from the vngodly, doth Rom viii blynd, and harden theyr hertes, but vnder- standing by faythe, to be in the number of the electe, and knowyng that god saueth not but by mercye, and damneth not but iustlie, so much the more are they moued to lyue in pure feare, to humble them selues, & render thankes to god, to whom be euer all laude, honour, and glorie, through Jesu Christ our Lorde. Amen.

¶ Howe God dothe dispose his grace: the twelfe Sermon.

Her are many whi- che thinke that god to e- uery one cōtinually doth offer his grace, and that it is in the power of man to accepte it or not, as though they had it in a boudget, & were in their arbitremēt to ope & take at their owne wil. And ÿ of this their dead, false, & erroni- ous opinion, groweth ÿ they liue most wic- kedly, thinking & saiyng, god neuer fayleth with his grace, and it is at our choyse to re- ceyue it at our wyll.

Q.ii   Thore

The twelfe Sermon.

Therfore we map take leisure & lyue a vicious life after our owne way, for we shal be saued alwaies, a moment of time is enough for vs to repent & be saued, sence it is in our power. Therfore for to flye such an euell, I haue iudged it good to shewe ý it is not so. It is no doute ý god hath created the world for his electe, so that if god had forsene that none should haue bene saued, he would not haue created it. For the also he dyd preserue it, to them he hath geuen the Aungels for kepers, and of them as a father he hath molte singuler care & prouidece. God wyl not suffer ý they be tepted aboue their power, yea eueri thyng worketh & serueth well to their saluacio. Sene times in a day ý iust shal fal, & ryse againe, because God is with the, and helpeth them in such sorte, that the more thei are in great perils & necessitie, so muche the more is god beneficial to them. For the god gaue the lawe to the world, sent Moses and the Prophetes, them he calleth inwardly in suche maner, that they heare his voice, and answere him of them he molitieth the herte, and draweth them to Christ, as the adamat doth Iron: If they erre, he dothe correcte and chasten them as chyldren, as it is read of Dauid, to them he doth not impute their sinne, he doth quicken and glorify them, and finally al that god hath wrought, and shall

worke

Heb.ic.c.
Cor.i.
Rom.viii.

Prou.xxiiii.

Psal.xxxi.
Ihon.x.
Ihon.ix.

worke for hym selfe, is for the electe, for the
he sent Chrift, and when he came, for them
he toke vpon hym their finnes, only for the
he prayed, for them he wepte, preached, and
dyd miracles, for them he fhed his bloude,
dyed, rofe, afcended into heauen, fent the ho
ly gofte, and fhal come to iudge the quicke
and the dead : yea all that he hath fuffered,
wrought and fhall worcke, is for the electe,
whom he loueth in fo exceffiue maner, that
he doth attribute to him felfe al that is done
to them. God then beyng gratified with the   **Ibon.r.**
electe in Chrift, doth geue vnto them his fpi
rite, the lyuely lyghte of hym, faythe, hope,
with all the refte of vertues & graces effen-
cial & neceffary to faluacion. And moreouer
he geueth them grace to vfe in the honor of
god, and be ferued in his glorye, of all the
gyftes and graces which maye be comune
both to the good, & to the euel, to be vfed wel
& euel, as riches, honour, dignitie, healthe,
long lyfe, chyldre, frindes, fciece, the giftes
of the tonge, to do miracles and fuche lyke.
Of them in parte, Paule made mencion,
wryting to the Corinthes. And alfo geueth **i.Cor.xij.**
them grace to vfe in his glorie, pouertie, ignominie, infamie, infirmitie, with all aduer
fitie, and the priuacion of lyke gyftes, euen
to the death, god geueth them fuche grace y
with euery wind, they faile to the porte, and

        G.iii.   they

they knowe that they are no lesse bounde to
thanke god when they are without such giftes, and in all aduersitie , then when they
haue suche thinges wyth the prosperitie of
the worlo, sence that bi the grace which god
geueth them, all thinges worke to good.
¶Therfore they are euer contented to bee in
the state which pleaseth the Lorde, neither
wolde they chaunge it, if they myght (without the wyll of god) and onlye for that they
fele the diuine goodnes, no lesse in aduersi-
rie then in the worldly prosperitie. In thend
when they are fallen to any sinne , god ope-
neth theyr eies, & maketh the se, not only the
euell ý they haue done, but also ý he hath so
permitted it for their benefit, to thend they
maye the better know theyr owne miseries
and the bountie of god. But speaking of the
reprobate, J saye, that it is enough for vs to
knowe that god is not bonde, nor necessited
to geue them his grace for theyr good worckes: because that the grace findeth not good
worckes, but doth make them to be done.
¶God neither hath, nor may haue any bonde
wyth his creatures . The bondes are all
oures wyth god , and so muche the more, as
that we beyng all loste in Adam, he myghte
iustly, not only abandon vs, but damne and
punyshe vs . He is not also compelled of
his

hys perfecte goodnes, mercie and charitie, to not haue created the worlde, he myghte nowe brynge it to nothinge, and dispose all creatures after his owne waye, beinge styl molte perfectlye iuste, as he is nowe, and was from without beginning, before he did create the worlde. God maye geue of his grace as much as it pleaseth him, when & to whome he thinketh good, yea, and not to geue it without beyng vniust, or doinge any iniuric. God also hath ben of power, without doyng any vnrighteousnes, to create the reprobate, foreseynge theyr damnacion, to serue his owne turne, and to vse them for in strumentes, or exercise the elect in vertue, to the ende that their victories and triumphes, and likewise Christes, myght be the more glorious, and finally all for his owne grea ter glorye.

And moreouer I saye, that Christe hy deth hym selfe and his grace manye times frome persons, so that althoughe they seeke hym, crie after hym, and recommend them selues to hym, they fynde him not, nor he heareth them not, notwythstandynge those such as are not moued to seke him, or commit them selues to him, by the spirite, nor for the zeale of the honoure of God, but for their proper interest, yea and mani times he doth

Math.xx

Iho.vij.

Prouer.j.

G.iiii.　　blinde

blinde and indurate the people, and all is
most iustlie done . And although it be writtē
that God hath cure of all, calleth all, wolde
saue al, died for al, doth illuminate al, dothe
taine and power his grace vpon all, & lyke
sentences: J saye, it is to be vnderstand, that
he hath cure of al ingeneral, but of the elect
in special, and so he calleth al, with a vocaci
on vniuersall, but the elect with an inward
and singuler. When Paule saide also, that
he wold saue all, he vnderstode that, to be of
euerie sorte of persones. His death also was
sufficient to saue all, but it is not effectuous
but to the elect, and so where it is written, y̌
he doth illuminate and geue grace to al, it is
vnderstand of the elect, of those that are illu
minate . Therfore saide Christe to the Apostels, to you it is geuen to knowe the miste-
ries of the kingdome of heauen, Paule said
likewise , that the faith which is the gifte of
God, is not al mēs. It is well true also, that
God doth illuminate al, in asmuch as there
is no person that hath not had some lighte &
knowledge of God . Let vs then geue him
thanckes , sence that of his mere goodnes,
he hath conumerat vs among the elect, and
praye we him that he geue vs so much light
of his goodues, that in euery place and time
we mai render him perfecte laude , honoure
and glorye, by Jhesu Christe oure Lorde.
　　　　　Amen.

Math.xiii.
Ihō.ii.
Tessa.ii

Ome myght thinke it superfluous for a christiane, to thynke whether he be fre or not, but that it is inough to force him self to make all possible resistence agaynst euell, and his best power to do wel, geuyng al honor & glory to god, because that in suche a case, they walke to god surely, neither falling into the depth of idlenes. But herein cōsisteth the difficultie, in geuing all the glorie to god. Pea it is not possible that man whyple arrogātly he presumeth of hym selfe (thinkyng to do that whiche he doth not) can geue al the glory to god. Therfore haue I iudged it necessarye to shewe what man can do, to thend ſ beyng able to knowe and discerne betwene that which in dede is his, and that that is goddes, he can and maye tender all prayse and laude vnto him to whom of duty it belongeth. Ffyrst, although the beyng of the creatures, compared to the beyng of god (by beyng infinitely far from the perfecciō of the diuine essence) is but a shadowe, pea rather no beynge, so Roma. iiii that truly it may be sayde that god only is that which is; neuertheleſſe wyth al this, it Exo. iii can not

can not be sayde but that the creatures haue
a beynge, although imperfect, in compari=
son of the diuine. And so is it true, that they
haue vertue, during the whiche they worke,
although principally in the vertue of god.

Therfore when the Lord had created the
world, he comaunded the earth to spzynge,
and the waters to bzinge forthe. Then false
is the opinion of them that Imagine that
god, & not the sunne dothe geue lyght, & god
not the fyze doth geue heate, and so of al the
reste of thinges created, that God dothe
worke in thē, & not the creatures, but euery
creature euen to the moste vile, hath his pro
per vertue, duringe the whiche, it worketh.
True it is, that in the creatures inferiour to
man, there is no libertie at all, because that
beinge not let, they muste of necessiti worke
accozding to the vertue that thei haue in the
disposition of thinges possible oz sufferable,
directlye set befoze them as it is sene in bur=
ninge, and so it is necessarye, they moue ac=
cozdinge to theire vertue, strength, and ape=
tite, the whiche is seene in the waters, that
runne to the sea, nether it is in the power of
liuinge soules vnresonable, to moue oz not
to moue weaklye oz stronglye, to the obiec=
tes that they apetite oz desier. Take away
the impedimentes, they muste of necessitie
moue them selues there ynto, after the mea=
sura

sure of the strength, and apetite they haue.
Cherfore in them is no libertie at al, as ther
is in man, in whome J consider fiue sortes
of mouinges, and operacions. The first are
mere naturalas if a man shuld voluntarely
throw him selfe downe, it shuld not be in his
lybertie to withholde him selfe, but shulde
be vp his weighte, compelled lyke a stone to
discende euen to the earthe. True it is, that
the same faul was in his liberti, in as much
as he mighte not haue throwen him selfe
downe at all. The seconde mouinges, that
J consider in me, are vegitatiue, as the grow
inge when they are childzen, and nurishinge
and suche like, the which also doth plantes.
And speakynge of those, J saye that they
are not in the libertie of man, sauynge that
he maye kyll him selfe, and depziue him of
that lyfe whych the trees can not do.

The thyzde are operacions animall, as
to see, heare, and taste, and suche lyke, of the
which speakinge, J saye, that albeit, it be in
the power of man, not to heare a voyce that
is present wythout closinge his eares, and
so of the other lyke operacioys, neuerthelesse it is in hys libertie to shut vp those sen-
ces, in the presence of the obiectes oz present thynges y delyght hym, & to withdraw
hym selfe frome them, and so not to moue,

Qz

or to moue to one side or another, softlye or
ſtronglie, as he will , the which the other a-
nymalles or liuinge ſoules can not do , beinge neceſſitate, to moue according to theire
apetites . But ſpeakinge of the foure operacions whiche are humaine , as to thincke
one or an other thinge , to ſpeake or not , in
this maner or in that, to lerne this or that ſci
ence , to gouerne him ſelfe or others in this
waye or in the other, yea not to do, or elſe to
do, alwayes more or leſſe, to this or that per-
ſon, (in caſe he haue goods in power) to faſt
watch , praye , to heare the word of God, to
communicate or not , and ſo of all the other
like operacions, I ſaye , that they are in the
power of man, that is that men (without o-
ther ſpecial grace and miracle but only duringe the generall influence of God) haue
in their power to do them , & alſo not to do
them, and alwaies they ſhal do them, if thei
effectuouſlye ſhal wil to do them, not being
letted of God, or of ſome other ſtronger then
they , and ſo alſo ſhall they not do them beinge not forced, and not willinge, to do the,
men are not images . Yea that they are free
in thinges humane, it is ſo cleare, that it can
not be declared by a rule more knowne , but
ſpekeinge of the laſte worckes , that are holie, ſpiritual and deuine, the which are grat-
full and acceptable to God, as to haue liue-

lye

lie lyght, and spirituall knowledge and vn¬
derstandinge of god, to haue in him firme
fayth & hope to loue him, honour hym, laud
hym, and reuerence hym, with all hy hert,
to order all thy lyfe to his glory, to obey and
commit hym selfe wholy to his gouernaūce
wyth mortifiyng and denying him selfe, the
fleshe and his owne prudence, and to loue
hys neyghbour as him selfe, euen to his ene
mies for the loue of god, wyth the herte to
praye for thē, and do them all the good possi
ble: And finallye to do suche workes to the
glorie of god is not in the libertie of them
that are carnall, & not regenerate by Christ,
because that it is not in theyr power to haue
the supernatural knoweledge of god, sence
it is aboue all their myght.

It is not also in theyr power to haue liue
ly fayth in god, hope, and charitie, for as
muche as they are the gyftes of god, diuine
vertues & supernatural. Therfore it is not in
theyr libertie to honour god in any wyse as
is due to hym, and that thys is true, let thē
proue to make experience in them selues, in¬
deuoringe them to haue more knoweledge
of god then they haue, to haue in hym grea¬
ter fayth and hope, and to loue hym more,
and they shal perceue that it wyl not come
to effecte: wherof it foloweth that being not

iii

in ẏ power of infidels, and not regenerate
by Chriſte to loue God with al theire harte
no noꝛ aboue al other thinges ,that alſo it is
not in theire power , not to loue the thinges
created, but in Chriſte and by Chriſt, nether
is it in theire power , not to loue them ſel
ues diſoꝛdinatelpe, oꝛ theire parentes , frin
des, dignitie, honoure, goodes, pleaſures, ꝗ
the reſte of thinges that are to them pꝛofita
ble ,commodious and delectable , and moꝛe
ouer it lieth not in theire power, not to hate
their enemies, ſo that thou maiſt ſe, how it is
in theire power, to loue them ſpeciallpe ſpi
rituallpe in Chriſte :and to the gloꝛi of God
ſuche like paſſiones and effectes , are not in
oure power, as euerpe one hath experienc
continuallpe in hpm ſelfe .

A wpcked man mighte abſteine frome
killinge his enempe , when he mighte do it,
pea and do his beſte to healpe him , but it
ſhoulde not be in his power , to loue him
in his herte , and muche leſſe in Chriſte and
to God.

Therefoꝛe all be it , it is in his libertie,
not to kpille his enempe , and ſo to do him
good, neuertheleſſe it is not in his power, to
refraine frome kpllinge hpm , oꝛ to do hpm
anpe benefite foꝛ the gloꝛpe of God. The vn
goblpe

godlye mighte, wyth all his conninge and
power consider all those thynges that serue
to the dyspraise of the worlde, to the morti-
fyinge of theyr selues, to the louinge of theyr
neighbour and also God: yet by no meanes
should they come to suche syght of the good
nesse of God, of theyr owne miseries and
vanitie of the worlde, that they should loue
God, to the hate of them selues, and dis-
prayse of the worlde, as he is bounde to do.

It is not then in the libertie of the carnall man to do worckes spirituall, he hathe
neede of the grace of God, of fayth, and
knowledge supernaturall, nor it is not in
hys power to gette, neyther in all nor in
parte, anye gyfte of God, grace or spirituall
vertue. Yea before that by Christe he bee
regenerate, he can not neyther wyth thyn-
kinge, desyringe, or workynge, nor by anye
other meanes dispose or prepare hym selfe
neyther whole nor partelye, to one of the
leaste graces of God: so that by those hys
thoughtes, desyres, or worckes, he maye be
worthye, or haue in all or in parte deserued
that grace.

And moreouer I saye, that as before hys
regeneracion he is vngodlye & wicked, euen
so is sin al his thoughtes, desires, & workes
and

and this is, bicause that while he is carnall,
beinge the seruaunte of sinne and concupi∫
sence whiche reigneth in him , he is deade to
God , and aliue to him selfe, he nether doth
worcke nor can worcke, to the glorye of god
as he is bound, for want of ÿ liuely light of
him, but being as he is carnal & in his owne
loue he is moued to worcke , onlye for his
owne intereste, he sinneth then , not for doinge almoste and like worckes , but for that
he doth them not for the glorie of God. And
althoughe the ungodly absteine some times
from robbinge and killinge, with suche like
wicked iniquities, yet alwaies he sinneth(al
though not so muche)not in absteining , but
that he absteineth not for the loue of God
as he is bounde to do, but for his owne proper accompte intereste and utilitie .   And
so is it true in carnall man, while he is carnal, sinne doth euer reigne, for that he can not
but sinne , yea and euer doth sinne continuallye , because that althoughe he absteineth
from homicide, thefte and committing such
like iniquities, neuerthelesse he sinneth euer
continuallye , in leauing behind him the loue
of God with all his herte, as he oughte to
loue his neighboure as him selfe , to worcke
for the helth of his neighboure , and the glorie of God, as he is bounde, absteininge for
his honoure from all sinne . Theire sinne

Rom. vi.
Roma.ii.
Rom. vii.

are then innumerable , and yet they thincke
in confession to number them al beinge then
al the woozkes of the carnal sinne and woz-
thye of punishmente : see howe they can by
any meanes be wozthi to be rewarded ,and
howe they may be true pzeparacions, oz disposicions to grace? Therfoze as a dead man
can not raise him self, oz woozcke toward his
resurreccio, noz he that is not, woozcke to his
creation , so the carnall man , that in Adam
is deade, and as though he were not can not **Ephe.ii.**
woozcke towardes his regeneracio and crea **Roma,iiii**
tion , yea euen as a humane boDye wythout
the soule can not moue but downewarde, so
the dead soule without the spirite & Chzilte,
his life can not lifte him selfe vp . but multe
of neceſsitie descende euer downe ,in regar-
dinge his own interelte. Therfoze he ca not **Jhon.iii.**
but sinne,he must be boone again to do woz-
kes spirituall and holye , and by oure selues
we can not be regenerate by no meanes,foz
it is onlye the woozcke of God. It is nedeful
then that God creatinge in vs a cleane hert
do geue vs a new hert ,as Dauid did pzaie **Pſal.l.**
and God did pzomiſe bi his pzophetes withoute me ,saithe Chzilt, ye can do nothinge,
that is spirituall, holi and gratefull to God.
Chzilte then is wholye our rightuouſnes,&
this is the moze riche noble and happi rightuouſnes, the if we were iuſte bi our selues,

H.i.   ye

pea none ſhuld be iuſte, if our iuſtice dpd in
anp part depēd vpō vs noz our owne glozp
excluded, as Paul and Moſes wplieth it to
be. There are manp that thinke that as men
choſe to ſerue a Prince, ſo we choſe to ſerue
god, but he him ſelfe in the contrarp, where
he ſapd, pou haue not choſen me, but J pou.
Likewiſe thep thinke, as thep that beſt ſerue
obtein moſt fauour of their lozd, & thoſe that
haue loſte it, the moze thep humble them ſelues, the ſoner thep recouer it: ſo thep thinke
of vs with god. Thus thep build thep2 good
lpfe, not vpon Chziſte, but on them ſelues,
and fall frome the diuine grace. And alſo it
is clene contrarp: foz not foz that we repent,
humble vs, and do good wozckes, therfoze
he geueth vs his grace: but becauſe he geueth vs his grace, therfoze we do wozckes
that are holpe. So that, not foz that the
good thpefe vpon the croſſe dpd confeſſe
Chziſt, therfoze he dpd illuminate him, but
foz that Chziſt did illuminate and touch his
herte, therfoze he dpd confeſſe him: and the
lpke happeneth of all vs.

And what good wozke dpd Paule when
Chziſt conuerted him? He was moſt ſtrong-
lpe agapuſte his honoure, euen as we were
befoze he called vs. Theſe that are not regenerate, bee wpth Sainete Peter in a darcke
· pziſon,

prison, bounde with manye cheynes, in the
power of the Deuyll, a slepe in sinne, and
wylte thou that they bee saued by them sel
ues? No, the Lorde him selfe muste needes
awake hym, the euell tree can not bzynge
foz the good frute, as Chziste sayde, no moze Math.vii.
canne the vngodlye good wozckes. Befoze
wee are by Chzist regenerate, we are fleshe,
and that whiche spzyngeth of the fleshe, is
fleshe. Therefoze canne we do no spirituall Jho.iii.
wozckes, yea euen as Paule sayethe, all the
effectes and despzes of the fleshe are death,
vncleane are all oure wozckes whych pzo-
cede of our corrupte nature, and finally he
that is not wyth Chziste, is agaynste hym.

¶God at the beginnynge made man free,
but in sinninge he was made in suche sozte
the seruaunt of sinne, y not only he can not,
neither in all noz in parte, merite befoze god
any grace, but he can not in his lyght do o-
therwyse but sinne: yet not foz this he shuld
leaue to heare the woozde of God, to pzaye,
to take counsayle, to seeke to bee corrected,
to do almes and lyke woozcke, not foz that
he dothe deserue grace but punyshemente,
euen as he that by fozce is compelled to
humble hym selfe, and aye pardon of hys
enempe, foz that fayned humilitye, he
meritethe not to bee pardoned, but should

H.ii.   merite

merite so muche the moze to be punished, as
that, hauinge bniustli offeded him, he ought
with his herte, to haue humbled him, and
asked pardon, and hath not done it. Now so
the bngodlpe, in askinge mercie of God, do
eth sinne, foz he that asketh not foz his glozy
as he is bounde, but foz his owne gaine, noz
therfoze he ought to ceasse from asking help
of God, foz that he sinneth not in pzayinge
but foz the not pzayinge in spirit, foz the glo
rie of God, and with al due circumstances
in that case he did partlpe obey God, foz if
he did not pzaye he should sinne much moze
greuouslpe. The Samaritane not onlpe deserued not to haue grace of Chzyste, foz asking him water, but foz that her demaund,
she deserued to be punished, bicause she did
it not in faithe, and to the glozpe of God.
Neuerthelesse Chziste would that she shuld
aske, and that it shulde passe bp those meanes. Now so he wil that sinners aske grace,
and do those wozckes that he hath commau
ded them, albe it thei do them not to the glozpe of god, beinge blinde to diuine thinges,
pea darckenes it self, as wziteth saint Jhon.
But after the sinners are regenerat bi chzist
then as childzē of god, thei are free, and not
the seruauntes of the deuell noz of sinne because that althoughe in them remaineth the
concupiscence of sinne, neuerthelesse thp do
                                                    not

Jhon.r.
Joh.biii.

not consente to it, they obey not vnto it. It
dothe not reigne in them: but they haue so
much lyght of god, & so much spirite (which
helpeth their infirmitie) that they are stirrer
to the glorie of god, thoughe not wholy as
they wolde, for because of the repugnaunte
flesshe. Therfore said Paul. I do not ý good
that I wold do, but the euell that I wolde
not. But suche defectes are not imputed to
them, for that they are vp fapthe graffed in
Christe. The regenerate bi Christe are prone
and readie to the good, god hathe illustrate
their mind and tottched their herte, in suche
maner that with all their soule, voluntarely
frely, and gladly, they do holpe worckes, to
the glory of god, so that as god counsailed
the soules of them that did electe Dauid to
content the selues in their herte to haue him
for their kinge, so he moueth the hert of the
regenerate, wyllinglye to haue god for thepr
god, to comit them to his gouernaunce, and
to delight to be gouerned of him, with hono
ringe him as a celestial father. So the as the
sonnes of Adam, before they be regenerate,
are the seruauntes of sinne, for that they ca
not but sinne, & therfore because they can not
worcke, wyl, desire, nor styrre in any wape
to the glory of god, as they are holden, but
only for their carnal comoditie, vp ý which
al men not regenerate, are called flesshe, not

only

Roma. vii.

Rom. vi.

Rom. vii
Psalm. xxxi.
Roma. viii.

only the body, but the soule, the wyl, desires
and thoughtes, with al the rest, so after that
they are regenerate, they be fre from sinne,
(for that they can worke to the glory of god)
and are seruauntes of ryghteousnes. Therfore although, as concerning the substaunce
and beyng of the bodie and of the soule, thei
remayne the same : neuertheles. where before they wer called fleshly men, and fleshe,
for that they sought not but theyr owne proper thynges, afterward they are called spirituall men and spirite, in as muche as they
seke the glory of God, the which they maye
do, for that God hathe geuen them by mere
grace liuely lyght and spiritual feling, and
knowledge of his goodnes, yea duringe in
them that perfect light, not only they are fre
from sinne, for that thei be able not to sinne,
but also they can not sinne, for that they cã
not but loue god & worke to his glory.

And this is the perfecte libertie, the
bringe fre frome the power to sinne, and beinge not of power to sinne, is not to sinne.
Otherwyse, neither the saintes that are in
the other lyfe, nor the Aungels shoulde bee
perfectly fre, neither Christ nor god, for thei
cã not sinne. It is very true this, ÿ god some
time doth let his electe & holy men fal, with-
drawing his diuine light for a time (yet for
their benefites) therfore we are not absolute
lye

lie and wholy fre from the power to sinne,
as we shal be in the life to come, but thei are
fre frõ power to sinne with this cõdiciõ, du-
ryng in thẽ the liuely & actual lyght of god.
So then as the carnal, before their regenera
cion are in such sort the seruauntes of sinne,
that they cã not but sinne, not therfore absolutely & without condicion, but so long as
they haue not the holy light of god, so the re
generate are in lyke maner fre frõ sinne that
they cã not sinne, yea they can not chose but
worke wel, yet not absolutely, but during in
thẽ that liuelie & actual light of god. And w
al this, neither the wyl of the fleshe is violẽ-
ted to wyl euel, nor the wyl of the spirite to
wyl wel. And this is, for that the wyl cã not
worke, but of wyl (therfore wyllingly) but
if it were possible that of any outward pow
er it were forced thẽ by that violẽce, it shuld
worcke not voluntarilye. And on the other
syde, it should worke willingly for y it coulde
not worke but of the same wil y it is : therefore it should worke unwillingly & willingly
the which in a maner is unpossible, & imply-
eth cõtradictiõ and gainsaiyng. So thẽ as if
one being a slepe were throwen doune from
a hyghe place, and in the fallinge should a-
wake, percepuinge hys falle, should wyllingly contente him selfe, and haue pleasure
so to fal doune to the botome, when he were

H.iiii.   at

at the ground, he were well worthy to haue
shame & punishement, not for that he might
in his fal withhold him selfe, for it was not
in his choyse nor libertie, but for that he did
so delight and cõtent him self with, that fal,
with his ful wyl, & would it wyth the herte,
in such sorte, that albeit he myght haue had
the power to restraine that fal, he wold not
haue done it. Euen so the lyke becõmeth of
al the chyldren of Adam, that by pnge fallen
in him, although when thei come to y peres
of discression, & begyn to discerne the good
frome the euel, they perceiue the sinnes that
they do, euery way they do thē volũtarilye,
delighting therin, so that althoughe they be
not of power, not to do thē, they ar neuerthe
les worthy of ponishmēt, for y they in sorte
cõmit thē wyllingly, that if they had pow
er not to do them, yet euery waye they wold
do them, bringe their wyll so malignaũte, as
it is. Their wyll then is not violented or
forced to do euel of ani outward power, but
of his owne proper & entiere or inward malyce: And so the other partie, the regenerate
by the glaũsome, entier, liuelye, & enflamed
light that they haue of the boũty of god, thei
are forced to eleuate thē selues, tõ an amo-
rous violẽce (Therfore volũtarily, & tõ perfect liberti) to god, to whom for euer be all
Laud, honor, and glory, through Iesu Christ
our Lorde. Amen.

℄ Of the effectes wrought bi the
spirite of god when it entrethe in
to the soule : the .xviii. Sermon

Wen as Christ entring into the
holye citye of Jerusalem, the
whole citie was moued, so mo
ueth the citie of the soule when
Christe entreth therein, speci-
allp, tence from that as from a fort & strong
municioneð rocke he hath the greate deuyll
to chase away. And if in ÿ lunatike son, ther
was a greate comocion, when Christ out of
his body wold haue drawen the malignaut
spirite that had possessed hym : thinke what
comocion there is, when he chaseth hym frõ
the soule, in the which he dwelleth more wil
lyng ly. And knowe, that it maketh a comõ-
cion not onli outward in ceremonies, as do
comonly ÿ false christianes when it is nere
Easter, but there is a comocion within the
very bowels of the soule, and inward parte
of the herte, there is nothing that so cã perce
the soule, as doth the spirite of god, when it
entreth into it by speciall slidinge. Not on
ly it spoileth vs of the olde Adam with hys
concupiscence, & doth cloth vs wyth Christ,
with all his vertues, but also maketh vs to
be borne a new, that as if a poore man were
sodenly made an Emperoure, he shulde be
wholy chaunged, so he that of a vile sinner,

Math. xxi

Luke. xi.
Luke. ix

Roma. xiii.
Jhon. iii.

15

is made the sonne of God chaungeth though
tes, effectes, desires, and wyll, chaungeth
frenshipes, practises, wordes, workes, and
life, and of humaine, beastly, carnall, earthe,
and deuelishe: he becommeth heuenly, spi
rituall, angelicall, and dēuine as did Paul,
goinge to Damasco, when Christ did enter
his herte. There was a mutacion, from the
righte hande of God. When the spirite of
the Lorde entreth in a person, he is chaun
ged into another man, for that dieng to the
worlde, he beginneth to liue to him self. And
if when Christe did enter in to the temple he
purged it from those that bought and solde,
thincke if when he entreth into the spiritual
temple, he clenseth it from euery vnclennes
of sinne, there restith not in it any thinge of
dampnacion, he healeth it moste perfectlye,
so that if the vncleane woman was healed,
at the touche of the hemme of Christes gar
ment, ȳ mayst thinke what it is when Christ
in spirite entring in to the soule, and the per
son with lyuely faythe, imbraceth him who
ly for his. Also as when the sonne beames
enter into thy house, thou perceiuist in the
ayre, euē to the smalest mote which ȳ coul
dest not se before, so whē in the soule do en
ter the beames of lyght of the diuine grace,
the sinnes are perceiued in more cleare ma
ner. Yea, as the prodigal sonne neuer knew
nor perceiued truly his own errour, til with

Actes.ix
Psalm.lxxvi.
i.Reg.xi.
Math.xii

Rom.vii

Luke.xv.

such pitie he was imbraced of his father, ¶
had profe how great was the fatherly good
nes and charitie whiche he had offended:so
the sinner when he conuerteth ¶ beginneth
with the spirite to taste the diuine goodnes,
he beginneth also to know his malice, pride,
and ingratitude with the rest his vnlawful
sinnes. He restoreth to Zacheus that which **Luke.xvi.**
is not his, if Christ enter into his house and
dispenseth the superfluous thinges, yea beyng ryche with the treasures of Christe, he
leaueth al with vnmeasurable loue. He can
not partici pate or take parte of the bountie
of god that doth not communicate ¶ distribute
to others. The liuely flame muste needes
breake forth, or els beinge smoudered it que- **Iho.vii.**
cheth ¶ the fountaines ᵱ continuallye receiue
runing water must of force ouerflowe:so thei
that haue in the ᵱ holy gost, by ᵱ testimonie **Roma.viii.**
wherof they are sure to be the sones of god,
haue continuallye one such ¶ so entire, sincere,
and pure gladnes (whiche groweth of the
liuely knowledge ᵱ they haue of the greate
goodnes of god) ᵱ thei cā not expresse it, nor **i.Pet.i.**
thei cānot comprehēd thē selfes. Therfore not
being able to vᵭ hold thē selues, they springe
¶ leape for ioye wᵗ Jhon Baptist, wᵗ his mo- **Luke.i.**
ther they make exclamaciō, ¶ as to Zacha- **Exo.iiii.**
rie, so are their tōges losed: so ᵱ although in **Acte.iiii.**
praising of god thei perceiue wᵗ Moses that **Math.vii.**
they stāmer and are of an vnlearned tonge,

Math.vii.

neuertheles with the Apostels, they can not
kepe scilence of that which they haue heard,
sene, & felt, with the spieite, they must nedes
speake lyp the superabundaūce of loue, that

Ihon.iiii

they haue, they despre with the woman of
Samarye, that euery one should taste that
which they them selues haue had experiēce
of. And although for preaching the gospell
they be persecuted, for al that they to not de
siste and leaue of, but triumphing in al, they

Roma.v.

perseuer and go turth euen to the death, thei
feele in such sorte in the herte the charitie of

Actt.v.

god, that not onlie it is swete to them to suffer for his loue, but with the apostels they
reioyce therin. And for that they participate
of that greate charitie of Christe, by beynge
his members. Therfore with hym they par
don al men, beyng ready to shed their bloud
and put theyr lyfe for their enemies, & with

Roma.ix
Actt.vii.

Paul also to be accursed from Christe. And
this, because that as to Steuen, so the heauens are opened to them, in suche sorte, that
in spirite with clere & supernatural lyght of
fayth, they see the glory of god, in hauing ge
uen his only begottē & dearely beloued sone
for them vpon the crosse, they rest also quiet
as the shyp when Christ entred into it, they
haue the peace of cōscience, knowyng with

Mat.vi
Roma.v.

certeine fayth, that god by Christe & by hys
mercie, hath pardoned them. They haue also

so quietnes of minde, in suche maner. that
thoughe they were in al the perils & necessi-
ties of the world, yet alwayes aprouing for
iuste, the iudgemetes of god, knowyng that
he is their only father, that he hath most singuler cure of them, & that euery thynge fer-
ueth them to faluacion, they stand most fuer
ly, quiet, in peace, & tranquillitie. These suche
for that they walke according to the vocaci-
on of god, haue honour of euery enterpaife
that they take in hand, they can not be letted
or resisted, no more then god. Yea it is force
that euerye one feare them, as Herode feared Sainte Jhõ Baptiste, for that he had in
him the spirit of the Lorde, & as Abimelech
did Abrahã & Jsaac. They are dayly more
firme & stablyshed in good purposes to do
euer better, beyng lyfted vp cõtinually to a
greater perfeccion with Paule, althoughe
their minde be conuerfaunt in heauẽ, neuerthelesse, descending vp chriltian pitie, to fele
the miseries of their brethern, they laboure
also to drawe them to Christ, and moue thẽ
to haue the spirite, & to be in veritie Christianes, & not Jpocrites. As ý very grape doth
moue the birdes to taste therof, and not the
pyctfal. And finally, although with the Apo-
stelles, they euer remaine wyth Christe and
wyth the Cananite, whiche woulde not departe for his vngentle wordes, neuertheles

tyey

Gene.xxi.
Gene.xxvi.

i Cor.i.

Jhon.vi.
Math.vii.

The .xiiii. Sermon.

they are promte and readie for his honoure
and glorpe, to leaue wyth the Samaritane
hys sweete presence.

And what is more to be sayde when the
spirite of God dothe enter into a soule, he
suffereth it not to slepe, nor stand in idlenesse, but maketh it worcke thynges
merueplous and inexplicable, for
the loue of God: to whome be
euer all laude, honoure
and glorie by Jesu
Christe oure
Lord Amē.

(˒˒)

Imprinted at

London by John Day
dwellynge ouer Aldersgate, ⁊
Wylliam Seres, dwellyng in
Peter Colledge.

Cum priuilegio ad impri-
mendum solum.

CERTAYNE
Sermons of the
ryghte famous and excellente
Clerk Master Barnardine Ochine,
Borne within the famous vniuersitie of
Siena in Italy, now also an ex
ple in thys lyfe, for the
faithful testimony of
Jesus Christe.
Faythfully translated into
Englyshe.

※

Psalme cxvii.
❧ I wyl not dye, but lyue and declare
the workes of the Lord.

❧ Imprinted at London by
Jhon Day: dwelling ouer Alders
gate beneth S. Martins.
❧ These bookes are to bee tolde at hys
sho, in Chepesyde, by the litle
Counduit at the sygne of
the Resurrection.
Cum priuilegio ad imprimendum
solum, per septenium.

The Contentes of thys Booke.

FINIS.

Ho wel consydereth where
vnto we are created (good
Christen Reader) shall fynd
that of al our trauailes ther
resteth no fruite, as proueth
the holy spirite of prophecy
by the mouthe of Salomon sayinge. I
haue looked vpon al the thynges vnder
the sunne, and haue founde none other
but vanity. Onely reserued the Image
of God in vs, beyng the spirit that sus-
tepneth not the natural lyfe alone, but
also al the holy and vertuous thoughts,
which God hath created immortal vnto
his own likenes, as thou maiest wel par-
cepue, if thou consider the substaunce of
the natural body, that hauyng the spirit
is al liuely, & not only moueth ech finger
hand, foote, eye & toung materiallp, but
also wyth the thoughte penetrateth the
heauens, and in maner conceiueth a sub
staunce in the immortality of Gods euer-
lastyng kyngdom, and wanting the spirite, resteth dead priuate of al those vertues, though wel thou shalt se that it lac
keth nether hand, foote, eye, tunge nor
other member. Thys I saye vnto thee
(gentle reader) to the entent that thou
shouldest know that the almyghty crea-
tour is serued not of vanities, that is to

A.ii.   saye.

say, of bodely or worldly exercises, but
of spirituall thoughtes , whyche are the
iuste and true sacrifyces vnto God. And
therby to draw the to remember the mar
uaile of hys workes, and to thinke more
vnto thine end thē to thy life. Disposing
thy selfe to learne the sciences that this
lytle boke shal teach the, which treateth
of none other but of the spiritual thynges, and beareth in it the substaunce of
the holy scripture wyth so vehemēt reasons, and so good perswacions , that it
sufficeth to draw frō the thy stony hart,
and to reneu in the a carnal hart, if thou
be one of them, to whom God hath deter
mined to gyue hys grace . One of thē (I
say) þ wyth lyuely fayth confesse Christ
the son of god, to haue suffered for their
synnes. As the Authour hereof sufficiēt-
ly perswadeth the, who (being a man of
great peares, and wonderful reputaciō)
for the loue of Christe and of the truthe,
hath rather chosen exyle and persecuci-
on, then contynuaunce of wealthe , ho-
nours and frendshyp. A man of profoūd
learnyng. The most notable preacher of
al Itali. Famous for the great example
of hys good lyfe . Estemed and honored
of all Princes, not for hys age onely (be
yng a man of .lxx. peares, or therabouts)
but

The Preface.

but also for hys infinite vertues and mo
desty. And fynally so beloued of al peo=
ple, that in what place so euer he prea=
ched, ther hath euer bene founde greate
pleafe of audyence. All thys notwyth=
ftandyng at length' becaufe he fyncere=
ly folowed the true Gofpel, and did not
forbeare to repreheno the publyke abu=
fes of the Romifh church) he was perfe
cuted of Paul the thyrde, and conftray=
ned to forfake Italy, ꝙ to flee into Ger=
mani. Wher he hath not ceafed with his
penne to folow the vertuous exhortacy
ons, that before tyme wyth hys mouthe
he preached. And now God of his merci
hath brought hym hither vnto vs, ꝙ prea
cheth in the Italyan toung, whyche all
men vnderftand not, I haue tranflated
vi. of hys Sermons out of hys toung in
to Englyfh. Intendyng to tranflate the
reft very fhortely if thefe fhalbe thanke
fully receiued) to the entent that hys na
tyue toung therby may be made oures:
and that the glory of God may the
better be fet forth. Unto whõ
al honour is due worlde
wythout end.
So be it.

A.iii.

IT is commou-ly the custome of men in their testamētes, and last wols to sai: I leaue. I bequeath, I geue, wythoute once sayinge I take oz cari with me wherein certes they be farre deceiued because they take that, whych they ought to leaue be hynde thē, and go wythoute caryinge that whych e is very beholeful and ne cessary. Wherfore to the entent they shuld no moze erre on þ behalfe. I wold we shuld conspder and weyghe how a true Christian shuld make hys wpll.

Men that be either fooles, mad, phrantyke, neyther cā, noz yet know how to make a wpll, by reason they haue not wytte to descerne good from euyll, what is theires, oz what is not, what to take, noz what to restoze oz be queath, noz pet to whome noz in what maner. And if happely they go about

to

to make the pꝛ testamēt, it ſhuld be but vain
and of no foꝛce God alloweth it not as a
thing made of a parſon witles. Wherefoꝛe
he that is willing to make a teſtament effec
tual (as expedient is to him that will be ſaued) behoueth to haue verp good ſpiritual
iudgment, a liueli faith in Chꝛiſt, and an vn
derſtanding and light aboue a natural mā,
he muſt alſo be the ſonne, and lawful hepꝛe
of God.

And then he map ſap: J found of mpnde,
and readp of ſpirit and remembꝛaunce, albeit as touching mp fleſh ſpck make mp teſtament, and hēqueath ſpꝛſt of al mp being
and ſubſtaunce to god: he gaue it to me and
alſo pꝛeſerued it, and of hpm J recogniſe to
haue it, and foꝛ it J render him thanckes. J
leaue to him likewiſe the giftes, graces, benefites tempoꝛal, bodelp and goſtlp, that J
haue had, oꝛ ſhall heare after recepue: foꝛ
thep'de his, and from hpm vp grace J acknowledge to haue recepued all, as Paule
ſapeth, what haſt thou, that thou haſt not re
ceiued at gods handes. Pea foꝛ aſmuch as
al the ſlaunders, miſrepoꝛtes, perſecuciōs,
ſickenex, and misfoꝛtunes, which J haue al
readp oꝛ ſhal from hencefoꝛth ſuffer, and e-
uen death ſelf, J confeſſe (by the vnderſtan
ding that the Loꝛd hath geuen me) that thei
haue

haue bene and shalbe his giftes and graces
geuen and graunted of a great loue for my
wealth and profit:wherfore as his deuyne
rewardes I graunt to haue had the of god,
for them I thancke him . and as hys owne
I leaue and restore them to him.

And for so much as I canot but acknow
ledge that I haue gone alwaies backward
from him so often as I wolde rule my selfe
by my blynde iudgement, folyshe wisdome
and deuelishe spirite, nether did so much as
go one steppe forthe toward God, but whe
I was moued, dryuen, and thrust forwarde
of his holy spirit. Wherefore I commit to
the highest God my most deare father, and
to his gouernance, al the world and special
ly my self, in him (as I may) I wil help my
selfe with myne owne wytte, and fredome,
namely by makynge it obedyent to hym.

Moreouer if euer I haue spoken or shal
from hence forth vtter any word, if I haue
done or shal do any worcke,that is to hym
pleasaunte, if I haue had or after this tyme
shal haue thoughte desyre or wil, that good
is, I geue it to God, and at hys handes I
professe that I haue had al my goodnes, so
that if it were gods wil,to take from me al
that he hath geuen me,there shuld in me re
mayne nothynge but onely sinnes;those are
myne

mp ne own, and al other thinges be his.

Thus be mp sinnes if I shuld go before
gods presence, I were but dampned, if I
were mynded to make satiffaction I could
not, no nor pet anpe sapncte that euer was,
ther is none whose loue is so greate to take
mp sinnes vppon him and satiffp for them,
and appeale gods anger saue Christ alone,
wherfore to him I bequeath mp spnnes. I
leaue to hpm mp pride, vnkindenes, vnbe-
true, mistrust, arrogancp, enup, wrath, am-
bitio, and al mp vnnumerable wickednes,
I geue to him mp euil thoughtes, affectios,
and desires: to be short I make one fagot &
boundel of al mp offences present, past and
to come, and geue them to Christ haupnge
sure faith, and stedfast hope, that he wil ac
cept them for his own, and hath euen alrea
dp taken them, and for them hath satiffped
on the crosse, hps father layed them on hps   **Esaye.liii.**
necke, and he did not ones agapn sap it, but
of great loue allowed them for bps, and to
consume and burn them in the flame of his
deuine loue, he bore them on his innocente
shoulders vppon the crosse, (as Peter wri-   **i.Peter.ii.**
teth) and so was offered a sacrifice for vs.

Now seing I haue left al mp sins to Christ
and geuen to God mp substaunce, and being, withal other giftes and graces, that he

        D.i.   be-

bestowed on me. J remayn naked wythout
eyther good oz euyl, and truly to say, J am
rather nothyng. Jn that J haue restozed to
God my beinge that J hadde by creatyon
and byzthe.

But foz becaule it is impossible that he
shuld saue me wythout being, and so it is y
he wil saue me, therfoze first J carye wyth
me Christ him selfe, which is my life. God
hathe so loued me, that he hathe geuen hym

Jhon .iii. selfe to me. ffoz so hath God loued y wozld
that foz theyz syns he hath geuen vs his on.
ly begotten sonne. J cary also with me hys
spirit, that was of his eternal father geuen
me of his most roial liberaliti, as wel decla
reth Paule, wher he sayeth, God hath sent

Gala.iiii. the spirit of his sonne into our hartes wher
by we cry and cal father, father.

And in that he hathe geuen me hym, he
hath restozed me to myself and former be.
ing. With a new substance and nature spi.
ritual, so that foz the possibility of my salua
ciõ. J haue a being: but yet lacke J treasure
to discharge my great dets, and to appeare
rych in goddes syght, in consideraciõ wher
of J beare with me Christes watching, ab.
stinences, trauayles, pzaiers, persecutions,
slaunders, J take with me hys teares, hys
swet, hys bloud, and al that euez he dyd oz
suffered

suffered in thre and thirty yeres is myne e=
uery deale, and with liuely faith J embrace
it as for mine own, J cary beside this with
me hys pacyence, meknes, loue, and al o=
ther hys deuyne vertues, his gifts and gra
ces, hys treasures, and al that he hath mere=
ted and deserued, hys lyfe, passion, deathe,
resurreccion and assenfion be mine, ye all ý
euer he hath done or shal from hencefoorthe
do is mine, and what nedeth more to say, if
God haue geuen vs his owne sonne, howe
hathe not he with him geuen vs al thynges **Rom.viii.**
wherfore with faithe J embrace my sweete
Jesus for mine owne, he is my rightwysenes, wysdom, raunsome, and holines, he is **i.Corin.i.**
my strengthe, he is my spirite, my lyghte,
lyfe, hope, and al my goodnes, euen Christ
him selfe in hys laste wyl bequethed me all
ý he had of the father. Wherfore he sayth:
J entertayne you at my table as my father
hathe vsed me, as my father hath made me **Luke.xxii.**
hys heyre so nowe J ordein you. J wil that
as you be my brethren so you shalbe my fo=
lowers. And in another place he sayeth: J
haue loued you, as mi father hath loued me
sithen J am nowe through Christe so ryche
of treasures, vertuouse, and graces, J shal
be hable not onely to satisfy for my dettes,
but also to purchase infinite paradise, when

D.ii. soeuer

soeuer they shalbe soulde.

Who shalbe nowe either to accuse or condemne me, after that Christ hathe thus clothed me with his innocensy, rightwisenes, holynes, loue, with all his vertue, graces, treasures, merites, and with his own selfe. I may with no lesse boldenes and suretye, then Christ, appeare before God, I am his sonne, as he is, and heyre of heauen, semblably I am innocent as Christ is now that he hathe satisfied for me, and payed my raunsome, and rewarded me wyth his innocency, Christe saied: I hallow my self that they also maye be holpe, euen he is oure holynes and we be his members. Wherfore it is as possible for God not to loue me, as it is possible that he shuld not loue Christ, by reason wherof Paule sayeth: who shall deuide me from the loue of God that is in Christe Jesu. It must nedes be that he be saued which wyth lyuynge faythe embraceth Christe for hys owne. And consideringe that the treasures, and merites of Christe are infinite, and able to enryche a thousande worldes, I entende not to carye with me anye other merites, nor spirituall ryches saue those that Christe hathe proupded for me, for they be not onlye sufficient for me, but also ouer aboundaunce and vnmesurable.

Then shoulde I do no small iniurye to Christe,

Roma. viii.

Chriſt,if J ſhuld ſearch to ſtore my ſelfe by
any other meane oꝛ ſhift,although J might
do it neuer ſo eaſely,nay rather wyth Paul
wyl J recken al other thynges as myꝛe and
dyꝛt ſo that J haue Chriſte,wyth whome a- Philip.iii.
lone J wil appeare befoꝛe God,and of and
by hym wyl J gloꝛye and make boaſte, yea Galath.vi.
God foꝛ byd,that J ſhuld make my auaūte
of any thing,ſaue of the croſſe of our Loꝛde
Jeſu Chriſt of whome only hangeth al our
health.And albeit al the ſaintes be ryche by
meane of Chriſt,neuertheles,if they had me
rytes of theyꝛ owne moſte plenteouſe,and
wolde geue them to me, yet wolde J none,
my Chriſt is inoughe foꝛ me,with him had
J rather ſuffer, then take pleaſure and ioye
without him. Jt would be a thing pleaſaūt
to me,if euerye man ſhulde make pꝛaper to
God foꝛ me,not becauſe J myght purchaſe
oꝛ haue anye other treaſures then thoſe that
J haue of Chriſt,but that J might by liuely
faith euery day acknowledge,poſſeſſe and
embꝛace thoſe p̄ J haue receyued of Chriſte
and counte them foꝛ myne and ſo enfoꝛme
my ſelfe,J my ſelfe were it not by Chriſte,
ſhoulde not knowe what to aſke,foꝛ in him
is al and without him al other things be but
mere vanitie,onely this peticion J make to
him,that he bouchſafe euery dai to geue me
light and vnderſtandinge,that J may haue

wpt to accounte and take hps treasures for
mine owne. Wherfore if anp man wil pray
for me let hpm not tarpe tpll J be deade, for
then J canne no more encrease in lighte and
grace. Let him pray now, that J map grow
in faith and more and more instruct mp self
of Christes riches. J am wel assured that in
purgatorpe J shall not come, bothe because
there is founde no other purgatorpe but
Christe in whome at the full be purged and
punished al the spnnes of the elected, and al
so because in case there were one, pet Christ
not bp mp merites, but bp hps mere goodues dothe satisfie for al mp spnnes, trespas-
ses, and papnes, and for as muche as hope
neuer made anp man ashamed, nor confoun
ded anpe persone, that hadde it in hps harte
(as Paul wrote) therfore am J sure and see-
ker that he wpll saue me without other pur-
gacion. We cannot promesse oure selfes to
muche of goddes goodnes, no we neuer can
be hete bs so much, but he wpll recompence
muche more, J wpl not suffer therefore that
after mp lpfe anpe good be done for me.
  Truth it is that if J haue anp goodes them
must J leaue to the poore flocke of Christe,
not because thep shoulde prape for me, that
am al readpe saue d . but for the vse of other
that lpue, and shalbe borne, as Christe dpd
and also because the rather thep mape lpue

Rom .iii.

Jhon. vii

godly, and knowe that they shal neuer lack
that be hys, and put theyr trust in hym. To
whom be alwayes, honoure and
glory through Jesu
Christ our Lord
Amen.

☞ The. viii. Sermon.

Howe we shoulde answer the de
uel when he tempteth vs & name
lye in the ende of oure lyfe.

The Deuel (as Peter wrpteth) seketh al
waye to deuoure vs but chefelye he is
busye at the houre of death, by reason
then it standeth hym in hand so to do for his
owne behooue. and our greater endomage
and harme. Then vseth he al myght, power
slepghte, decepte, and malice: wherefore I
thynke good that we shulde search howe to
make hym aunsweare and by the assistence
and ayde of gods grace to vnderstand him
aud get the vpper hande of hym.

He is constrayned speciallye when wee
aproch nere to oure death, to throw vs into
a bisse and pit of desperacion, or els to set vs
in pride and presumpciō: if he shal perceyue
that thou either put trust in thy self, or confidence in thyne owne worckes, he will not
goo in hande to make the despayre and mi-

D. iiii. trust

i. Peter. v.

trust gods mercy, but rather stablishe the
in that erronpouse opinion of pryde of thy
dedes, on the other syde if he fele that thou
hast all thy hope in God: then wyl he shew
the on the one partie the multitude and wic
kednes of thy synnes, and on the other partie goddes wrathe and seuere iustice, he wyl
tell the how thou art in a maze and perpler
itie not able to be shaken of, or wonden out
of, and by makyng the to fele thyne offences, otherwise then euer thou dyddest in thy
healthe wyll go aboute to take oute of thy
harte the passion of Christ, and all the great
goodnes, mercy, and loue of God, & finallp
to proue the damned, he wyl bryng for hys
purpose, euen the holy scriptures.

But I wyll that al hys temtacions serue
the to the honour of God and saluacion of
thy soule as they do serue the turne of the e-
Roma.viii. lected, to whom all thynges woorke to gether for they wealth, fyrste of all I warne
the, that thou maintein not thy self for good
but admit and graunte all the euill that he
shall reherse of the and thynke, that he hath
i.Jhon.ii, not saied so muche, but that it is much more
and thanke God that now at laste he hathe
bene so fauorable, to make the consider thy
sinnes, wherin he vseth the deuel for an instrument, to the entent that by the knowing
of them, thou shuldest take occasion to hum
ble

ble thp felfe, and to cal Chriſt to thp remembraunce, whpche to ſcoure and clenſe them
hath not onlpe reputed them foz hps owne,
but alſo dped foz them bpō the croſſe, graūt
thou hardelp that thou art a greate rpbalde
and noughtpe withoute erculpnge thp felfe
in anp wiſe, and that thp ſinnes are immume
rable. Confeſſe that thou could neuer ſatiſ-
fpe foz one alone, and that thou were the
moſt damned ſinner of the wozld if Chriſte
had not deliuered the, and ſtpl prompte thp
felfe with thoſe matters, whpche mape further the to come into deſperacion of thp ſelf

But if the deuel wait to bzpng the to deſpapze of Chriſt, thou map in no wpſe cōſent
therto, but ſtedfaſtlp put thp truſt in hpm.
And mp mpnd is that thou ſap to him thus:
Jf it were good foz me to miſtruſt Chriſt, ꝑ
neuer wouldeſt haue perſwaded me therto
but rather haue dzawen me from it, wherefoze in that thou woldeſt putte me in mpnde
to miſtruſt Chriſt, thou makeſt me ſtronger
in mp hope and truſt.

Thou ſhalt ſap to him, that when he cau-
ſed iniuſtlp Chriſt to dpe, whpch was an innocent, he loſt al his interpriſe and iuriſdic-
tion, that euer he had oz poſſible might haue
ouer man. And if he procede fozth to induce
the to deſpapze, hp ſettpnge befoze the thp
greate ſpnnes, J wpll the to ſapto hpm. Go
to

Jhon. ii. to Christ, which (as Jhon wryteth) is myne
attournei and aduocate, he can make the an
aunswere for me, reason there with hym, if
thou haue any claime or title in me, as thou
sayest, doest thou not know that he hath taken my synnes for hys owne, and hathe for
them made satisfactyon most plentuously,
therfore hast thou no ryght in me at al.

If he chaunce to say his death is not i-
nough to sane the, answere him: if Adam by
tasting one apple with one only sinne was
hable to damne me: how is it that so manye
holy workes of Christ, which tasted for my
sake of great loue the most bytter death, be
not sufficient to saue me. If the disobedience
Roma . vi. of Adam had power to condemn me, much
more the obedyence of Christe is stronge i-
nough to saue me, yea the gift of Christ is a
boue and excedeth the synne of Adã, Christ
hath more auapled and holpen vs, then A-
hain annoied and harmed vs, by reason the
light of Christ is of more force & effect then
the darkenes of our fyrst parent, the goodnes of Christes surmounteth and passeth ý
malice of man, and his vertue preuaileth a-
boue oure frailty: one teare of Christe hathe
bene more pleasaunt to God, thẽ al the sins
of the world be displeasaunt, Christ hath be
able to do more to appeace hym, then we to
prouoke hym to anger, Christes liuing was

more

more formal and ordinary, then oures was
out of order and frame. Christ hath doone
more to the honour of God, then we haue
done to his dishonoure. Wherfore I maye
wel say, Christ that is my wisdom, rightwis
nes, holynes, and redempcion is sufficient i. Corin, i.
inough to saue me.

And if haply he shuld say, it is not sufficient for thy saluacion to beleue in Christe, the
behoueth to keepe his commaundementes,
thou must loue God wyth al thy hart, & thy
neyghbour as thy self, and desire nor couet
any thing worldly, which thinges because
thou doest not, ergo, thou art dampned, if
fayth only wer inough I also and al the deuels shuld be saued, because (as it is writte)
euen the deuels beleue and feare. They be-   Jacob. ii.
leue that God made and created heauen and
earth, and that Christ came, dyed, rose, ascended into heauen, that he sent the holy ghost,
and that he shal come to iudge the quicke &
dead, and yet are not we therfore saued, and
that because we obserue not his deuine preceptes. Wherfore thou also art but lost, he
wyl thus labour to bring the vnder the law
to thinke that thou must be iustified not by
Christ, but by perfourminge and fulfillinge
of the lawe, to the end y thou shuld despair.

But I wyl that thou make answere and
say: if thou diddest beleue as by gods grace

I beleue:that is, that God for thy wealthe
hath created the worlde, and semblably pre
serueth it, in such sort that thou couldest fele
in the creatures the loue of God, and lyke=
wyse wold beleue firmely, that Christ came
and dyed for thy sinnes, for to saue the, and
for thy sake and profit, and in lyke manner
of the other articles, thou also should be sa=
ued, and then, when thou haddest a liuely fe
ling of the goodnes and loue of God thou
woldest loue hym, and thy neyghbour like=
wyse, and beynge rauyshed into God woul
dest begynne to set litle store by the world as
al good Christen men and women do. If it
fortune that he say: he is cursed that kepeth
not and obserueth the lawe, wherfore thou
arte one of myne, saye to hym agayne, for
that cause Christ dyed on the crosse, for to
delyuer me from all curses, and in so much
as I am alreadye of Christ, I am deade to
the lawe.

Agayne if he replye saying: wher be thy
workes, wherby thou trustest to be saued?
answer, I trust not to be saued bi mi works
for they be such that if I shuld haue regard
or respect to them, I feare me to be damned
yea I were surely acertained of my damna
cion. I hope only to be saued by Christ, and
hys workes, whyche be myne owne, and so
much rather myne, then they I dyd mysele

Deu.xxvii.

Galath.iii.
Roma.vii.

Rom.viii.

A.v.

as that the spirite of Christe geuen to me is
more enper to me then mpne own life or a
np other thyng.

Further if he shulde endeuour to proue
the to be none of the elect, bp reason of the
innumerable, and outragiouse spnnes that
thou haft cnmmitted, for prosperites, or ad=
uersities thou haft had, for the great euplles
wherin thou art founde at thp deathe, or for
the temptacpons thou hafte suftepned, sap=
inge, that God preserueth his elected from
the lyke eupls. Make hpm answer and sap:
rather dothe God practpse them in diuerse
such manners, albeit of euerpthing thep be
certified to the honoure of God, thou shalt
morcouer sap to hpm thus. I geue more cre
dite and trufte to Christe, whiche when he
was deade for me on the crosse, tould me I
was saued, then to the, that arte alwapes a
lyer and father of erroures. I wpll thou tel
hpm, how thou geuest more sapth to Christ
alone, then to al the reasons and authorities
of the world: thou map vp spde thps sape to
him, the spirit of God beareth witnes to mi
spirit, that I am the sonne of god and to him
muste I rather trufte then to the. When he
shall sape, if thou were the sonne of God he
would not leaue the in such punishmentes,
as thou art in, but would geue the some re=
lease and easement, answere hpm: In case it

wer

were as thou fapest Chriſt ſhulde not haue
bene the ſonne of God,ſithen on the croſſe
he had no comfort,nor ſenſual taſt or feling
ſo that he ſapd: mp God,mp god why haſt

Mark,xb. thou forſaken me ; it ſufficeth to me that he
ſheweth me ſo much fauoure,for J am contented with all that pleaſeth hpm, as Chriſt
alſo was,pea in his ſufferinge,he felt exce-
dinglp the infinite loue of the father.

Beſide theſe if he ſap :thou art the ſonne

Ephes.ii. of Adam,ergo thou art accurſed, Anſwere
thou thus : J am bleſſed agapne bp brpnge

Jhon.i. borne of God,and bp meane of that bleſſed
ſede Chriſt as God long agone promiſed A

Gene.xii. dam when he ſaped;Jn thp ſede al nacpons
ſhalbe bleſſed,thou ſhalt tel hpm:how thou
art deſpoiled and bereft of the old Adam, ẽ

Roma,xiii. clothed with Jeſu Chriſt as Paul teacheth
and aduertiſeth the,

What time as he ſhal declare to thẽ that
Chriſt is wroth, angrp and ſharp:make him
anſwere how Chriſt is not ſuch one , for he
is the health and hope of ſinners, and whp-
leſt we be in this life preſent he is bttered to
bs,pitifull, ſweete,and oure Jeſus,that is,
our ſaiuoure , and al be it he ſeine to ſpeake
ſharpe,and cruel wordes to the woman of

Meth.xv. Cananp:pet in heart he gaue her confidẽce
and boldnes,and ſhewed him ſelf to her ful
of ſwetenes and loue. Jn dede at the dap of
Judgmẽt

iudgement to the damned ſhall he be ſhew=
ed angry, & wrathful but in the meane tyme
till that day while we be here in this preſent
life, he is ſhewed pitiouſe to al, and pryncy=
pally to the greate ſynners.

And if it ſo were that he wolde ſaye thou
art not truly confeſſed, nor haſt rehearſed al
thy ſynnes, and the circumſtaunces of the
ſame, ne haſt examyned ſufficiently thy con
ſcience, nor yet haſte not that pure perfecte
greate and vnfayned ſorowe for thy ſynnes
that thou of dutye ſhuldeſt haue, thou haſte
not ſatyſſyed for theſe ſo great an innume=
rable dettes, that thou haſte towarde God,
make hym thys aunſwere and ſay: thou art
a ſeruaunt and not a iudge: or to ſaye more
truly, thou art already iudged and condem
ned, ſeing thou beleueſt not in Chriſt, & wol Jhon.iii.
deſt thou iudge me: trouble thy ſelfe no lon=
ger in prouynge that I haue failed in al, for
ſure I am, and fully I beleue to be ſaued,
not by workes by reaſon they be vnperfect
nor yet by the worthynes of my fayth, for in
that alſo I am not perfect, becauſe I beleue
not with ſo great a faith as I oughte, but I
beleue I ſhalbe ſaued by Chriſte, and not
by my workes.

He wyl ſay: thou art not worthy to be ſa=
ued, ſay thou to him for a ful anſwer: the vn
worthy be ſaued ſo often as they acknowe=
ledge

kedge theyr owne vnworthines, go hartelye
for healpe to Chriſte, by whoſe meane they
be come worthye.

Where as he ſhal laye to thy charge that
thou arte one of the worſte of the world, ſay
to hym on thys wyſe: oure inſpꝛꝛꝛꝛmptyes be
but ſmall in compariſion of the infinite merites of Chriſte, and of the incomprehenſy-
ble mercye of God: and the moꝛe great that
my ſinues be and without number, ſo much
greater ſhalbe hys gloꝛye in deliuering me,
and J with ſo muche the greater truſt pꝛay
as that if he wyll heare me, it ſhall be moꝛe
to hys honoure and gloꝛye. And when J cō
ſyder and call to remembꝛaunce, that my
ſweete and louinge bꝛother Jeſus Chriſt the
ſonne of God, whyche foꝛ my ſake dyed on
the croſſe, and wolde agayne innumerable
tymes foꝛ me, if neede were, and that J am
hys owne foꝛ ſo manye cauſes, and that he
may determyne of me after his own mind.
Foꝛ ſo muche as hys father hathe geuen
hym full power in heauen and earth: when
J conſyder thys, J ſay, J canne in no wyſe
doute of my ſaluacion.

If he efte ſoones reaſon thus: thou haſte
done no penannce foꝛ thy ſynnes, anſweare
on thys manner: that can J neuer doo, if J
ſhoulde alwaye ſtande in the fyꝛe, Chriſte
hathe done that foꝛ me on the croſſe moꝛeouer.

rer Chrifte is myne, the father hathe geuen
hym to me wyth al his merites, al the good
woorckes, that euer he dyd are myne, wherefore I maye with his deuine riches, and tre-
sures satiffy for al.

After thys manner I wolde thou shulde
aunswere him, when so euer he setteth afore
the thy sinnes, and infinite dettes, that thou
oughtest to God for the benefites, thou haft
recepued wyth dyuerse and sundrye vyces
whyle he tempte the, but specyallye wyth
desperacion, wherwith he tempteth euen ŷ
sayntes he wyll put the in mynde and my-
trufte that Chrifte hathe forsaken the: but
make answere that he neuer forsoke person
that trufted in hym, but becaufe he wold forsake none of vs, he was mynded to be forsaken him selfe on the croffe, and if he shuld
at anye tyme forsake and refufe vs (the whi
che is a thinge impoffible) it shoulde be for
more glorye of God, and we oughte not on
lye to be contented, but alfo to take it for a
synguler priuiledge and prerogatyue. It be
houeth vs to ftande ftronge in the faythe,
and thynke that afore God the paffyon of
Chrift can do more to caufe him to loue vs,
then oure synnes canne procure hys hate to
ward vs, we had nede to bewel armed with
spirite, faythe, and grace, for learning suffi-

F.i.   ceth

ceth not to know how to answere, and witte
thou well that Christe was tempted, and
specyallye at the ende, wherefore he sayeth:
the prynce of thys worlde is common, but he
hathe gotten nothynge of me.

Jhon .xb.

And if he canne not wyth these armoure
hurte the, he wyll tourne ouer the leafe, and
saye thus, and al because to deceiue the. Go
to thou haste all readye banqupshed me, I
was mpneded to bring the into desperacio,
but I coulde not. Thou art saued: & by & by
wil y angels come to set the. He wil appere
to the lyke an aungel of light, and say to the
as he did to saynte Hilarion. Haste thou serued God so longe, haste thou done so many
good deedes so greate penaunce, geuen so
many good ensamples, saued so mani souls
and albeit thou haste committed sinnes? yet
arte thou confessed of them, thou haste done
penaunce, thou haste taken pardons, thou
haste gone for indulgences, thou kepeste the
commaundementes, and besyde these done
manye boluntarye workes that thou wast
not bounden to do, wherfore why shuldeste
thou feare. Thou shalte be safe and sure, if
thou be not saued, then shall none be saued.
yea thy good workes be ouer plusse, more
then sufficeth, whiche thou maye sel or geue
to other, whiche if thou do not the church of
Rome

ii. Cor, xb.

The Diuel
is a lyar.

Rome shalbe the heyre, and thou shalt en- *Thou. still*
rich their treasury of indulgence. What fe-
rest thou therfore: hast thou happely gone a
nother path or way. Albeit thou haue admit
ted synnes, yet seest thou not how thou art
wel disposed at the last, only stād stoutly in
the trust of these thy great and many good
workes suffer thys sycknes, and death for
the remission of thy synnes, and thou shalt
be more then saued, only ofte remember thy
self. Of thy good workes. Then it is expedi
ent for the to say thus. Thou wouldest that
I shuld trust in my workes, and I haue no
feare of being dampned, wer it not for my
workes., I geue thankes to my Lord Christ
Jesus, whych hath geuen me the grace to
counte my workes for a thing of nought, &
for such, that euery one of them I deserue to
be punyshed, thou magnifiest my workes,
to draw me backe from the confydence of
Christ, but by gods grace, thou shalt not be
able to do it, I fynde that I am vpon a litle
bourd in the sea tossed with myghty wynds
and haue embraced and be clepped a strōg
pyller or rocke, and thou councelest me to
leaue it, and to sticke to the rotten thynges
whych if I shuld do, the windes would carye bothe me and them into the sea. Rather
I wyl perish with Christ which is a thyng
F.ii.   imposs

The.viii.Sermon of

impossible J then ipue wpthout hym, no J can not put mp trust holp in Christ vnles spit al together J dispapre of mp selfe and mpne own workes. Wherfore it is necessary that we despoile our selfes of al trust in our own workes, and bp fapth and hope, clothe vs and arme vs with Christ and in hpm put our hope, and although we haue not that great fapth, pet in no wple ought we to despapre, because if at the first he do not, pet at length he gruith it to hps elected at thep death, as the Prophet Abacucke told a fore hand, when he saped, Lord when thep shal be neare to the death at the latter ende, betwene thps wap and the other, thou wplt make knowen to them Christ and his great benefits, and wilt epen to them the boome of thp graces bp Jesu Christ our Lord.

Amen.

The.ix.Sermon.

Howe aunsweare is to be made at the iudgment seat of god

A felon or gpltp person, that canne not flpe, but of necessitp must appeare at the sessions assise, or law dap afore barre, ppcketh out and choseth him for hps aped and succoure, attourneps, protectours and counsellers, and goeth deuising how he

map be defended , namely in a matter tou=
ching life and death:which thing it standeth
vs in hand more to do. In so much as, that
we being ful of sinnes, must appeare before
the high iudgment seat of gods iustyce, and
when iudgment by definitiue sentence is geuen against vs, we shal lose paradise, soule,
grace, God, and al goodnes without reco-
uery, and be throwen into the depe pit of hel
therto remain and abide in fyre euer lasting
ly. Wherfore me semeth it wer expedient to
imagin what way to take, what answere to
make, with what reasons to arme vs, that we
may haue the matter to passe on our syde. Roma .v.

First of al an vndouted matter is it, that
we al haue sinned in Adam, and beside the o
riginall sinne haue innumerable actuall, ne
can be saued, onles first we be absolued and
forgeuē, and that must nedes be whilest we
be in thys lyfe for afterward is no more re
demcion at al . To the glotten was denyed Luke. xvi,
one droppe of water.

Wherfore necessary is it to know ý ther
be two iudgment seates of God: the one is
of ryghtwisenes, the other of mercy, grace,
pitie, goodnes, loue swetenes, and liberali=
ty: as Paule speakynge of thys laste sayth:
Let vs go boldly to the trone, and bench of Heb.iiii,
gods grace at the first bench sitteth God, &
E.iii.   Chrise

Christe kepeth residence at the second. Now as for the spinners, if they wil be saued they must go al to the bench of mercy to aske and cal for pity, and not iustice, for fauour & not strayghte reconyng, because we haue al ben vniuste, and withall oure rightwisnes, and good workes be not hable to withstad gods rightwisenes, wherfore Dauid sayed, Lord none can be iustified in thy syght, if there thou wilte see a reconinge, and in a nother place. Lord if thou wilt punish our iniquities, who shalbe hable to abide? & Job saith I knowe that man can not be iustified if he stande face to face a fore God. And in a nother place, what thing is man that he shuld be cleane? the heauens be not cleane in hys syght. And Jeremye wryteth thus: If thou washe the wyth Nitrus thou shalt neuerthe les be stayned. And Esaye sayeth: our right wisenes be lyke the clothes of an vncleane woman: and Salomon witnesseth the same, sayinge who is he that can saye my heart is cleane. I am pure and innocent from sinne wherefore sayth God by Jeremy, why wyl you striue with me in iudgment: As though he shulbe saye you are fooles, if you thynke your selfe hable to wythstande the iustice of God, seinge your ryghtwysenes is vnclene and that so muche vnclener, as that not only the

Psal. cxliii.

Psal. cxxix.
Job. ix.

Job. xv.

Jeremi. ii.

Prouer. xx

the moorkes, but also the berpe inwarde thoughtes, affections, and despies shalbe examined, and tryed. Therfore sayeth God, I wyl searche, trye and proue Jerusalem wyth lanternes, it is moste profitable to go to the benche of mercy. And say with Dauid, Lorde I shall come afore the, not wyth the multitude of my workes, but of thy mercye, and incase thou be somemoned and called to the throne of iustice. Appeale to the other benche of mercye, for as from the iudgmente of a Lorde subiecte to the Emperour a man maye appeale to Cesars iudgemente seate: so may a man appeale from the bench of iustice to the trone of merci as to the higher courte. In as muche as James wryteth mercye excelleth iustice: it is seene that Ezechias, after sentence was geuen vpon him at the benche of iustice, because he appealed to the other trone of mercye had graunted to hym, that he shuld lyue fiftene yeres longer And Dauid by appealynge to mercye caused the sentece to be reuoked, whiche was geuen that he shulde dye. And what tyme that seruaunte of whome the gospell speaketh, sayed, haue pacience wyth me and geue me respyte: he appealed to mercy and was herd Jn lyke manner is it and hathe be of al sinners that be saued.

Sopho.i.

Psalm.xb.

James.ii.

iiii.Reg.il

ii.Reg.x.i.

Math.bii.

E,iiii,   Nowe

Nowe muſte we doo in the ſame wyſe, J
meane when we be cyted to the court, of iuſtyce to render and yelde an accompte, then
muſt we appeale to mercy, and ſaye: we be
deade throughe Chriſte to the law, and ther
Rom.vii. fore to iuſtice alſo, which iudge after ỹ law
are we deade, then hathe iuſtyce no iuriſdic-
tion vppon vs at all, no thoughe it were the
greateſt ſynner of the worlde, ſaye thou to
God, J am Chriſtes, thou gaueſt me to him
as Chriſte ſayeth, they were thine, and thou
Jhon.xvii. haſte geuen them to me. Moreouer Chriſte
hathe redemed me, therefore am J hys for
manye cauſes, J wyll therefore ſtand to his
iudgemente, thou haſte geuen hym all pow-
Mat.rviii. er in heauen and in earthe as hee hym ſelfe
ſayeth, to me is geuen all power in heauen
and in earthe, wherefore he maye doo wyth
me the thynge that lyketh hym, and as to
hym ſemeth good, he is my iudge as Chriſt
hym ſe lfe ſayeth, the father hathe geuen all
Jhon.rii. iudgmente to the ſonne, it is therfore his du
ty to iudge me. But as in a nother place he
ſayeth he came not to iudge but to ſaue the
worlde, ſaye therefore to Chriſte, doo thyne
offyce, ſaue me, for thou cammeſte, and thy
father dyd ſende the for that intente, J feele
all readye thy voyce, and in my hearte thou
ſayeſte to me, that becauſe J truſte in the,
thou

thou wylte saue me, all readye bp thy grace
haue J put in the mp confidence and hope,
and he that beleueth in the, can not be damp Exodi. xix.
ned, saue me therfore accozding as thou art
bounden bp a couenaunt made. And al be it
thy conscpence accused the, and all the deuels besyde layed to thy charge, pea though
iudgement wer geuen against the, pet so long
as thou art in thys present lyfe, it is alwaye
lawful to appeale to the mercy of God.

And if it wer so, that bp force thou shuld
be drawen to the court of iustice, crpe oute
wpth Esay, & say to Christ: O Lozd J suffer
biolence, make answere foz me, healpe me, Es. xxxviii.
forsake me not, J chose and wol haue the foz
mp attozney and speach manne: not because
thou shuld defend mp iuste accomptes, and
true reckenpnges, foz J haue none such, but
to the intente thou shuld take mp synnes foz
thyne, and reward me with thine innocency
holpnes and ryghtwysenes. Thou hast all
readye satisffied foz me on the crosse and ap
popnted me bp a dopcion to be the sonne of
God, wherfoze J can not be damned, no not
one shalbe found that dare accuse me, being Rom. viii.
one of goddes electeb.

Moreouer if thou be mpnded and wpl-
lynge to appeare wpthoute daunger at the
benche of goddes ryghtewysenes byspople
                                    first

Colloss. iii.

stryse thy selfe of the olde Adam, and apparel the with Christe (as Paul exhorteth vs) & thou shalbe safe. For in so muche as thou haste embraced him for thine own, thou can not be damned although thou haddest committed al the sinnes of the worlde. As a wo-

Apoca. iii.

man greate with childe cannot be punished no more canthou, if thou haue Christ in thy harte, or rather (as Christe sapeth) he that be-

Jhon. iii.

leueth in the son is not iudged he is so assured of hys saluacion, that there nedeth no examinacion to be hadde of him, he is one of Christes mēbers, and hath his spirit, wherfore he can no more be dampned then Christ because he is knit to him by liuelye faythe.

If it be so that God woulde make there with the a reckenynge, saye to hym howe

Esaye. liii.

thou hast made it wyth Christ, for as he put on Christ al our iniquities and sinnes (as Esaye sapeth) and with greate loue accepted them for hys owne, and bounde him selfe to make satisfaction for them. Wherfore thou shalt say, Lorde if thou haste anye reconing or matter agaynste me, make it with Christ he knoweth wel how to answere and can declare that he hathe satisfied for them.

In case be that any must be dampned for the synnes I haue doone, it is Christe, that muste be dampned, and not I good Lorde,

for

for albeit J am he that commytted them, ne
uertheles Christe bounde hym selfe to satisf=
fye for them, and that by consente and good
wyll of hys father, wherefore who so euer
beleueth symelye in Christe is all to gether
safe and sure.

Besyde thys if God wolde needes make
the audite and accompt wyth vs, and wold
saye: J am not contente wyth Christes satis
factpō for you. J wil that your selues make
recompence for that you haue offeded (whi=
che is a thynge impossyble) all readye from
the beginninge he is contented, and hath ac
cepted that deuine sacrpfyce of the vndefy=
led lambe Christe Jesus, whyche dyed on
the crosse to be obedyente to hys father (as Phillip, ii.
Paule hathe wrytten) al readye is the right
wyseues of God satpsfyed by Christe more
then suffycyente, we be all readye consyled
wyth God, and made his sonnes, and so con
sequentlye hys heyres he hath al readye ge=
uen vs paradyse, and when God hath once Roma. ri
geuen a gyfte it neuer repenteth hym: wher
fore the gyfte canne not be called agayne by
reason God is not chaungeable, J neuerthe
les althoughe (as J sayed) he shulde saye:
J wyll that thou thy selfe satisfye. Answere
hym on thys wyse: Lorde if J were as dere
beloued to the, as is Christe, and had done
and

and suffered longyng lye for thy honoure. All that Christ did and suffered, in this case wolde thou not holde thy selfe sufficiently satiffyed for me: in case he grannted thereto. Thou shulde make hym this answer. Then is it all readye done. For in that Christ suffered I my selfe suffered, By reason I am chãged into Christ. Yea the true Christians, ÿ haue Christ in theyr heartes (as Paule sayeth let Christe dwel in our harts) maye pitiouslye lamente and complayne to of God, and saye to him: thou hast punished vs more bytterlye then we haue deserued, cõsidering that we offended and not Christe, reasone wolde thou shulde haue punyshed vs, oure wyll, and oure lyfe and soule, and not that innocent and vndefiled lambe Jesus Christ and thou hast punished Christ which is the lyfe of my soule. The harte of my heart, the spirite of my spirite (as Dauid sayth) God my flesh and my hearte. God of my hart. Thou shuldest, if my deathe had not bene inoughe for my synnes, tourned me into nothynge, and letten a loue that innocent, and iust Christ more deare and intier to me then myne owne soule wherefore I feele more that, that he suffered for me, then I shoulde haue felt, if I had suffered al ÿ torment possible on mine own body, but wel wyst thou
that

Rom. viii.

Psal. lxxiii

that J could not bp reason of mp fraplty, a
bpde and suffer al, that J had deserued for
mp synnes, and therfore thou chose ẙ mpgh
tp and strong Christ to suffer for them in mi
steade, and moreouer hast set him in mp hart
to the intent that J shuld not onlp feele that
he suffered also, but also that he mpght geue
me strength to be able to suffer,

Thou maiest also sap: Lord albeit J haue
synned. J am regenerate and born again bp
Christ, J am no more ẙ mā that synned, but
J am a new creature: wherfore thou cannot
iustlp punish me, because that spirit of mine
that sinned, is dead, and Christ liueth in me, *Galath. ij.*
J lpue no longer mp selfe, but Christ in me.
Punpsh, kpl, and turne to nonght that spp-
rite of mpne, that wpll of mpne, spoile from
me that olde Adam, that sensulialitp, and al
that in me hath synned: and punpsh not me,
sithen bp the newe spirite, that J receiued of
Christ J am his most innocent creature.
Moreouer thou Lord hast geuen me Christ *Rom. biij.*
withal his diuine treasures and graces, and
that to be more surelp mpne, then J am mp
selfe, and in so much as he is mpne entper J
am able to satisfp for al mp dets.

What fearest thou then O synful soule. *Heb. ij.*
Seest thou not that as the blud of Abel cried for vengaunce, so this bloud of Christ cal
leth

leth for mercy and he cā not but muſt nedes
be heard, one depenes calleth on a nother J
meane the buttomeles abiſſe of my ſpnues

Pſalm.xli. hath neede of the abiſſe of Chriſtes paſſyon
and the abiſſe of Chriſtes paſſyon calleth

Pſalm.x. to the abiſſe of the mercye of God. Saye
therfore to Chriſt, O Lorde make thy mar-
cye maruelous and wonderful, thou ſaueſt
them that truſte in the, cry ſaue me for thy
mercye ſake, take and embrace thine ꝑ right

Pſalm.vii wyſenes of Chriſt, and then canne J be con
tented thou ſay. Judge me Lord accordyng
to my rightwiſnes. Let euery man therfore
go to the court of the mercy of God, and if
we be called to the barre of iuſtice, let us ap
peale alwayes to mercy, and ſee that neuer
a man appeare before the throne of iuſtyce
except fyrſt he be clothed w Chriſt through
fayth and then he may be preſented boldly,
as he that is armed with innocency ꝗ truth
may bepreſented afore any place of iudgement, And God ſhal accept them for ryght-
wyſe. To whome be all honoure and glory
through Jeſu Chriſt oure Lorde. Amen.

¶The.x.Sermon.
By what meane to come
to heauen.

Exp.

Experpence proueth that euerpe creature hathe naturallpe a despre and ap
petite to resort to it own proper place
and manspon, and namelp man, because he
is the most souerem creature of al other.
And for so much as our natpue countrp is $\quad$ Heb.ro.
not heare vpon the earth, but in heauen is $\quad$ Collossi. i.
our place of rest (considering that al men
haue thps despre to go to heauen) J take it
to be expedpence to weigh and ponder how
we mape go together.

God hathe geuen vs Christ for an oulp
mirrour, glas, squier, Maister, and guide,
wherfore who so is willinge to walke thp-
ther J meane to heauen, muste go the same
path, that he hathe gone and troden before
vs, because he knoweth p̃ map most perfect
lp, and taught it to vs wpthout anp gile as
wel bp his examples, as bp his woros, therfore he that entedeth, to go to heauen must
follow him. And firste as he bepnge in the
shape and fourme of God was not proud,
nor an arrogat vsurper, nor ascribed to him
self that he mpght conuenientlp haue done, $\quad$ Phillip. ii.
but contrariwise, was louelp humble, of no
reputacion, and toke vpo him the shape of
a seruaunte, or rather of a spnner, and God
layed on hpm all oure wpckednesse, pe and $\quad$ Esap. liii.
most louinglp admitted and allowed them
$\hfill$ for

for hys own, as though he had commytted
them hym self.

Now in lyke maner, a Christen man being al ready regenerate and born agayn by
Christ, & graffed into him by a liuing faith,
commeth down from heauen, that is from
hys own pryde, and false excellency, for (as
Christ sayeth) no man goeth vp into heauen
but he that commeth down, that is the son
of man and hys members. Wherfore by &
by as a Christen man hath a liuely tast and
feling of Christ, and his great benefyt he is
humble, counteth him self of no halue & nothing in his reputacion, for whē he seeth by
deuine influence, the mekenes of Christ, his
liberality, pacience, loue, goodnes, innocē-
cy, wyth other of his vertues, he is of force
constrayned to feele his own pryde, vnkind-
nes, vnpacientnes, wyckednes, vngodly-
nes, and his other iniquities. And as God
put vpon Christ al our synnes, and he wyth
most tender loue receiued them: so wil this
Christen man ascribe to him self al the offe-
ces of the world: by reason that he perceu-
eth, that if God had wyth drawen frō him
hys grace and had not born him vp, but mi
nistred to him occasion and oportunity to
offend, ther had not ben a syn in al ẙ world
but he had don it wherfore he wyl attribute

to

to hym self al, as though he had committed
them in dede so that albeit in Christ, and by
Christ he perceiueth him self innocent and
safe, not withstanding of him self he taketh
it, that he is most damned, and greatest synner of al the world and is forced to say that
(whych Paul spake long a go) Christ came
into the worlde to saue synners, whereof I l. Timo. l.
am one of the chefe.

The second act of Christ was, that, after
he was thus humbled, clothed wyth oure
fraple nature, borne, and shewed forth to y
world, he liued al together for hys neyghbour, and sought only y glory of his father
and saluacyon of hys brethren, without any
regard or respect to hym self (& cause whyt Jhon. l.
is) for that he was so full of loue, grace, fauour, truth, godlines, and all light, vertue,
and perfeccion, wherfore considering he had
no nede to enryche hym self, he lyued holp to
the wealth and benefyte of others, as Paul Collossi. l.
sayeth Christ hath not pleased hym selfe he Rom. xb.
was inflamed in such wyse wyth a feruent
desyre to saue the world, for the glory of his
father, that he being cleane swalowed vp in
God, had no mynde nor consyderacyon of
hym self. Nowe in semblable sorte that true
Christen man, that seeth hym self the sonne
and heyre of God, as Lord of all studyeth,

ff.i.   not

not to lyue to hys own vse, but is holp bent
to the benefitinge of hys brethren for gods
glory, and beinge as it were chaunged into
theyr nature feeleth al theyr good, and euyl
as Paule dyd.

Next ensueth the thyrd acte, that lyke as
y world persecuted Christ, so it pursue hym
and that because in sauynge his neighbour
and sekyng the glory of God, he auaunceth
and set forthe the grace, the gospell, and the
great mercy of God: thrusting down, sub-
mittyng, throwing down to the ground, &
makyng nothynge of man: and because the
world reppneth at thys, therfore immediat
ly foloweth persecutyon, in lyke case therefore as the hoole life of Christ was one con-
tynual persecution because it was godly, so
chaunceth fytly and agreablyp to a true christian, that magnifieth the greate benefyte,
whych we haue receiued by Christe, which
thing is open and manifest in sundry places of the Actes of the Apostles. ffor imme-
diatlyp as the Apostles had preached the gospel, they wer pursued, and so the case goeth
in thys our time. More ouer as Christ was
done on the crosse, from whence, he wolde
not come down, althoughe in scorne it was
sayed to hym, that if he were the sonne of
God, he shoulde come downe of the crosse,
and

Actes. ir.

Mat. rrbii

and they woulde beleue hym, but becaue
he was the onne of god, he wolo not come
downe, but abyde there, and wyth his own
death make perfect our aluacion, in lyke
maner alo a Chriten man mut be tran-
formed and changed into Chrit crucified,
o that wyth Paule he may ay I am crucified with Chrite, in uch wie alo knitte to
hym on the crole, that nothinge is hable to
part me from the loue of God, whych is in
Chrite Jeus.

Furthermore as Chrit dyed on y croe
o a Chriten man, that lyueth in Chrit, di-
eth to the world in uch ort, that he palleth
not of riches, honour, dignity, kinred, freds
worldly pleaures, or properity cõidering
that he eeth by fayth that he is afe, happy,
and onne, and heyre of God, yea euen as
Chrit was buryed, o is he, o that y world
counteth him not only for a thing dead, but
rotten, tynkyng and lothome, wherfore he
mut ay wyth Paule, the world is crucify-
ed to me, and I to the world. He beyde this
mut ryle with Chrite in newnes of lyfe, liuing after another maner then he did before
that he was regenerate by Chrite, becaue
he is become piritual he lyueth to the
glory of God.

And thus finally with Chrit he acedeth into

Galath. ii
Rom. viii.
Rom. vi.
Galath. ii
Rom. vi.
Collo. iii.

f. ii.

into heuē stāding, as touching his thoughts,
affeccions, and despres, aboue in his celesti=
Phillip.iii. al countrp, so that he sap with Paul our con=
uersacion is in heauen, where he eniopeth &
taketh pleasure and comforte in God. To
whome be alwapes al honoure and glorpe,
through Jesu Christ our Lord. Amen.

The .xi. Sermon.

Howe God hathe satysfied for oure synnes and hathe purchased Paradyse for vs.

God by hys absolute and free power
mpght haue saued vs without any sa=
tisfaction at al: In as much as the iu=
stice of God is contented and pleased of al
that is liking his good wil: neuerthelesse he
hath appointed from euerlasting bp his de=
upne minde and wisdom, neuer to saue sin=
ner, onles first he wer fully satisfied, and se=
then he percepued that we coulde not dooe
it our selfes, he was minded to send into the
world his sonne to make for vs satisfaction
and layed on hym the iniquities of vs al, as
Esap. liii. Esap wrot, And he right louingly, although
he were a verpe innocent, toke them for hys
own, and was contented to satisfy for oure
offences, to suffer that we had deserued, and
dye bpon the cros, according to his Fathers
wpl,

wyl, as Paule wryteth he toke our infirmi=
ties for his own and he hath borne oure ini=
quities and miseries, bi reason he came into
the world as though he had ben an offender
he toke a similitude of sin to serue our turne
on the behalfe of our sinnes ↄ as though we
had ben most innocent, and he committed al
the sinnes on his wil was to go alone to the
death, and therfore he sayed to hys disciples Esay. xliii.
in the garden: stand there in peace, rest, and
wythout care, and suffer me alone to enter Mat. xxiiii
into the battaple, and abyde on my boones
that you haue deserued. And metynge the
multitude he sayd to the: whom seke you, they Jhon. xiii.
answered, Jesus of Mazareth as thoughe
they shuld haue said, we seke for him, which
hath vpon him al the sins of the world. And
Christ made answere. J am he, J haue take
oume al the sinnes, loue hath layed them on
my shoulders, therfore if you seke for me as
a man in whom be al the synnes let my dysci-
ples and my elected passe as innocentes,
ease, satisfy reuenge, ↄ do your wurst to me
which am cotented to suffer for al one cause
also, wherfore Christe beinge accused at the
iudgment seat of Jerusalem, made no aunswere was to shewe that they had agaynste
him all actyons, in so much as he had embraced for hys owne al our synnes. Jt pleased
                              f.iiii.   hym

hym also to be crowned wyth thornes, as
kinge of al miseries, & set bettwene.ii.thefes
as the starkest errand thefe of all, lykewyse
was he contented to be striken and beaten.
for our synnes, as (Esay sapeth)he was smi
ten for our infirmities and brused for our i-

Esaye. liii. niquities,and offences:God hath chastised
and beaten him for the sinnes of hys people
and by his wounds, & passions we be made
hole,he payed that he owed not,(as Dauid

Psa. lxviii saied)I haue paied those things that I toke
not. And Esay also dyd say in the parson of

Esay.xliii. Christ,you haue put me to trouble for your
iniquities . He was contended that vppon
hym shuld come al those infirmies, slauders
& rebukes,which we haue deserued for our
synns,which thing Dauid signified in spi-

Psa.lxviii. rit in the parson of Christ where he sayeth,
the rebukes,and reproches,wherwith they
slaunderd the,fel al vpon me,yea and those
curses also, that wer due to vs fel vpon him,

Galath. iii (as Paule sapeth)he hath redemed vs from
the curse,in that he became a curst for vs.
And lyke a godly shepherd hauyng on hys

Esap.vi. backe the lost shepe(for he hath his kingdo
vpon his shulders)hath he born our synnes

i.Peter. ii. on the crosse,(as Peter sapeth)he hath born
our synnes in hys body vpon the crosse and
tree. Vpon it as it had bene an altar, to con
dempne

dempne our synnes, wyth the syn that was
imputed to hym, was he offered as a sacrifice to be burned in the fyre & flame of gods
loue, and to the Corinthians Paul wryteth,
he that knew no syn was made syn for vs. ii. Coriu.b.
Jt was gods wyl and mynd, that he which
was most innocēt should be don on ŷ crosse
as though he wer not only a synner but euē
syn it self and thus (as Daniell prophesyed
was iniquity consumed) and in one day god
toke it out of the world, accordyng to ŷ pro-
phesy of Zachary, wherfore saynt Jhon sai Zachar.b.
eth he appeared to take away our syns, and Jhou. iii.
saynt Jhon Baptist sayeth of Chrift that he
is the lambe of God ŷ taketh away the sins
of the world. Therfor when Chiist suffered Heb. i.
most louingly al that, which we haue deserued, he satisfied for vs, and purged vs from
our synnes. He after the manner of the pro-
dygal sonne, of an excedyng loue, ŷ he bare
to the soul, when he had geuen hys deuyne
treasures of grace to the very open synners
and harlots and had taken to hym selfe our
synnes, as if he had done them hym self, he
made prayer to hys father that he wold par
don them to hym, and to hym he pardoned
them, for we were not worthy: nether wold
he yeld vp hys spirit tyl fyrst he had bowed
down hys head that is vntyl he had moued

ff. iiii. God.

God, whyche is (as Paul wryteth) his head
to pardon vs to Chrilt therefore were our
sins ascribed so that iustly he meryted that
death for hys syns, not because he committed them, but because he admitted them for
his own & so hath he satisfied for thē, not only sufficiently, but also more thē was requi-
site. For to God is one teare of Chrilt more
pleasaunt, then al the sins of the world vns-
pleasaunt, and that lyfe & death of his were
more to the honour of god, thē our life was
to his dishonour, yea he hath not only satis-
fyed for our synnes, but hath purchased for
vs lyfe euerlastynge.

But happely wylt thou say, then nede I
to take no paynes nor trauail to satisfy for
my sins, nor to deserue paradise. I mai take
myne ease, or do what euil that liketh me geuing me to plesure, and good chere, for if it
be as thou saiest, I cannot but be saued. I
answere thus. First I say y truth it is thou
oughtest not to labour thy self for the entēt
to satysfy for thy syns nor yet to deserue paradyse: for that is only Chrilles offyce, nor
thou canst haue any such entent without doing greate iniurye and wronge to God, but
wheras thou sayest, y thou wold lyue ydel-
lye or do euel, after that Chrilt hath now delyuered the from al euil, and purchased the
the

the greatest felicitp: J make the answere on
thps wple. Jf case wer, that one were led to
the gallowes for hps rpbaldrp and nough-
tpnes, and hps Lorde or maister of mere fauour and good wil shuld delpuer hpm, and
count him for his sonne, and pet would sap:
Mp Lord or master hath deliuered me fro
al euell, and taken me for hps sonne & hep re
therfore wpl J go mp wap and be idle, and
in folowing mpne own lustes, and wpll do
hpm wronge: how thinke pou, in this case,
be not these wpcked wordes ? euen the lpke
sapest thou, Christ hath delpuered me from
hel, and made me the son of God, and hepre
of heauen, wherfore J wpl stand lpke an i-
dle parso, or rather do more euil, Chrift certes died not for the, nor satisfied for thp dets
nor pet merited for the paradise to the intet
thou shulde stand idle, commit spn, and become a starke rpbald, but that thou, sepnge
hps great loue, and how greatlp spnne dps-
pleased hpm seeing he was willpnge to dpe
because to take them out of the world, shuld
no more do spn, but honour hpm, loue him,
thanke hpm, put thp trust in hpm, and work
vertuous and good works plenteouslp, not
as a bonde seruaunte to escape hel, spthen
Chrift hath deliuered the, ne pet to get para
dpce, the which Chrifte hathe purchased for
the

the, but as a natural sonne for the glorye of
God, moued thereto by mocion of fapthe,
loue, and spirit, not by mans wytte, sensualitie, or thy behofe or comoditp. More ouer
epther thou beleuest that Christ hath satisfied for the or not, if thou beleue not, that he
hath delyuered the from hel and gotten the
Paradise. if thou be wyse, thou wylt search
to healpe thy self, and so wylt thou not be p-
ble, muchles wylt thou commit sinnes : but
rather enforce thy selfe to make satisfaction
for thy selfe and to deserue paradise, which
is a thing impossible, but if thou beleue liue
lpe, that he had so loued the, that to saue the
he died on the crosse, thou shuld be constrained to loue hym agayne, and to doo for his
glorp, maruelous workes plenteouslp and
redilp to beleue that we are saued by Christ
maketh not vs negligent and naughtype but
feruente and holpe.

Let vs therefore render thankes to oure
Lorde God, seinge he hathe wyth so
greate loue saued vs by so hyghe
rych, happp, & gloryous meane.
To whome be alwaye all honoure, laude and glorpe
through Jesu Christ our
Lorde.
Amen.

.

S. Harding, del.   H.R. Cook, sc.

ANNA LADY BACON.

daughter of Sir Anthony Cooke Knt. & Wife of Sir
Nicholas Bacon, Lord Keeper of the great Seal.

From an Original Picture in the Collection of
Viscount Grimstone, at Gorhambury.

An Apologie

or anſwere in defence of the
Churche of Englande,
with a briefe and plaine
declaration of the true
Religion profeſſed
and vſed in
the ſame.

Londini, Anno Domini
M·D·LXIIII.

To the right honorable learned and vertuous Ladie A. B, M . C. wissheth from God grace, honoure, and felicitie.

ADAME, ACCORDING to your request I haue perused your studious labour of trāslatiō profitably imploied in a right cōmendable work. whereof for that it liked you to make me a Iudge, and for that the thinge it selfe hath singularly pleased my iudgement, and delighted my mind in reading it, I haue right heartely to thanke your Ladiship, both for youre owne well thinking of me, and for the comforte that it hathe wrought me. But far aboue these priuate respectes, I am by greater causes enforced, not onely to shewe my reioyse of this your doinge, but also to testify the same by this my writing prefixed before the work, to the commoditie of others, and good incouragement of your selfe. You haue vsed your accustomed modestie in submittinge it to iudgement, but therin is your

prayse

prayſe doubled,ſith it hath paſſed iudgemēt
without reproche . And whereas bothe the
chiefe author of the Latine worke and I,ſe-
uerallye peruſinge and conferringe youre
whole tranſlation , haue without alteration
allowed of it,I muſt bothe deſire youre La-
d iſhip, and aduertiſe the readers , to thinke
that wee haue not therein giuen any thinge
to any diſſemblinge affection towards you,
as beinge contented to winke at faultes to
pleaſe you,or to make you without cauſe to
pleaſe your ſelfe: for there be ſundry reſpe-
ctes to drawe vs from ſo doinge, although̄e
we were ſo euil minded , as there is no cauſe
why we ſhould be ſo thought of. Your own
iudgement in diſcerning flatterie,your modeſtie in miſlikinge it , the layenge open of
oure opinion to the world, the truth of our
friendiſhip towardes you,the vnwillingneſſe
of vs bothe(in reſpecte of our vocations) to
haue this publike worke not truely and wel
tranſlated,are good cauſes to perſwade,that
our allowance is of ſincere truth and vnderſtanding: By which your trauail(Madame)
you haue expreſſed an acceptable dutye to
the glorye of G.O.D , deſerued well of this
Churche

Churche of Chrifte, honourablie defended
the good fame and eftimation of your owne
natiue tongue, fhewing it fo able to contend
with a worke originally written in the moft
praifed fpeache : and befides the honour ye
haue done to the kinde of women and to
the degree of Ladies, ye haue done pleafure
to the Author of the Latine boke, in deliueringe him by your cleare tranflation from
the perrils of ambiguous and doubtful con-
ftructions: and in makinge his good woorke
more publikely beneficiall : wherby ye haue
rayfed vp great comforte to your friendes,
and haue furnifhed your owne confcience
ioyfully with the fruit of your labour, in fo
occupienge your time : whiche muft needes
redounde to the encoragemente of noble
youth in their good educatiõ, and to fpend
their time and knowledge in godly exercife,
hauinge deliuered them by you fo fingular
a prefident. whiche youre doinge good
Madame, as God (I am fure) doth accept and
will bleffe with increafe, fo youre and ours
mofte vertuous and learned foueraigne Ladie and Maftres fhal fee good caufe to commende : and all noble gentlewomen fhall

(I

(I truſt)hereby be alured from vain delights
to doinges of more perfect glory. And I for
my part (as occaſion may ſerue)ſhal exhort
other to take profit by your worke,and followe your example: whoſe ſucceſſe I beſeche
our heauenly father to bleſſe and proſpere.
And now to thende bothe to acknowledge
my good approbatiō, and to ſpread the benefit more largely, where your Ladiſhippe
hathe ſent me your boke writen,I haue with
moſt hearty thankes returned it to you (as
you ſee)printed : knowing that I haue therin done the beſte, and in this poynte vſed a
reaſonable pollicye:that is, to preuent ſuche
excuſes as your modeſtie woulde haue made
in ſtaye of publiſhinge it . And thus at this
time I leaue furder to trouble youre
good Ladiſhippe.

M.  C.

An Apologie or aun∫were in defence of the Church of England, with a briefe and plaine declaration of the true Religion *profe∫∫ed and u∫ed in the ∫ame.*

T HATH BEEN AN olde complaint, euen from ƥ firſt time of ƥ Patriarks & Prophetes, and confirmed by the writinges and teſtimonies of e= uery age, that ƥ Truth wandereth here and there as a ſtraunger in the world, & doth redily fynde enemies and ſlaunde= rers amongſt thoſe that knowe her not. Albeit perchaunce this may ſeeme vnto ſome a thinge harde to bee beleeued, I meane to ſuche as haue ſcante well and narowly taken heed thereunto, ſpecially ſeing all mankind of natures very mo= tion without a teacher doth coueite the truth of their owne accorde : and ſeinge oure Sauioure Chriſte hym ſelfe, when

Tertull. in Apolo= getico.

A.i.   he

he was on earthe woulde bee called the Truthe, as by a name moste fytte to expresse all hys diuine power : yet wee, whiche haue been exercised in the holie scriptures, and whiche haue bothe redde & seene what hath happened to all godly menne commonly at all tymes, what to the Prophets, to the Apostles, to the holie Martyres, and what to Christe hym selfe, with what rebukes, reuilings and dispightes they were continually vexed whyles they heere lyued, and that onely for the truthes sake: wee (I saye) do see, ý this is not onely no newe thinge or harde to be beleued, but that it is a thing already receaued and commonlye vsed from age to age. Nay truly, this might seeme muche rather a meruayle and beyonde all beleife, yf the Diuell, who is the Father of lyes and ennemye to all truthe, woulde nowe vppon a sodaine chaunge his nature, and hope that truthe might otherwyse be suppressed, then by belyeuge yt : Or that he would
beginne

Iohn.8.

beginne to eſtabliſhe his owne king=
dom by vſing now any other practiſes,
then the ſame whiche he hathe euer vſed
from the beginning. Foꝛ ſince any mans
remembꝛaunce, wee canne ſkante finde
one time, either when Religion did firſt
growe, oꝛ when it was letled, oꝛ when
it did a freſhe ſpꝛinge vp againe, wher=
in truth and innocencye were not by all
vnwoꝛthy meanes and moſt diſpitfully
intreated. Doubtleſſe the Dyuell well
ſeeth, that ſo longe as truth is in good
ſauety, hym ſelfe cannot be ſafe, noꝛ yet
maintaine his owne eſtate.

Foꝛ lettinge paſſe the auncient patri=
arkes and Pꝛophetes, who, as we ſayd,
had no parte of their lyfe free from con=
tumelies and ſlaunders. Wee knowe
there were certaine in tymes paſt, whi=
che ſaid & commonly preached, that the
old aũcient Jewes (of whom we make
no doubt but thei wer the woꝛſhippers
of the onely and true God) did woꝛſhipp
J.ii.　　either

Cornel. Tacitus.

eyther a fowe oz an affe in Gods fteede, and that all the fame Religion was nothinge els, but a facriledge and a plaine contempt of all godlynes. We know alfo that the fonne of God, our Sauioure

Mar. ii.

Jefu Chrifte, when hee taughte the truthe, was coumpted a Jugler and an enchanter, a Samaritan, Belzebub, a decciuer of the people, a dronkard, and a Glutton. Againe, who wottetļ not what woozdes were fpoken agaynfte Sainct Paule the moft earneft and vehement preacher and maintainour of ſtruth: Somtime that he was a feditious and bufy man, a raifer of tumultes, a caufer of rebellion : fonitime againe that he was an heretique, fometime þ he was mad: Somtime that onely vppon ſtrife and ſtomacke he was bothe a blafphemer of Gods lawe, and a defpiſer of the Fathers ozdinances. Further who knoweth not howe Sainct Stephan after he had thzoughly & fincerely embzaced the truth, and beganne frank-

ly

lye and stoutly to preache and set forthe
the same as he ought to do, was immedi
atlye called to aunswere for his life, as
one that had wickedly vttered disdainful
and haynous wordes against the lawe,
against Moyses, against the Temple,
and against God: Or who is ignorant
that in tymes past there werre some
which reproued the holye Scriptures
of falsehood, saying they conteined thin
ges both contrary and quite one against
an other: and howe that the Apostles of
Christe did seuerallye disagree betwixt
them selues, and that S. Paule did vary
from them all: And not to make rehear-
sal of al, for that were an endles labour:
who knoweth not after what sorte our
fathers were railed vpon in times past,
which first began to acknowledge and
professe the name of Christe, howe they
made priuat conspiracies, deuised secrete
councels against the common welth, &
to that end made earelie and priuie meetinges in the darke, kylled yonge babes,

Marcion
ex Tertul-
Aeliued
Lactantio.

Eusib. li.5.
capit.
Tertull. in
Apologe.3.
Idem.1.2.
3. & 7.8.9.

A.iii.　　　fedde

fedd themselues w mens flesshe, and lyke
sauage and brute beastes, didde drinke
their bloude? In conclusion, howe that
after they had put out the candels, they
committed adulterye betweene them=
selues, and without regarde wrought
incest one with an other, that Brethren
laie with their sisters, sonnes with their
Mothers, without any reuerence of na=
ture or kynne, without shame, without
difference: and that thei wer wicked men
without all care of Religion, and with=
out anye opinion of God, being the ve=
ry ennemies of mankinde, vnworthy to
be suffered in the worlde, and vnworthie
of lyfe?

All these thinges wer spoken in those
daies against the people of God, against
Christ Iesu, against Paul, against Ste=
phan, and against all them whosoeuer
they were, which at the first beginninge
imbraced the truthe of the Gospell, and
were contented to be called by the name
of Christians; which was then an hate=
full

full name amonge the common people.
And although the thinges whiche they
said, wer not true, yet the Diuel thought
it shoulde be sufficient for him, yf at the
least he coulde bringe it to to passe, as
they might bee beleeued for true: and
that the Christians might bee brought
into a commō hatred of euery body, and
haue their death and destruction sought
of all sortes. Hereupon kings and Princes beinge ledde then by suche perswa-
sions, killed all the Prophetes of God,
lettinge none escape: Esai with a sawe,
Jeremy with stones, Daniell with Lyons, Amos with an yron barre, Paule
with the sword, & Christ vpon ꝑ crosse,
and condemned all Christians to impri-
sonmentes, to tormentes, to the pikes, to
be throwne downe headlong from rocks
& stepe places, to be caste to wild beastes
and to be burnt, & made great spies of
their quicke bodies, for ꝑ only purpose to
giue light by night, & for a very scorne &
mockinge stocke; and didde compt them

Tertull.
in Apolo.
cap. j.

Suetoni
in Tran-
quil. in
Nerone.

A.iiij. no

no better then the vileſt fylth, thoſſcou=
ringes and laughing games of y whole
worlde. Thus (as ye ſee) haue the Au=
thors and profeſſours of the trueth euer
ben entreated.

Wherefore wee oughte to beare yt
the more quyetlye, which haue taken vp
pon vs to profeſſe the Goſpell of Chriſt,
yf we for the ſame cauſe be handled after
the ſame ſorte: and yf wee, as our foreſa=
thers weare longe a go, bee lykewyſe at
thys day tormented & bayted with rap=
lings, with ſpitefull dealinges and with
lyes, and that for no deſert of our owne,
but onely bicauſe we teach and acknow
ledge the truthe.

They crye out vpon vs at thys pre=
ſent euery wheare, that we are all here=
tiques, and haue forſaken the fayth, and
haue with newe perſwaſions and wic=
ked learninge vtterly dyſſolued the con=
corde of the Churche, that we renew, &
as it weare, fetche againe from hell, the
olde and many a daye condempned he=
reſyes:

resyes: that we sow abroade newe sects,
and suche broyles as neuer yearst weare
hearde of: also that we are already deui=
ded into contrarye partes and opinions,
and coulde yet by no meanes agree well
amonge oure selues: that wee be cursed
creatures, & lyke ƥ Gyauntes do warre
againste God him selfe, and lyue cleane
without any regarde or worshippinge
of God: that we despise all good deedes:
that we vse noe discipline of vertue, no
lawes, no customes: that we esteeme nei=
ther righte, nor order, nor equitie, nor iu=
stice: that we geue ƥ brydell to al naugh
tines, and prouoke the people to all ly=
cenciousnes and lust: that we labour &
seke to ouerthrowe the state of Monar=
chies and Kyngdomes, and to bringe al
thinges vnder the rule of the rashe incō=
stante people and vnlearned multitude:
that wee haue seditiously fallen from ƥ
Catholique Churche, and by a wycked
schisme and diuision haue shaken the
whole worlde, and trobled the common

A.b.   peace

peace and vniuersal quiet of the church:
and that as Dathan and Abyron con-
spired in times past against Moises and
Aaron, euen so wee at this day haue re=
nounced the Byshop of Rome without
anye cause resonable: y̌ we set nought
by the aucthoritie of thauncient fathers
and Councels of oulde time: that wee
haue rashly and presumptuously disanul
led the olde cerimonies, which haue ben
well alowed by oure fathers and forefa=
thers manye hundreth yeare past, bothe
by good customes and also in ages of
more puritie: and that wee haue by our
owne priuate head, without the auctho
ritie of any sacred and general Councell
brought new traditions into y̌ Church,
and haue don all these thinges not for
Religions sake, but only vppon a desyre
of contention and stryfe.

But that they for theyr parte haue
chaunged no maner of thinge, but haue
helde and kepte still suche a nomber of
yeares to this verye day all thinges as
                                    they

they were deliuered from the Apostles, and well approued by the most auncient Fathers.

And that thys matter shoulde not seeme to be don but vppon priuie slaun= der, and to be tossed to and fro in a cor= ner, onely to spyte vs, there haue ben be= sides wylely procured by the Byshop of Rome, certaine parsons of eloquence ynough, and not vnlearned neyther, whiche shoulde put theyre helpe to thys cause now almost despaired of, & should polyshe and set furth the same, both in bookes and with long tales, to the end, that when the matter was trymlye and eloquently handled, ignorant and vnskil full persons mighte suspecte there was som great thing in it. In deede they per= ceiued that their owne cause did euerye where go to wracke, that their sleightes were nowe espyed and lesse esteemed, & that their helpes did dayly fayle them, & that their matter stoode altogether in great neede of a conninge spokesman.

Now

Now as for those things which by thē
haue been layed against vs, in part they
be manifestly falſe & condempned ſo by
their owne iudgementes whiche ſpake
thē, partly again, though thei be as falſe
to in deede, yet beare thei a certain ſhew
and colour of truth, ſo as the Reader (if
he take not good hede) may eaſily be trip
ped and brought into errour by them,
ſpecially when their fine and cunninge
tale is added thereunto: and part of them
be of ſuche ſorte, as wee oughte not to
ſhunne them as crimes or faultes, but
to acknowledg & profeſſe them as thin=
ges well done, and vpon very good rea=
ſon.

For ſhortly to ſay the truth, theſe
folke falſely accuſe and ſlaunder all oure
doinges: yea the ſame thinges whiche
they themſelues can not deny but to be
rightly and orderly don, and for malice
do ſo miſconſtre and depraue al our ſay=
inges and doinges, as though it were
impoſſible, ẏ any thinge could be right=
ly

ly spoke oz don by vs. They ſhould moze
plainly & ſincerely haue gon to wozke
if thei would haue dealt truely, but now
they neither truelye noz ſincerelye : noz
yet Chriſtianly, but darklye and craftely
charge and batter vs with lyes, and doe
abuſe the blindenes & fondenes of the
people, together with the ignozaunce of
Pzinces, to cauſe vs to be hated, and the
truth to be ſuppzeſſed.

This, lo ye, is the power of darkenes, and of men which leaue moze to the
amaſed wondering of the rude multitude and to darknes, then they doe to ᵱ
truth and light: and as S. Hierome ſaieth, which doe openly gainſay the truth,
cloſing vp their eyes, and wil not ſe foz
the nonce. But wee giue thankes to the
moſt good & mighty God, ᵱ ſuch is our
cauſe, wher againſt (whē they woulde
fayneſt) they were able to vtter no di-
ſpite, but the ſame which might aſwell
bee wzeſted againſte the holye Fathers,
againſt the Pzophetes, againſt the Apoſtles

ſtles, againſt Peter, againſt Paule, and
againſt Chriſt himſelfe.

Nowe therefore, if it be leeſull for
theſe folkes to be eloquent and fine ton=
ged in ſpeaking euil, ſurely it becōmeth
not vs in our cauſe, being ſo very good,
to be dumme in anſwering truelye. For
men to be careleſſe what ys ſpoken by
them and their own matter, bee it neuer
ſo falſelye and ſlaunderouſelye ſpoken,
(eſpeciallie when it is ſuche, ẏ the Maie=
ſtie of God and the cauſe of religiō may
therby be dammaged) is the part doubt=
les of diſſolute and retcheles perſons, ⁊
of them which wickedlye winke at the
iniuries don vnto the name of God. For
although other wrōges, yea oftentimes
great, may be borne and diſſembled of a
milde ⁊ Chriſtiā man, yet hee that goeth
ſmothelye awaye and diſſembleth the
mater when he is noted of hereſy, Ruffi=
nus was wont to deny that man to be
a Chriſtian. We therefore will do the
ſame thinge which all lawes, which na=
tures

tures owne voyce doth comm and to be
don, and whiche Chꝛiste him selfe did in
like cale when he was checked and reuis
led, to the intent we may put of from vs
these mens ſlaunderous accuſations, and
may defend ſoberly and truely our own
cauſe and innocencie.

For Chꝛiſt verelye when the Phary=
ſies charged him with ſoꝛcery as one ꝑ
had ſome familiar Spirites, ⁊ wrought
many thinges by their helpe, I ſaide he,
haue not the Dyuell, but dooe glorifie
my Father: but it is you, that haue diſ=
honoꝛed me, and put me to rebuke and
ſhame. And S. Paul when Feſtus the
Lieutenaūt ſcoꝛned him as a mad man:
I (ſaide he) moſte deere Feſtus, am not
madde as thou thinkeſt, but I ſpeake
the woꝛdes of truth and ſobꝛenes. And
the auncient Chꝛiſtians when they wer
ſlaundered to the people foꝛ mākillers,
foꝛ adulteroꝛs, foꝛ committers of inceſt,
foꝛ diſturbers of common weales, and
did perceaue that by ſuche ſlaunderous
accuſations ꝑ Religion which they pꝛo=
ſeſſeꝗ

felled, might be brought in queſtion, namely if they ſhould ſeeme to hold their peace, and in māner to confeſſe the fault: leſt this might hinder the free courſe of the Goſpell, they made Oꝛations, they put vp ſupplications, and made meanes to Emperoꝛs and Pꝛinces, that they might defend them ſelues and theyꝛ fellowes in open audience.

But we trulye, ſeeing that ſo many thowſandes of our bꝛethꝛen in theſe laſt twenty yeares haue boꝛne witnes vnto the truth, in the middeſt of moſt painfull toꝛmēts that could be deuiſed: and when Pꝛinces deſirous to reſtraine the Goſpel ſought many wayes but pꝛeuayled nothinge, and that now almoſt the whole woꝛlde dothe begynne to open theyre eyes to behold the light: we take it that our cauſe hath already ben ſufficiently declared and defended, and thinke it not needfull to make many woꝛdes, ſince ꝑ verymatter ſaith inough foꝛ yt ſelfe. Foꝛ yf the Popes woulde, oꝛ els if they could

weigh

weigh with their own selues the whole
matter, and also the beginning and pro
cedinges of our Religion, how in a ma=
ner al their trauail hath com to nought,
no body driuing it forwarde, and with=
out any wordely helpe: and howe on the
other side, our cause, againste the will of
Emperoures, from ý beginning againſt
the willes of so many Kynges, in spite
of the Popes, and almoste maugre the
head of all men, hath taken encrease, and
by little and little spredde ouer into all
countries, and is com at length euen in=
to kings courtes and Palaices. These
same thinges me thinketh might bee to=
kens greate ynough to them, that God
him self doth strongly fight in our quar=
rel, and doth from heauen laugh at their
enterprises: & that the force of the truth
is suche, as neither mans power, nor yet
hell gates are able to roote it oute. For
they be not all mad at this day, so many
free Cities, so manye Kynges, so manye
Princes which haue fallen away from

B.i.   the

the Seate of Roome, and haue rather
ioyned themselues to the Gospell of
Christe.

And although the Popes had neuer hetherunto leasour to consider dili-
gentely and earnestly of these matters, or
thoughe some other cares do nowe lett
them and dyuerse wayes pull them, or
though they coumprehet to be but comen
and triesinge studies, and nothinge to
appertain to the Popes worthines, this
maketh not why oure matter oughte
to seeme þ worse. Or yf they perchaunce
will not see that whiche they se in deede,
but rather will withstande the knowen
truth, ought wee therefore by and by
to be coumpted heretikes, bycause we o-
bay not their will and pleasure? Yf so be
that Pope Pius were the man (we say
not which he would so gladly be called)
but if he were in deede a man that eyther woulde accoumpte vs for his bre-
threne, or at least woulde take vs to be
men, he woulde firste diligently haue examined

amined our reasons, and woulde haue
sene what might be saied with vs, what
againste vs, and woulde not in his Bull
whereby he lately pretended a Councel,
so rashely haue condēned so great a part
of the worlde, so many learned and god=
ly men, so manye common wealthes, so
many kyngs, and so many Prynces, on
ly vppon his owne blynd preiudices and
foredeterminations, and ý without hea=
ring of them speak, oz without shewing
cause whye.

But bycause he hath alredy so no=
ted vs openlye; least by holdynge oure
peace we should seme to graunt a fault,
and specially bycause we can by no mea=
ne haue audience in ý publik assembly of
the general Councel, wherein he would
no creature should haue power to geue
his voice oz declare his opinion, excepte
he were sworne and straightly bounde
to maintaine his aucthoritie.

For wee haue had good experience
hereof in his last conference at the coun=

B.ii.   cell

cel at Trident, where the embassadours
& diuines of the Princes of Germany
and of the free Cities were quite shutte
out from their company: nother can we
yet forget, how Julius the third, aboue
ten yeares past, prouided warely by his
writt, that none of our sorte shoulde bee
suffered to speake in the Councell (except
there were som paraduenture y wolde
recante and chaunge his opinion). For
this cause chiefly we thoughte it good
to yelde vp an accoumpte of oure faith
in writing, & truely and openly to make
aunswere to those things wherwith
wee haue ben openly charged, to thende
the worlde may see the partes and foun=
dacions of that doctrine, in the behalfe
whereof so many good men haue litle
regarded their owne lyues. And y al men
may vnderstand what manner of people
they be, and what opinion they haue of
God and of Religion, whome the Bys=
shop of Rome before they were called
to tell theire tale, hath condemned for he=
retikes,

retikes, without any good consideratiõ, without any exaumple, & vtterly without lawe oz righte, onelye bycause he hearde tell that they did dissente from hym and his in som pointe of Religion.

And although S.Hierome would haue no bodie to be patient when he is suspected of heresy, yet we wil deal herein nether bitterly noz brablingly, noz yet be caried away w̃ angre & heate, though he ought to be reckned neither bitter noz brabler y̌ speaketh y̌ truth. We willing ly leaue thys kynde of eloquence to oure aduersaries, who whatsoeuer they say against vs, be it neuer so shrewdly oz dispitefully sayde, yet thinke it is sayd modestely and comely ynough, and care nothing whether it be trew oz false. Wee neede none of these shyftes which do maintaine the truthe.

Further, yf wee do shewe it plaine that Gods holie Gospell, the aunciente Byshops and the primatiue Churche do make on our syde, and that wee haue

B.iii. not

not without iuſt cauſe left theſe men, and
rather haue retourned to the Apoſtles
and oulde catholique Fathers. And yf
wee ſhall be founde to doe the ſame not
coulorably or craftely, but in good faith,
before God, truly, honeſtly, cleerely and
plainly: and yf they theſelues which fye
our doctrine and woulde be called Ca-
tholiks, ſhall manifeſtly ſee how al thoſe
titles of antiquitie whereof they boſte ſo
much, ar quite ſhaken out of their hãds,
and that there is more pith in this oure
cauſe then they thoughte for, wee then
hope and truſt that none of them wil be
ſo negligent and careles of his own ſaluation, but he will at length ſtudye and
bethinke him ſelfe, to whether parte hee
were beſt to ioyne him. Undoubtedlye,
excepte one will altogether harden his
hearte and refuſe to heare, he ſhal not repent him to geue good heede to this our
defence and to mark well what wee ſay,
& how truly and iuſtly it agreeth with
Chriſtian Religion.

For where they call vs Heretikes,

It is a crime so haynous, ẏ onles it may
be seene, vnles it may be felt, & in māner
may be holdē with hands and fingers,
it ought not lightly to be iudged oʒ bele=
ued when it is laide to the charge of any
Chriſtian man. Foʒ hereby is a forſaking
of ſaluatiō, a renouncing of Gods grace,
a departing from the body and ſpirite
of Chriſte. But this was euer an olde
and ſolempne propretye with them and
theire foʒefathers, yf any did complaine
of their errours and faultes, and deſired
to haue true Religion reſtored, ſtreyghte
waye to cōdemne ſuch one foʒ heretikes,
as men new fangled & factious. Chriſte
foʒ no nother cauſe was called a Sama
ritan, but onely foʒ ẏ he was thoughte
to haue fallen to a certaine newe Religi=
on, and to be the Aucthoʒ of a newe ſect.
And Paul thapoſtle of CHRISTE was
called befoʒe the Iudges to make aun=
ſwere to a matter of hereſy, and therfoʒe
hee ſaied: Acoʒdinge to this way whiche
they call Hereſye , I doo woʒſhippe
the God of my Fathers , beleeuinge

B.iiii,   all

all thinges which be written in the law
and in the Prophets.

Shortely to speake. This vniuersal
Religion whiche Christen men professe
at this day, was called firste of the heathen people a Sect & Heresy. With these
termes did they alwaies fil princes eares,
to thintent when they had once hated
vs with a foredetermined opinion, and
had coumpted all that wee sayed to bee
faction and heresy, they might be so ledd
away from ytruth & rightvnderstãding
of the cause. But the more sore and outragious a crime heresye is , the more it
ought to be proued by plaine and strong
argumentes, especially in this time, whē
men begin to geue lesse credite to theyre
wordes, & to make more diligent searche
of theyr doctrine then they were wont
to do. For y people of God ar otherwyse
instructed now then they were in times
past, when all the Byschopps of Romes
sayenges were allowed for Gospell, &
when all Religion did depende only vp-

Tertull in
Apologe-
tics.

on

on their aucthoritie . Nowe a daies the
holie scripture is abroad, the writinges
of the Apostles & Prophets ar in printe,
whereby all truth and Catholyke doc=
trine may be proued, and all heresie may
be disproued and confuted.

Sithens then they bring furth none
of these for them selues, and call vs ne=
uertheles Heretiques, which haue nether
fallen from Christ nor from ý Apostles,
nor yet from the Prophets, this ys an
iniurious and a very spitefull dealinge.
With this swozd did Christe put of the
Dyuel when he was tempted of him: wt
these weapons oughte all presumption
which doth auaũce it selfe against God,
to be ouerthrowen and cõquered. For al
Scripture, sayeth S.Paule, that cõ- 2.Tim.3
meth by the inspiration of God, is profi
table to teach, to confute, to instruct, and
to reproue, that the man of God may be
perfect and throughly framed to euery
good work. Thus did the holy Fathers
alway fight agaynst the heretikes with

B.v.   none

De Vnitate
Eccle.cap.3.
Et contra
Maximinū
Arrianorum
episcop.li.3.
Cap.14.

none other force then with ÿ holy scrip=
tures. S.Augustin when he disputed a=
gainst Petilian an heretike of ÿ Dona=
tistes : Let not these woordes, quod he,
be heard betwene vs: I say, or, you say:
let vs rather speake in this wise : Thus
sayeth the Lorde : there let vs seeke the
Church, ther let vs boult out our cause.

In primum.
caput Agg

Lykewise S.Hierome: All those things
(sayth he) which without the testimonie
of the scriptures are holden as deliue=
red from ÿ Apostles, be throughly smit=
ten down by the sword of Gods worde.
S.Ambrose also to Gratianus ÿ Em=
perour: Let the scripture (sayeth he) bee
asked the question, let the Apostles be as
ked, let ÿ Prophets be asked, & let Christ
be asked. For at that time made the Ca=
tholik Fathers and Bysshops no doubt,
but that our Religion mighte be proued
out of ÿ holy scriptures. Neither were
they euer so hardy to take any for an he=
ritike, whose errour they coulde not eui=
dently & apparently reproue by the selfe
same

ſame ſcripturs. And we verely to make
aunſwere on this wiſe as S. Paul did:
According to this way which they cal he
reſie, we do worſhip God and the father
of our Lorde Jeſus Chriſt, & do allowe
all thinges which haue ben written either in ŷ Law or in the Prophets, or in ŷ
Apoſtles workes.

Wherefore yf we be heretikes, and
they (as they woulde faine be called) bee
Catholikes, why do they not, as they ſee
the fathers which were Catholike men,
haue alwaies don? why do they not conuince and maiſter vs by the diuine ſcriptures? why do they not call vs agayn to
be tryed by them? why do they not lay
before vs howe wee haue gon away frō
Chriſt, from the Prophets, from the A-
poſtels, and from the holy fathers? why
ſtick they to do it? why are they afraide
of it? It is Gods cauſe: whye are they
doubtful to commit it to ŷ trial of gods
worde? yf wee be heretkes which referre
all our controuerſies vnto the holy ſcrip
tures

tures, & report vs to ý selfe same words,
which wee knowe were sealed by God
him self, and in comparison of them set
little by all other thinges whatsoeuer
may be deuised by men, howe shall wee
say to these folke I pray you, what mã
ner of men be they, & howe is it meete to
call them, which feare the iudgement of
the holy scriptures, that is to say, ý iudgement of God hym self, and do preferre
before them theyr owne Dreames, and
full colde Inuentions: and to maintaine
their owne traditions, haue defaced and
corrupted now these many hundred yeares the ordinances of Christe and of the
Apostles?

  Men say that Sophocles the tra-
gicall Poet, when in his oulde dayes he
was by his own sonnes accused before
the Judges for a dotinge and sottishe
man, as one that fondelye wasted hys
owne substaunce, and seemed to neede a
Gouernour to see vnto him: to thintent
he might cleere him selfe of the faulte, he
came

came into the place of Judgemente, and
when he had rehearsed before them his
Tragedye called Oedipus Coloncus,
which he had written at the verye tyme
of his accusation, maruelous exactly and
conningly, did of him selfe aske the Judges , whether they thought any sot-
tish or doting man could do the like peece
of worke.

In like manner, bycause these men
take us to be mad , and appeache us for
heretikes, as men which haue nothing
to do neyther with C H R I S T , nor with
the Churche of G O D, wee haue iudged yt shoulde be to good purpose and
not unprofitable, yf wee doe openlye and
frankely set furth our faith wherein we
stande, and shew al that confidence which
wee haue in C H R I S T E I H E S V, to the
intent al men may se what is oure iudgement of euery parte of Christian religion, and may resolue w them selues, whether ẙ faith which they shall see confirmed
by the wordes of Christ, by the writinges
of

of the Apostles, by the testimonies of the
catholique Fathers, and by the examples of many ages, be but a certain rage
of furious and mad men, and a conspiracie of heretikes. This therefore is oure
Belieffe.

WE BELEEVE that there is one certaine nature and diuine power, whiche
wee call G O D: and that the same is
diuided into three equall persons, into ÿ
Father, into the Sonn, and into the holy Ghoste, and that they all be of owne
power, of one Maiestie, of one eternitie,
of one Godhed, and of one substãce. And
although these three persons be so diuided, that neither the Father is the sonne,
nor the sonn is the holy Ghost or the Father, yet neuertheles wee beleeue ÿ there
is but one very God. And that the same
one God hath created heauẽ and earth,
and al thinges contained vnder heauen.

Wee beleeue that I E S V S Christe ÿ
onely Sonne of the eternall Father (as
long before it was determined before all
beginn

beginninges) when the fulnes of tyme
was com,did take of that blessed & pure
Virgin, bothe flesshe & all the nature of
man,that he might declare to the world
the secret & hid will of his father:which
will had ben laide vp from before all a=
ges and generaciõs . And that he might
full finisshe in his humaine bodie the mi=
sterie of our redẽption,& might fasten to
the crosse our sinnes,and also that hand=
writinge which was made againste vs.

Woe beleue that for our sake he dy=
ed, and was buried, descendyd into hell,
the third day by the power of his God=
hed retorned to lyfe and rose again, and
that the fourtyth day after his resurrectiõ,
whiles his Disciples beheld and loked
vppon him,he ascendid into heauen, to
fulfill all thinges,and did place in maie=
stie and glory the selfe same body wher=
with he was borne , wherin he liued on
earth, wherin he was tested at , where=
in he had suffred most painful tormẽts
& cruell kinde of death , wherein he rose
againe

Augustin.
tracta.50.
in Iohan.

againe, and wherein he ascendid to the
right hand of the father, aboue all rule,
aboue all power, all force, all Dominiõ,
and aboue euery name which is named
not onely in this worlde, but also in the
world to com. And that there he now sit=
teth, and shall syt, till all thinges be full
perfetted. And althoughe the Maiestie
and Godhed of Christ be euery wheare
habundauntly dispersed, yet wee beleue
ý his body, as S. Augustine saieth, must
needes be still in one place: ᴣ that Christ
hath geuen maiesty vnto his bodye, but
yet hath not take away from it ý nature
of a body: and that wee must not so affir=
me Christ to be God, that wee deny hym
to be man: and, as the Martyr Uigili=
us sayth, that Christ hath left vs as tou=
ching his humaine nature, but hath not
left vs as touchinge his diuine nature.
And that the same Christ, though he bee
absent from vs concerning his mãhood,
yet is euer present with vs concerning
his Godhed.

Actor. 3.

In Epist. ad Dardanum.

Contra Eutichen. lib. 1.

Fulgent. ad Trasis= mundum.

From

From that place also wee beleue that Christ shall com againe to execute that general iudgemēt, aswel of them whom he shall then fynde aliue in the bodye, as of them that be already dead.

Wee beleue that the holy Ghoste, who is the third persō in the holie Trinitie, is very God: not made, not creat, not begotten, but proceding from both the Father and the Sonne, by a certain meane vnknowen vnto men & vnspeakable, and that it is his propretie to mollifie and soften ye hardnes of mans heart, when he is once receiued thereunto, eyther by ye holsom preaching of the Gospell, or by any other way: that he dothe geue men light, and guide them vnto the knowledge of God, to al waye of truth, to newnes of the whole liefe, and to euerlastinge hope of saluation.

Wee beleeue that there is one Church of God, and that the same is not shutte vp (as in times past amonge the Iewes) into some one cornet or kyngdoine, but

C.i.   that

that it is catholique and vniuersall, and dispersed throughout the whole worlde. So that there is now no nation which can truly complaine that they bee shutt furth, & maye not be one of ȳ Church & people of God: And that this Churche is the kingedome, the bodye and the spouse of Christe: and that Christ alone is the Prince of thys kyngedome, that Christ alone is the heade of this bodye, and that Christ alone is the brydgrome of this spouse.

Furthermore that there be dyuerse degrees of ministers in the church, wher of some be deacons, some preestes, some Byshops, to whom is committed the office to instruct the people, and the whole charge and settinge furth of Religion: yet not withstanding we say that there neither is nor can be any one mā, which may haue the whole superioritie in this vniuersall state, for that Christe is euer present to assist his Church, and nedeth not any man to supply his roome, as his

onely

onely heyre to all his substaunce: and þ
there can bee noe one moztall creature,
which is able to comprehēd oz conceaue
in his minde the vniuersall Churche, þ
is to witte, all the partes of the wozlde,
muche les able to put them in ozdre and
to gouerne them rightly and duely. Foz
all the Apostles, as Cyprian sayeth, were *De Simpli,*
of lyke power among themselues, and þ *prælat.*
rest were the same that Peter was, and
that it was sayed indifferently to them
al, Feed ye: indifferentlye to them all, Goe
into the whole wozld: indifferently to thē *A d Euagriū.*
al, Teache ye the gospell: And as Hierom
saithe, all Byshoppes wheresoeuer they
be, be they at Rome, be they at Eugubi=
um, be they at Constantinople, be they
at Rhegium, be all of lyke preeminence,
and of like preesthood. And as Cypzian *De Simpli.*
saith, there is but one Byshopzike, and þ *prælatorum,*
a peece therof is perfitely & wholy holdē
of euery particular Byshop: & accozding
to the iudgement of the Nicene Counsel
wee say that the Byshop of Rome hath

C.ii.   nomine is

nomoze iurifdicion ouer the churche of
God, then the reſt of ẏ Patriarkes either
of Alexandria oz Antiochia haue. And
as foz the Byſhop of Rome, who nowe
calleth all matters befoze him ſelfe alone,
except he do his deuty as he ought to do,
except he adminiſter the ſacraments, ex=
cepte he inſtructe the people, excepte he
warne them and teache them, wee ſay ẏ
he ought not of right once to bee called
a Byſhop, oz ſo much as an elder. Foz a
Byſhop, as ſaith Auguſtine, is a name
of labour and not of honour: bycauſe he
would haue that man to vnderſtand him
ſelfe to be no Byſhop, which wil ſeke to
haue preeminence, and not to profyt o=
thers: And that neither the Pope noz a=
ny other wozldly creature, can nomoze be
head of the whole Church oz a Byſhop
ouer all, then he can be the brydegrome,
the lighte, the ſaluation, and lyfe of the
Church. Foz theſe priuileges and names
belong onely to Chriſte, and be propzely
& onely ſyt foz hym alone. And that no
Byſhop

Byſhop of Rome did euer ſuffer hymſelfe to be called by ſuch a prouder name
and title befoze Phocas themperoures
time, who as wee know, by killing hys
owne ſouerain Morice the Emperour,
did by a traiterous byllanie aſpire to
Thempire. which was about þ ſirt hū-
dreth & thirtenth year after Chriſt was
bozne. Alſo the Councell of Charthage   c4.47.
did circumſpectly prouide, that no Byſſhop ſhould bee called either the higheſt
Byſhop oz chiefe preeſte. And therfoze
ſithens the Byſhop of Rome wil now
a daies ſo be called, & chalēgeth vnto him
ſelf an aucthozitie, þ is none of his : beſides þ he doth plainly contrary to þ āū-
tiēt Coūcels & cōtrary to þ old Fathers.
We beleue that he doth giue vnto him-
ſelfe, as it is written by his owne com-   Gregor.epi-
panyon Gregory, a preſūptuous, a pro-   ſtola. li.4.
phane, a ſacrilegious and Antichriſtian   ept.76.
                                          78.80.
name: that he is alſo the kinge of pryde, Et lib.7
that he is Lucifer, which preferreth him- epiſt.6.6.
ſelfe befoze his bretherne : that he hathe
           C.iij.   foꝛſaken

forsaken the faith, and is the forerunner of Antichriste.

Further wee saye, that the Minister ought laufully, duely, and orderly to be preferred to that Office of the church of God, and ꝑ no mā hath power to wrest himself into ꝑ holy ministery at his own pleasure & list. Wherefore these persons do vs ꝑ greater wrong, which haue nothing so common in their mouthe, as ꝑ wee do nothing orderly and comely, but al thinges troublesomly and without ordre: and that wee alow euery man to be a preest, to be a teacher, and to be an Interpretour of the Scriptures.

Moreouer we say, ꝑ Christ hath geuē to his ministers power to bind, to loose, to open, to shutt, and ꝑ the office of loosing consisteth in this point, that ꝑ Minister should either offer by ꝑ preaching of the gospel the merits of Christe & full pardō, to suche as haue lowly & contrite hearts, and do vnfainedly repent thē, pronoūcing vnto ꝑ same a sure & vndoubted forgiuenes

forgeuenes of their sins, & hope of euerlasting saluation. Or els ŷ the minister,
when any haue offended their brothers
mindes with a greate offence, & with a
notable & open fault, wherby they haue
as it were bannyshed and made themselues straungers from the common fel-
loship, and from the bodye of Christe,
then after perfitte amendement of suche
persons, doth reconcile them, and bringe
them home againe, and restore them to
the company and vnitie of the faithfull.
We say also that the minister dothe execute the aucthoritie of binding and shutting, as often as he shutteth vp the gate
of the kingedome of heauen againſt the
vnbeleeuing and stubborne persons, de-
nouncing vnto them Gods vengaunce
and euerlastinge punishmente. Or els
when he doth quite shut them out from
the bosome of the Churche by open ex-
communicatiō. Out of doubt, what sentence so euer the Minister of God shall
giue in this sorte, God him selfe doth so

well

well alowe of it, that what soeuer here
in yearth by their meanes is loosed and
bounde, God him selfe wil loose & binde,
and confirme the same in heauen.

And touchinge the kayes wherewith
they maye either shut or open the kyng=
dome of heauen, wee with Chrysostom
saye, they be the knowledge of the Scri=
ptures: with Tertullian we say, they be
the interpretation of the lawe: and with
Eusebius we call thē the worde of God.

Moreouer that Christes Disciples
did receiue this aucthoritie, not that they
shoulde heare priuate confessions of the
people, and lysten to their whisperinges,
as the cōmen Massing preestes do euery
where nowe a dayes, and do it so, as
though in that one poinct laye all the
vertue and vse of the kayes: but to thend
they should goo, they should teache, they
should publishe abrode the Gospell, and
be vnto the beleuing a sweete sauour of
lyfe vnto life, and vnto the vnbeleuing
and vnfaithfull, a sauour of death vnto
death.

death: and that the mindes of godly per=
sons being brought low by the remorce
of their former lyfe and errours, after
they once begonne to looke vp vnto the
light of the Gospel, and beleue in Chrst,
might be opened with ý worde of God,
euē as a dore is opened with a keye. Cō=
trariewise, that the wicked and wilfull
folke, and suche as woulde not beleue
nor retorne into the right waye, shoulde
be lefte still as fast locked and shut vp,
and as S. Paul sayeth, waxe worse and
worse. This take we to be the meaning
of the keyes: and that after this fashion
mens consciences eyther to be opened or
shut. We saye that the preist in deede is
Judge in this case, but yet hath no ma=
ner of right to chalenge an auctoritie or
power, as saith Ambrose. And therfore
our Sauiour Jesu Christ to reproue ý
negligence of the Scribes and Phari=
seis in teaching, dyd with these wordes
rebuke them sayng: Wo vnto you Scri=
bes and Pharisies, whiche haue take a=

2.Tim.3.

De panitentia
dist.1.cap.
Verbum Dei.

Luk.11.
Math.23.

C.b. waye

waye the keyes of knowledge, and haue
shut vp the kyngdome of heauen before
men. Seing then the keye whereby the
waye and entery to ẙ kingdom of God
is opened vnto vs, is the worde of the
Gospell and thexpounding of the Lawe
and Scriptures, we say plainely, where
the same woorde is not, there is not the
keye. And seyng one maner of worde is
geuen to al, and one only keye belongeth
to al, we say there is but one only power
of all ministers, as concerning opening
and shutting. And as touching the Byssop of Rome, for all his Parasites flateringlie singe in his eares those wordes,
To the will I geue ẙ keyes of the kingdome of heauen, (as though those keyes
were syt for hym alone and for no body
els) except he go so to woorke as mens
consciences maye be made pliaunte, and
be subdued to the worde of God, we denye ẙ he doth either open or shut, or hath
ẙ keyes at all. And although he tought
and instructed the people (as woulde to
God

God he might once truely do, and per=
fwade him felfe it were at the leafte fome
pecce of his ducty)yet we thinke his keye
to be neuer a whit better oz of greater
fozce then other mens. Foz who hath fe=
uered hym frō the reft?who hath taught
him moze cōningly to open, oz better to
abfolue then his bzetherne?

We fay ꝑ matrimonie is holy and hono
rable in al fozts ⁊ ftates of perfones, in ꝑ
patriarches,in the pzophetes,in the apo=
ftles,in holy martyzs,in ꝑ minifters of ꝑ
Churche,and in Byfhopps, and that it
is an honeft and laufull thinge(as Chzy=
foftome faith)foz a man liuing in matri=
monie, to take vpon hym therewith the
dignitie of a Byfhop.And as Sozome=
nus faith of Spiridio n:and as Nazian=
zen faith of his owne father,that a good
and diligent Byfhopp doth ferue in the
minifterie neuer the woze foz that he is
maried, but rather the better, and with
moze ablenes to do good. Further we
faye,that the fame lawe whiche by con=
ftraincte

Chryfoft. in epift. ad Titum Hom.11.

Eufeb lib.10. Cap.5. Nazianzen. in monodia de Bafilic.

ſtrainte taketh awaye this libertie from
men, and compelleth them againſt their
willes to liue ſingle, is the doctrine of
Dyuells, as Paule ſaith: and that euer
ſince the tyme of this lawe, a wonderful
vncleanes of lyfe and maners in goddes
miniſters, and ſundrie horrible enormities haue folowed, as the Byſſhop of
Auguſta, as Faber, as Abbas Panormi-
tanus, as Latomus, as the Tripartite
worke whiche is annexed to the ſeconde
Tome of ꝑ Councelles, and other chã-
pions of the Popes band, yea and as the
matter it ſelfe and al hiſtories do cõfeſſe.
For it was rightly ſayd by Pius the ſecond, a Byſſhop of Rome, that he ſawe
many cauſes why wiues ſhould be takẽ
awaye from Preiſtes, but that he ſawe
many moe, and more weightye cauſes
whye they ought to be reſtored them
againe.

    We receyue and embrace all the Ca-
nonicall Scriptures, both of the oulde
and new Teſtament, geuing thankes to
                                    our

(marginal note:) i. Tim. 4.

(marginal note:) Platina in
vita Pij
Secundi.

our God, who hath raiſed vp vnto vs
that light whiche we might euer haue
before our eyes, leaſte eyther by the ſub=
tiltie of man, or by the ſnares of the Dy=
uell we ſhoulde be caried awaye to er=
rours and lyes. Alſo that theſe be the
heauenly voices, wherby God hath ope=
ned vnto vs his will, and that onely in
them mans hearte can haue ſetled reſte:
that in them be habundantly and fullye
comprehended all thinges what ſoeuer
be nedefull for our ſaluatiō, as Origene,
Auguſtine, Chryſoſtom & Cyrillus haue
taught: That they be ẏ very might and
ſtrength of God to attaine to ſaluation:
That they be the foūdations of the Pro=
phetes and Apoſtles, whereupon is
buylte the Churche of God: That they
be ẏ very ſure and infallible rule, wher=
be may be tryed whether ẏ Church doth
ſtagger or erre, and wherunto all eccle=
ſiaſticall Doctrine ought to be called to
accompte: and that againſt theſe ſcrip=
tures neyther lawe nor ordinaunce, nor
                                        any

any cuſtom ought to be hard, no though Paule his owne ſelfe oꝛ an Aungell frō heauen ſhoulde come and teache the con-trarie.

Moꝛeouer we alow the ſacramētes of the Churche, that is to ſaye certaine holy ſignes & ceremonies whiche Chꝛiſt woulde wee ſhould vſe, that by them he might ſet befoꝛe our eyes the myſteries of our ſaluation, and might moꝛe ſtron-gely confirme our faith which we haue in his bloud, and might ſeale his grace in our heartes. And thoſe ſacramentes togither with Tertullian, Oꝛigene, Am-bꝛoſe, Auguſtin, Hierome, Chꝛyſoſtome, Baſill, Dionyſius, and other Catholi-que Fathers do we call figures, ſignes, markes oꝛ badges, pꝛintes, copies, foꝛ-mes, ſeales, ſignettes, ſimilitudes, pat-terns, repꝛeſentations, remembꝛaunces, and memoꝛies. And we make no doubt togither with the ſame Doctours to ſay, that thoſe be certaine viſible woꝛdes, ſeales of righteouſnes, tokens of grace:

and

and do expꝛeſly pꝛonounce, that in the
Loꝛds ſupper, there is truelye geuẽ vnto
the beleuing, the body and bloud of the
Loꝛd, the fleſhe of the ſonne of God,
whiche quickeneth our ſoules, the meate
that cometh from aboue, the foode of in=
moꝛtalitie, grace, truth, and lyfe. And ꝑ
ſupper to be the cõmunion of ꝑ body and
bloud of Chꝛiſt, by the partaking whcre=
of wee be reuiued, wee be ſtrengthened,
and be fed vnto immoꝛtalitie, ꞇ wherby
we are ioyned, vnited, ꞇ incoꝛpoꝛate vn=
to Chꝛiſt, that we may abide in him and
he in vs.

Beſides wee acknowledge there be
two ſacramentes, which wee iudge pꝛo=
pꝛely ought to be called by this name,
that is to ſaye Baptiſme, and the ſacra=
mẽtes of thankes giuing. Foꝛ thus many
we ſee were deliuered and ſanctified by
Chꝛiſt, and well allowed of the oulde fa=
thers Ambroſe and Auguſtine. We ſay ꝑ
Babtiſme is a ſacrament of the remiſſiõ
of ſinnes, and of that waſhing which we
haue

haue in the blood of Christe, and that no perso which wil professe Christes name, oughte to bee restraigned or kepte backe therefrom : no not the very babes of Christiãs, forsomuche as they be borne in sinne, and do pertaine vnto the people of God. We say that Eucharistia, the supper of the lorde, is a sacramente, that is to wytte, an euident token of the body and blood of Christe : wherein is set as it were before our eyes, the death of Christ and his resurrectiõ, and what act so euer he did whilest he was in his mortall body, to thende we may giue hym thankes for his deathe, and for our deliueraunce. And ꝑ by the often receauinge of this sacramente, wee may daily renewe the remembraunce of that matter, to thintent we being fedd with the body and blood of Christ, may be brought into the hope of the resurrectiõ and of euerlasting life, and may moste assuredly beleue, that the bodye and blood of Christe dothe in like manner feede our soules, as breade and

wine

wine doth feede our bodies. To this bã-
kett wee thinke the people of God ought
to be earnestly bidden, that they may all
communicate amonge them selues, and
openly declare and testifie both the godly societie whiche is amonge them, and
also the hope which they haue in Christ
Jhesu. For this cause yf there had ben a-
ny which would be but a looker on, and
abstaine from the holy Comunion, him
did the old fathers & Byshops of Rome
in the primatiue Church, before Private
masse came vp, excomunicate as a wicked persõ and as a Pagan. Neither was
there any Christian at that tyme which
dyd communicat alone whyls other looked on. For so did Calixtus in times past
decree, that after the consecration was
finished, all should communicate, excepte they had rather stande without
the Churche doores: bycause thus (saith
he) did the Apostles apoincte, and the
same the holye Churche of Rome keepeth still.

Chrysost. ad Ephe. hom. 3.

Dis. 2. Ca. Seculares.

De Consec. dist. 2. cap. Peracta.

D.i.   More-

Moreouer when the people commeth to the holy communion, the Sacrament ought to be giuen them in both kindes, for so both Christe hath commaunded, and the apostles in euery place haue ordayned, and all the auncient Fathers and Catholique Byshops haue folowed the same. And whoso doth contrary to this, he (as Gelasius sayth) committeth sacriledge. And therefore wee saye, that oure Aduersaries at this daye, who hauinge violentlye thruste out and quite forbidden the holye Communion, dooe without the woorde of God, without the authoritie of any auncient Councell, without any catholique Father, without any example of y primatiue Church), yea and without reason also, defend and maintaine their priuate Masses and the manglinge of the Sacramentes, and do this not onely against the plaine expresse commaundement and bidding of Christe, but also against al antiquitie do wickedly therin, and are very Church robbers.

De Const. dist.2.Ca. Comperi.

Wee

We affirme that breade and wine are
holy and heauenly mysteries of the bodie
& bloud of Christ, & that by them Christ
himselfe being y tru bread of eternal life,
is so presently giuen vnto vs, as that by
faith we verely receaue his body and his
bloud. Yet say we not this so, as though
we thought that the nature of bread and
wine is cleane changed and goeth to no=
thing, as many haue dreamed in these la=
ter times, which yet could neuer agree a=
mong themself of this their dreame. For
y was not Christes meaning y the whea=
ten bread should laye apart his owne na=
ture, & receaue a certain new diuinitie, but
y he might rather chaunge vs (& to vse
Theophilactus woordes) might trans= *Iohan.cap.6.*
forme vs into his bodie . For what can
be said more plainly then y whiche Am=
brose saith, Bread & wine remain stil the *De Sacra.*
same thei were before, & yet are changed *lib.4.cap.4.*
into an other thing: or y which Gelasius
saith, y substance of y bread , or y nature
of y wine, ceaseth not so to be: or y which

D.ii.   Theodoretis

Theodorete faith, After the consecratiō, the mysticall signes do not caſt of their owne propre nature : for they remaine ſtil in their former ſubſtaunce, forme and kynde . Or that whiche Auguſtine ſaith, That whiche ye ſee is the bread and Cuppe, and ſo our eyes tell vs, but that which your faith requireth to be taught is this, The bread is the body of Chriſt, & the Cuppe ys his bloud . Or ÿ whiche Origene ſaith: Bread which is ſanctified by the word of God, as touching ÿ material ſubſtaūce therof, goeth into ÿ belly and is caſt out into the priuey . Or that which Chriſt him ſelfe ſaid, not only after ÿ bleſſing of the cup, but after he had miniſtred the Comunion: I will drinke nomore of this frute of the vyne . It is well knowen that the fruit of the vyne ys wine, and not bloud .

And in ſpackyng thus, we meane not to abaſe the Lordes ſupper, or to teache that yt is but a could ceremonie onely, & nothing to be wrought therin: (as many falſely

In Dialogis
1 . & 2 .

In ſermone
ad infantes.
De conſecrat.
diſt.2.Cap.
Qui mandu.

Origene in
Mat.Hom.15.

falsely slaunder vs we theache) For wee
affirme that Christ doth truely and pre=
sently giue his owne selfe in his Sacra=
mentes: In baptisme,that wee may put
him on: and in his supper, that we may
eate him by faith & spirit,and may haue
euerlasting lyfe by his crosse and bloud.
And we say not this is done slightly and
couldely,but effectually and truely. For
although we do not touche the body of
Christ with teethe and mouth), yet wee
hold him fast and eate him by faith,by
vnderstanding, and by the spirit. And
this is no vaine faith whiche doth com=
prehend Christ: and that is not receiued
with colde deuotion,whiche is receiued
with vnderstanding,with faith,& with
spirit. For Christ him selfe altogither is
so offered & giuen vs in these mysteries,
that we may certainly know we be flesh
of his flesshe, and bone of his bones : and
that Christ continueth in vs,and wee in
him . And therefore in celebrating these
mysteries,ẏ people are to good purpose

D.iii.   exhorted

exhorted before they come to receaue the
holy communion, to lift vp their hearts,
& to direct their mindes to heauenward,
bicause he is there, by whom we must be
full fedde and liue. Cyrill saith, when we
come to receaue these mysteries, al grosse
ymaginations must quite be banished;
The councell of Nice, as is alleadged by
some in greeke, plainly forbiddeth vs to
be basely affectioned, or bent toward the
bread and wine which are set before vs.
And as Chrysostome very aptly wryteth: We say that the body of Christe is
the dead carcas, and we our selues must
be the Egles. meaning thereby, that we
must flie hye if wee will come vnto the
body of Christe. For this table as Chrysostome saith, is a table of Egles and not
of Ieyes. Cyprian also, This bread saith
he, is the foode of the soule, and not the
meate of the belly. And Augustine, How
shall I holde him, saith he, which is absent? how shall I reache my hand vp to
heauen to laye holde vpon him that sitteth

De con. dil. 1.
Ca. Quando.

Ad Obie. 71.
Theodoreti.

Chrysost. in 10
ad Corinth.

De Cœna
Domini.

In Iohan.
Tract. 50.

teth there? He aunswereth, Reache thy-
ther thy faythe, and then thou hast layde
holde on him.

We can not also away in our churches
with ẏ shewes & sales, & byeng & selling
of Masses, nor the carrieng about & wor-
shipping of bread, nor such other ydola-
trous and blasphemous fondnes, whiche
none of them can proue ẏ Christe or his
Apostles did euer ordaine, or left vnto vs:
and we iustly blame ẏ Bishops of Rome,
who wout ẏ word of God, wout ẏ authoritie of the holy fathers, without any
example of antiquitie, after a newe guise
do not onely set before ẏ people ẏ sacra-
metal bread to be worshiped as God, but
doe also carp ẏ same about vpon an ambling horse, whyther soeuer themselues
iorney, as in old time ẏ Persiās fier & ẏ
reliques of ẏ goddesse Isis were solemly
caried about in processiō, & haue brought
ẏ sacraments of Christ to be vsed nowe
as a stage play, & a solemne sight, to the
end that mens eyes should be fedde with

In libro de Ceremonijs Romanæ Ecclesiæ.

D.iiii.　　　nothing

nothing els but with mad gasinges and
foolishe gaudes, in the selfe same matter
wherein the death of Christ ought dili=
gently to be beaten into our heartes, and
wherein also the mysteries of our redép=
tion ought with all holines and reue=
rence to be executed.

Besides, where they say and somtime
doe perswade fooles, that they are able
by their Masses to distribute and applie
vnto mens commoditie al the merites of
Christes death, yea although many ty=
nies ý parties thinck nothing of ý mat=
ter, and vnderstand ful litle what is don,
this is a mockery, a Hethenyshe fansie,
and a very toye. For it is our faith that
applieth the death and crosse of Christe
to our benefite, and not the Acte of the
Massing priest. Faith had in the Sacramentes (saith Augustine) doth iustifie, &
not the sacramentes. And Origene saith:
Christ is the priest, the propitiation and
sacrifice, which propitiatio cōmeth to e-
uerie one by meane of faith. So that by
this

Origen.ad
Rom.4.cap.3.

this reconing we saye, that the sacramentes of Christ without faith, doe not once profite those that be alyue, a great deale lesse doe they profite those that be dead.

And as for their bragges they are wōt to make of their Purgatory, though we know it is not a thing so very late risen amongest them, yet is it no better then a blockyshe and an olde wyues deuise. Augustine in deed somtime saith there is suche a certaine place : sometime he denieth not but there maye be suche a one: sometime he doubteth, sometime againe he vtterly denieth it to be, and thinketh that menne are therin deceiued by a certaine naturall good wil they beare their frendes departed. But yet of this one errour hath there growen vp suche a haruest of these Massemongers, ꝑ Masses being sould abrod comonly in euery corner, the Temples of God became shoppes to get money, and selie soules were perswaded that nothing was more necessarie to be bought. In ded there was

Augustin. in psal.85.I Enchirid. cap.67. De Ciuit. li. 21. Cap. 26. Hypognost. 5a

D.v.   nothing

nothyng moze gainefull foz thefe men
to felle.

As touching the multitude of vaine
and fuperfluous ceremonies, wee know
that Auguſtin did greuouſly complain of
thē in his owne time : and therfoze haue
wee cut of a great numbze of them, bycauſe we know that mens conſciences
were cumbzed about thē, and the Churches of God ouerladen with them. Neuertheleſſe we kepe ſtill and eſteeme not
onely thoſe ceremonies which wee are
ſure were deliuered vs from the Apoſtls,
but ſome others too beſides, whiche we
thought myght be ſuffred without hurt
to the churche of God, becauſe we had a
deſire that all thinges in the holy congregation might (as Paul cōmandeth)
be don with comelines and in good oz-
der: but as foz all thoſe thinges whiche
we ſawe were eyther very ſuperſtitious
oz vnpzofitable, oz noyſome, oz mocke-
ries, oz contrarie to the holy Scriptures, oz els vnſemelie foz honeſt oz diſcrete
folkes.

Ad Ianuar.
epiſtola.119.

folkes, as there be an infinite numbre
now a dayes where Papiltery is vfed,
thefe I faye wee haue vterly refufed
without all maner exception, bycaufe
wee would not haue the right worfhyp=
ping of God any lenger defiled with
fuche folies.

We make our prayers in that tonge
whiche all our people, as meete is, may
vnderftand, to thend they may (as Paul
counfeleth vs) take commō commoditie
by common prayer: euen as all the holy
fathers and catholique Byfhops bothe
in the ould and new Teftament did vfe
to pray them felues, & taught the people
to praye to, leafte as Auguftin faith, like
parrottes and oufells wee fhoulde feme
to fpeake that we vnderftand not.

Neither haue we any other Media=
tour and Interceffour, by whome wee
may haue acceffe to God the father, thē
Iefu Chrift, in whofe onely name all
tyings are obteined at his fathers hād.
But it is a fhamefull parte and full of
infidelitie

infidelitie that we see euery where vsed
in the Churches of our aduersaries, not
onely in that they will haue innumerable sortes of mediatours, and that vterly
without the auctoritie of Goddes word.
So that, as Ieremie saith, the Saintes

Hiere. ca. 2
& 11.

be nowe as many in numbre, or rather
aboue the numbre of the Cities: a poore
men cannot tel to which Sainct it were
best to turne the first. And though there
be so many as they cannot be tolde, yet
euery one of the hath his peculiar deuty
and office assigned vnto him of these folkes, what thig they ought to aske, what
to giue, and what to bring to passe: but
besides this also, in that they do not only wickedly, but also shamelesly cal vpon

Bernardus.

the blessed virgine Christes mother, to
haue her remember that she is a mother,
and to commaunde her sonne, and to vse
a mothers auctoritie ouer him.

We saye also, that euery person is
borne in sinne, and leadeth his lyfe in
sinne: that no body is able truely to saye,

his

his hearte is cleane. That ý moſt rightu=
ous perſone is but an vnproſitable ſer=
uaunte: That the law of God is perſite,
and requireth of vs perfit and full obe=
dience: That we are able by no meanes
to fulfill that lawe in this worldly lyfe:
That there is no one mortall creature
whiche can be iuſtified by his owne de=
ſertes in goddes ſight, and therfore that
our only ſuccour and refuge is to flye to
the mercy of our father by Ieſu Chriſt,
and aſſuredly to perſwade our myndes,
that he is the obtayner of forgiuenes for
our ſinnes. And that by his bloud al our
ſpottes of ſinne be waſhed cleane: That
he hath pacified and ſet at one ail thin=
ges by the bloud of his Croſſe: That he
by the ſame one onely Sacrifice whiche
he once offered vppon the Croſſe, hath
brought to effect and fulfilled al things,
and that for that cauſe he ſayd when he
gaue vp the Ghoſte, It is finiſhed. as
though he woulde ſignifie that the price
and ranſome was nowe full payde for
the

the sinne of all mankind. Yf there be any
then that thinke this sacrifice not suffi=
cient, let them go in Gods name and seke
an other that is better. We verely, bicause
we knowe this to be the onely sacrifice,
are well contente with it alone , and
loke for none other: And forasmuche as
it was to be offered but once, wee com=
maund it not to be renewed againe. And
bicause it was full & perfite in all points
and partes, wee doe not ordaine in place
thereof anye continuall succession of of=
feringes.

Besides, though wee saye we haue no
meede at all by oure owne woorkes and
deedes , but apoint all the meane of oure
saluation to be in Christe alone , yet say
we not that for this cause men ought to
liue looslie and dissolutely : nor that it is
ynough for a Christian to be Bapti=
zed onely and to belieue, as though there
were nothing els required at his hande,
for true faith is liuely, and can in nowise
be idell . Thus therefore teache wee the
                                    people

people,that God hath called vs not to fo
lowe ryot and wantonnes, but as Paul
faithe, vnto good woozkes, to walke in
them. That God hath plucked vs oute
from the power of darkenes to ferue the
liuinge God : to cutte away all the rem=
nauntes of finne, and to woozke oure fal=
uation in feare and tremblinge, that it
may apere how that þ Spirit of fanctifi=
cation is in oure bodies,and that Chzift
himfelfe doth dwell in our heartes.

To conclude, we beleue that this oure
felfe fame flefh wherin we liue,although
it dye and come to duft,yet at the laft day
it fhall retourne againe to lyfe by the
meanes of Chziftes fpirite which dwe=
leth in vs, and that then berely whatfo=
euer we fuffer heere in the meane whyle
foz his fake,Chzift wil wipe from of our
eies all teares & lamentation, & that we
thzough him fhall enioy euerlafting life,
and fhall foz euer be with him in glozy.
So be it.

Beholde thefe are the hozrible herefies
foz

for the which a good parte of the worlde
is at this day condemned by the Byshop
of Rome , and yet were neuer hearde to
pleade their cause . He should haue com=
menced his sute rather againſt Chriſte,
againſt the Apoſtles, and againſt the ho=
ly fathers. For theſe thinges did not only
procede from them, but were alſo apoin=
ted by them : except perhaps theſe menne
will ſay (as I thinke they will in deede)
that Chriſte hath not inſtituted the holy
Communion to be diuided amongeſt the
faithfull : Or that Chriſtes apoſtles and
the auncient fathers haue laide Priuate
maſſes in euery corner of the Temples,
nowe tenne , now twenty togithers in
one day: Or that Chriſt and hys Apoſtls
banniſhed all the common people from
the Sacrament of his bloud: or that the
thing whiche them ſelues do at this day
euery wheare , and do it ſo as they con=
demne him for an heritike whiche dothe
otherwiſe , ys not called of Gelaſius,
their owne doctour plaine ſacriledge :or
　　　　　　　　　　　　　　　that

ỹ these be not ỹ very wordes of Ambrose, Augustine, Gelasius, Theodorete, Chrysostome, & Origene, The bread and wine in the Sacramentes remaine still the same they were before: The thing which is seene vpon the holye table, is breade: there ceaseth not to be still the substaunce of breade and nature of wyne: the substance and nature of bread are not changed: the selfe same breade as touchinge the materiall substaunce, goeth into the bellie, and is cast out into the pryuei: Or that Christe, the Apostles, and holy fathers prayed not in that tongue whiche the people might vnderstande : Or that Christe hath not performed all thinges by that one offering which he once offered: or that the same Sacrifice was imperfect, and so now we haue neede of another. All these thinges must they of necessitie say, onlesse perchaunce thei had rather say thus, that all lawe and right is locked vp in the treasurie of the Popes breaste, and that as once one of his sou-

E.i.   thing

thinge pages and clawbackes did not
sticke to say, the Pope is able to dispence
against the Apostles, against a councell,
& against the Canōs & rules of the Apostls,
and that he is not bound to stand neither to
the examples, nor to the ordināces, nor to
the lawes of Christ. We for our parts haue
learned these thinges of Christe, of the
Apostles, of the deuout fathers, and doe
sincerely and with good faith teache the
people of God the same. Whiche thinge
is the onely cause whye wee at this daye
ar called heretikes of the chiefe prelates
(no doubt) of Religiō. O immortal God,
hath Christ him selfe then, the Apostles &
so many fathers, al at once gon a stray?
were then Origene, Ambrose Augustin,
Chrysostome, Gelasius, Theodoret, for-
sakers of the catholique faith? Was so
notable a consent of so manye auncient
Byshoppes and learned menne nothing
els, but a conspiracye of heretiques? Or
is that nowe condemned in vs, whiche
was then commended in them? Or is
the

Dist.36,lect.
in Glosa.

Distinct.82.
Presbyter.

the thyng nowe by alteration onely of mens affection sodenly becôme schismatique, whiche in them was compted catholique? Or shall that whiche in times past was true, nowe by and by, bycause it liketh not these men, be iudged false? Let them then bring furth another Gospell, and let them shew the causes why these thinges which so long haue openly ben obserued, and well alowed in the Churche of God, ought nowe in thend be called in againe. Wee knowe well ynoughe, that the same worde whiche was opened by Christ, & spred abrode by the Apostles is sufficient, both our saluation and al trueth to vp holde & mayntein, and also to confounde all maner of heresie. By that Word only do we condemne all sortes of the olde heretiques, whom these men say we haue called out of hell againe. As for the Arrians, the Eutychians, the Marcionites, þ Ebionites, the Ualentinians, the Carpocratians, the Tatians, the Nouatians, and

Shortelie

shortelie all them which haue had a wic=
ked opinion eyther of God the Father
or of Christ, or of the holy Ghoste, or of
any other pointe of Christian Religion,
for somuche as they be confuted by the
Gospell of Christ, we plainly pronunce
them for detestable and cast awaye per=
sonnes, and defye them euen vnto the dy=
uell. Neyther do wee leaue them so, but
we also seuerely and straitely hold them
in by lawful and polittick punishemétes,
yf they fortune to breake out any where
and bewraye themselues.

In deede we graunt that certain new
and very straunge sectes, as the Anabap=
tistes, Libertines, Menomás, & Zuenk=
feldians haue ben stirring in the worlde
euersience the Gospel did first spring. But
the worlde seeth now right wel, thankes
be giuen to our God, that wee neyther
haue bredd nor taught, nor kept vp these
Monstres. In good fellowship I pray
the whosoeuer thou be, read our bokes,
they are to be sould in euery place: What
hath

hath there euer ben written by any of
our company, which might plainely beare
with the madnes of any of those heretiques? Nay I saye vnto you, there is no
countrie at this daye so free from their
pestilent infections, as they be wherein
the gospel is freely and comonly taught.
So that yf they wey the very matter wt
earnest and vpright aduisement, this
thing is a great argumet, ŷ this same is
the very truth of the Gospell whiche we
do teache. For lightly neyther is cockell
wont to growe without the wheat, nor
yet the chaffe without the corne. For frō
the very Apostles times, who knoweth
not how many heresies did rise vp euen
togeather, so soone as the Gospell was
first spred abrode? Who euer had heard
tel of Simon, Menander, Saturninus,
Basilides, Carpocrates, Cherinthus,
Ebion, Valentinus, Secundus, Mar-
cosius, Colorbasius, Heracleo, Lucia-
nus, and Seuerus, before the Apostles
were sent abrode? But whye stande wee

C.iii.   reckeninge

reackoninge vp these: Epiphanius re-
hearseth vp foure score sundrie heresies,
and Augustine many moe, whiche dyd
spring vp euen togeather with the Gospell. What then? was the Gospell therfore not the Gospell, bycause heresies
sprang vp withall? or was Christ therefore not Christ? And yet as we said, doth
not this great crop and heape of heresies
grow vp amongest vs, which do openly
a broade and frankely teache the Gospel?
These poysones take their beginninges,
their encreasinges and strengh emongest our Aduersaries, in blindenes and in
darkenes, emongest whom trueth is w̄
tyrannie and cruelty kept vnder, and cannot be hearde but in corners and secrete
meetinges. But let them make a proofe,
let them giue the Gospell free passage,
let the truth of Iesu Christe giue his
cleare light and stretche forth his bright
beames into all partes, and then shall
they furthwith see howe all these shadowes streight will vanyshe and passe
away

away at the light of the Gospel, euen as
the thick myste of the night consumeth
at the sight of ẙ sunne. For whilest these
men sit still and make mery, and doe nothing, we continually represse and put
backe all those heresies, whiche they falselye charge vs to nourishe and mainteine.

Where they say that we haue fallen
into sundrie sectes, and woulde be called
some of vs Lutherians, some of vs
Zuinglias, and cannot yet well agree a-
mong our selues touching ẙ whole substaunce of doctrine, what woulde these
menne haue said, yf they had bene in the
first times of the Apostles and holy Fathers, when one said: I holde of Paul,
an other I holde of Cephas, an other
I holde of Apollo: when Paule dyd so
sharpelye rebucke Peter: when vppon a
falling out Barnabas departed from
Paul: when as Origene mentioneth, the
Christians were deuided into so many
factions, as that they kept nomore but

the

the name of Christians in cōmon emōg them, beyng in no maner of thyng els like to Christians, when as Socrates saith, for their dissensions and sundrye sectes they were laughed and iested at openly of the people in the cōmon game-playes, when as Constantine the Emperour affirmeth), there were suche a nūber of variaunces and braulinges in the church, that it might iustely seme a miserie farre passynge all the former miseries: when also Theophilus, Epiphanius, Chrysostome, Augustine, Rufine, Hieronie, being all Christians, being all fathers, being all catholiques, did striue one against an other, with moste bytter and remediles contentions without end? When as saith Nazianzene, the partes of one body wer consumed and wasted one of an other: when the East part was deuided from the West, onely for leuened bread, and only for keping of Easter day, whiche were indyd no great matters to be striued for? And when in al Councels

new

new Credes and new decrees cõtinually
were deuised ? what woulde these men
(trow ye)haue said in those days?which
side would they specially thẽ haue taken,
and whiche would they then haue for=
saken?whiche Gospel woulde they haue
beleued ? whome woulde they haue ac=
coumpted for heretiques,and whom for
Catholiques?And yet what a stirre and
reuell kepe they at this time vpon two
poore names onely Luther and Zwin=
glius, bicause these two men do not yet
fully agree vpon some one poinct , ther=
fore woulde they nedes haue vs thinke,
that both of them were deceiued , that
neyther of them had the Gospell, & that
neyther of thẽ taught the trueth aright.
But good God,what maner of felowes
be these,which blame vs for disagreing,
and do all they themselues, weene you,
agree wel together?Is euery one of thẽ
fully resolued what to folow?hath there
ben no strifes,no debates amongest thẽ
at no time?why then do the Scotistes

and Thomistes about that they call
me ritum congrui, & meritū condigni,
no better agree togeather? Why agree
they no better amonge themselues con-
cernyng originall sin in ȳ blessed virgin:
cōcerning a solemne vowe, and a single
vowe? Whye saye the Canonistes that
auricular confession is appoincted by the
positiue lawe of man, and the Schole-
men contrarie wyse, that it is appoincted by the lawe of God? Whye doth Albertus Pius dissente from Caietanus?
why doth Thomas dissent from Lom-
bardus, Scotus from Thomas, Occa-
nus from Scotus, Aliēsis from Occa-
nus? And whye do the Nominalls disagree from the Realles? And yet saye I
nothing of so many diuersities of fryers
and monkes, howe some of them put a
great holynes in eatyng of fyshe, and
some in eating of heardes: some in wearing of shewes, and some in wearing of
Sandalles: some in going in a lynnen
garment, and some in a wollen: some of
thē called whit, some blacke: some being
shauen

haue bꝛoade, and ſome narowe: ſome
ſtalkinge abꝛoade vppon patens, ſome
barefooted: ſome girte, and ſom vngert?
They ought Iwys to remembꝛe howe
there be ſome of their owne companie
whiche ſay, that the body of Chꝛiſt is in
his ſupper naturallie: Contrarie other *Stepha. Gard.*
ſome of the ſelfe ſame companie denye *in Diabolica*
Sophiſtica.
it to be ſo: Againe that there be other of *Richardus*
them whiche ſaye, the bodye of Chꝛiſt in *Smith.*
the holy Communion is rent and toꝛne *De conſecra-*
with our teache, and ſome againe that *Recat. Beringe*
Schola, &
denye the ſame. Some alſo of them there *Gloſe. Cus*
be, whiche wꝛite that ẏ body of Chꝛiſt is *mundus.*
quantum in Euchariſtia, That is to ſay,
hath his perfite quantitie in the Sacrament: Some other againe ſaye naye.
That there be others of them whiche
ſaye, Chꝛiſt did conſecrate with a certain
diuine powec, ſome that he did the ſame *Thomas*
with his bleſſing, ſome againe that ſay *Aquinas.*
hee didde it with vtteringe fiue ſolemne
choſẽ woꝛds, and ſome with rehearſing
the ſame wooꝛdes afterwarde againe.
                                        Some

Some wil haue it that when Chrift did speake thofe fiue wooꝛdes, the materiall wheaten bꝛead was pointed by this demonftratiue Pꝛonoune, hoc: Som had rather haue that a certaine vagum indiuiduum, as they terme yt, was ment therby. Againe, others there bee that fay, dogges and myce may truely and in very deede eate the body of Chꝛifte: and others againe ther be that ftedfaftly denie it. There be others whiche faye, that the very accidentes of bꝛead and wine maye nurꝑſhe: others againe there bee whiche fay, how that the fubftance of the bꝛeade doth retourne againe. What neede J fay moꝛe? yt were ouer longe and tedious to recken vp all thinges, fo very vncertaine and full of controuerſies is yet the whole foꝛm of thefe mês religiõ and doctrin, euê amõgeſt thêſelues, frõ whence it did firſt ſpꝛinge and beginne. Foꝛ hardly at any time do they well agree betweene themfelues, excepte it be peraduentur as in times paſt the Phariſies and Saduees

Stephanus Gardinꝰ

De confe. diſt. 2. Spe. Gloſa.

Magiſt. Sent. & Schola.

cees: oz as Herod and Pylate did accozde
against Chzist. They were best therfoze
to go and sette peace at home rather a-
monge theeir owne selues. Of a truthe,
vnitie and concozde dothe best become
Religion, yet is not vnitie the sure and
certaine marke whereby to knowe the
Church of God. Foz there was the greatest consente that might bee amongest
them that wozshipped the Golden calfe,
and among them whiche with one boice
ioyntly cryed against our Sauiour Jesu Chziste, Crucifie him. Nother bicause
the Cozinthians were vnquieted with
pziuate dissensions, oz bicause Paule did
square with Peter, oz Barnabas with
Paule: oz bicause the Chzistians vpon
the very beginning of the Gospell were
at mutuall discozde, touchinge some one
matter, may we therefoze thinke there
was no church of God amongest them?
And as foz those personnes whom they
vpon spite cal Zwinglians and Lutherians, in very deede they of bothe sydes
be

be Chriſtians, good friendes & brethern.
They vary not betwixt themſelues vpon
the principles and foundacions of oure
religio, nor as touching God nor Chriſt
nor the holy Ghoſte, nor of the meanes
to iuſtification, nor yet euerlaſting life;
but vpon one onely queſtion, whiche is
neither weightie nor great : neither miſtruſt we or make doubte at all, but they
will ſhortely be agreed. And if there bee
any of them whiche haue other opinion
than is meete, we doubt not but or it bee
longe, they will put apart all affections
and names of parties, and that God wil
reueale it vnto them : ſo that by better
conſidering & ſearching out of the matter, as once it cam to paſſe in the Councel
of Calcedone, al cauſes & ſeedes of diſſen
ſion ſhall bee throughly pluct vp by the
roote, and be buried and quite forgotten
for euer. whiche God graunt.

But this is the moſte greuous and
heuye caſe that they call vs wicked and
vngodly men, and ſay we haue throwne
a waye

àway all care of religion. Though this
ought not to trouble vs muche, whiles
thei themselues ŷ thus haue charged vs,
knowe ful well how spitefull and false a
sayinge it is : for Iustine the martyr is
a witnes how that all Christians were
called ἄθεοι, that is Godlesse, assone as the
Gospell firste beganne to bee publisshed,
and the name of Christe to be openly de=
clared. And when Polycarpus stood
to be iudged, the people stirred vp the
President to sleye and murder all them
whiche professed the Gospell, with these
wordes, ἄιρε τὰς ἀθέος, That is to saye,
Ridde out of the waye these wicked and
Godles creatures. And this was not bi=
cause it was true that the Christians
were Godlesse, but bicause they woulde
not worshyp stones and stockes, whiche
were then honored as God. The whole
worlde seeth plainelye ynough alreadye,
what we and ours haue endured at these
mens handes for religion and our onely
Goddes cause. They haue thrown vs
into

into pzison,into water, into fyer,& haue
embzued themselues in oure bloude, not
bycause wee were eyther adulterers oz
robbers,oz murtherers,but only foz that
we confessed the Gospell of Jesu Chzist,
and put oure confidence in the liuinge
God. And foz that wee complained to
iustly and truely (Lozde thou knowest)
that they did bzeake the lawe of God foz
their owne moste vaine traditions: And
that our Aduersaries were the very foes
to the Gsopel,and enuemies to Chzistes
crosse, who so wittingly and willingly
did obstinately dispise Gods commaun=
dementes. Wherefoze when these menne
sawe they could not rightly finde faulte
with oure doctrine,they woulde needes
picke a quarel,and inuey & raile against
our manners, surmisinge how that we
do condemne all well doinges,how wee
sette open the dooze to all licenciousnes
and lust, and lead away the people from
all loue of bertue. And in very deede the
lyfe of all men,euen of the deuoutest and
moste

moste Chriſtian, bothe is and euermore hath been ſuche, as one maye alwayes find ſome lacke, euen in the very beſt and pureſt conuerſation. And ſuch ys the inclination of all creatures vnto euell, and the readines of al men to ſuſpect, that the thinges whiche neither haue been done, no̅z once ment to be done, yet maye bee eaſely bothe heard and credited for true. And like as a ſmall ſpotte is ſoone ſpyed in the neateſt and whyteſt garment, euen ſo the leaſt ſtaine of diſhoneſtie is eaſelye founde out in the pureſt & ſincereſt lyfe. Neither take we all them whyche haue at this day imbraced the doctrine of the Goſpell to be Angels, and to liue clerely without anye mote or wrinkle : nor yet thinke we theſe men either ſo blind, that yf any thing may be noted in vs, they ar not able to perceaue y̅ ſame euen through the leaſt creuie ; nor ſo friendly that they will conſtrue ought to the beſt: nor yet ſo honeſt of nature nor curteous, that they will looke backe vpon themſelues, and

F.i.   Neys

wey our fashions by their owne . Yf so
be we list to search this matter from the
bottome: we knowe in the very Apostls
times there were Christians , throughe
whome the name of the Lord was blas-
phemed and euell spoken of amonge the
Gentiles . Constantius the Emperoure
bewaileth, as it is writē in Sosomenus,
how that many waxed worse after thei
had fallen to the religion of Christe. And

Cyprian de
Lapsis.

Cyprian in a lamentable Oration setteth out the corrupt maners in his time:
The holsome discipline, saith he, whiche
the Apostles left vnto vs , hathe idlenesse
and long rest now vtterly marred, euery
one studied to encrease his liuelyhode,
and cleane forgettinge either what they
had done before, whiles they were vnder
the Apostles , or what they ought continually to doe hauing receaued the fayth:
they earnestly laboured to make greate
their owne welth wᵗ an vnsatiable desire
of couetousnes. There is no deuout religion, saithe hee, in Preestes , no sounde
faith

faith in ministers , no charitie shewed
in good workes , no forme of Godlinesse
in their conditions, men are become ef=
feminate, and womens bewty is coun=
terfeited. And before his daies, said Ter=
tullian, O how wreatched be we which
are called Christians at this time? For
wee liue as Heathens, vnder the name of
Christe. And without reciting of manye
mo wryters, Gregory Nazianzene spea=
keth this of the pitifull state of his owne
time: We saith he, are in hatred amõg ÿ
Heathen for our own vyces sake, we are
also becomme nowe a wonder not alone
to Aungels and menne , but euen to
all the vngodlye. In this case was
the Churche of God when the Gos
pell firste beganne to shyne, and when
the fury of Tyrauntes was not as yet
cooled, nor the sword taken of from the
Christians neckes. Surelie it is no new
thinge that menne bee butte menne, al=
thoughe they bee called by the name of
Christians.

F.ii.   But

But will thefe menne J praye you
thinke nothing at all of thē felues, whi=
les they accufe vs fo malicioufly, ꜩ whi=
les they haue leafure to beholde fo farre
of, and fee both what is done in Germa=
nye and in England ⸫ Haue they eyther
forgotten, or can they not fee what is
done at Rome⸫ Or be they our accufers,
whofe lyfe is fuche, as no man is able to
make mention thereof but with fhame
and vncomelines⸫ Our purpofe here is
not to take in hande at this prefent to
bryng to lyght and open to the worlde
thofe thinges whiche were meete rather
to be hyd and buryed with the workers
of them, Jt befemyth neyther our Reli=
gion, nor our modeftie, nor our fhame=
faftenes. But yet he which giueth com=
maundement that he fhoulde be called
the vicar of Chrift and the head of the
Churche, who alfo hearith that fuche
things be don at Rome, who feeth them,
who fuffereth them (for we will go no
further) he can eafily confider with him
felfe

selfe what maner of things they be. Let
him on Gods name call to mynde, let
him remembre that they be of his owne
Canonistes, which haue taught the people that fornication betwen single folke
is not sinne (as though they had set that
doctrine from Mitio in Terence) whose
wordes be: It is no sinne (beleue me) for
a yonge man to haunte harlottes. Let
hym remembre they be of his own which
haue decreed, ŷ a preiste oughte not to be
put out of his cure for fornication. Let
him remembre also, how Cardinall Cam-
pegius, Albertus Pighius and others
many moze of his owne, haue taughte ŷ
the preiste whiche keepeth a Concubine,
doth liue moze holily and chastelye, then
he which hath a wyfe in matrimonie. I
trust he hath not yet forgoten, that there
be many thousands of common harlottes in Rome: and that hym selfe doth
gather yearely of ŷ same harlottes vpō
a thirty thousade Duckettes by the way
of an annuall pension. Neyther can he

Iohan. de magist. De temperãtia.

3.4.7 lege Extra. de bigamis Qua circa.

F.iii.   forgets

forgette how himselfe doth mainteine o=
penly brothels houses , and by a moste
filthye lucre doth filthelye and lewdelye
serue his owne lust . Were all thinges
then pure and holy in Rome, when Io=
hane a womā rather of parfeit age thē of
parfect lyfe, was Pope there, & bare her
selfe as the head of the Church? And af=
ter that for two whole yeares in that
holye Sea, she had plaide the naughtie
packe, at last going in procession about
the Citie, in the sight of al the Cardinals
and Byshopps fell in trauaile openly in
the stretes?

The image
of this wo=
men Pope
lieng in tra
uel,ys yet
to be seene
in Rome.

But what neede one rehearse Con=
cubines and Bawds, as for that is now
an ordinarie , and a gainefull sinne at
Rome . For harlottes syt there now a
days, not as they did in times past with=
out the Citie walles, and with theire fa=
ces hid and couered, but they dwel in pa=
laces and fayre houses : they strey about
in Courte and market, and that wyth
bare and open face : as who saye they,
may

Pag.38.

In concilio.
delett. Card.
Tomo 3.

may not onely lawfully do it, but ought
also to be prayſed foꝛ ſo doing. What
ſhould we ſay any moꝛe of this: their vi-
tious and abhominable lyfe is now tho-
roughlye knowen to the whole woꝛld.
Bernarde wꝛiteth roundely and truely
of the Byſhop of Romes houſe, yea and
of the Byſhop of Rome him ſelfe. Thy
Palaice ſayeth he, taketh in good men,
but it maketh none: naughtye perſones
thꝛiue there, and the good appayꝛe and
decaye. And who ſoeuer he were which
wꝛote the Tripartite woꝛke annexed to
the Councel Lateranenſe, ſaith thus, So
exceſſiue at this daye is the ryote aſwel
in the Pꝛelates and Byſhoppes, as in
the Clerkes and Pꝛieſtes, that it is hoꝛ-
rible to be told. But theſe thinges be not
onely growen in bꝛe and ſo by cuſtome
and continuall tyme well alowed, as all
the reſt of their doinges in maner bee,
but they are now waxen old and rotten
ripe. Foꝛ who hath not hearde what a
haynous act Peter Aloiſius, Pope Paul

the

the thirdes sonne committed against Cosmus Cherius the Byshopp of Fauense: what John Casus Archebishop of Beneuentanus the Popes Legate at Uenyce wrote in the commendation of a moste abhominable sylthynes, and how he set furth with most lothesom wordes & wicked eloquence, ȳ mater which ought not once to proeede out of any bodys mouth. To whose eares hath it not come, that N. Diasius a Spaniard, being purposely sent from Rome into Germanie, did shamefulie and diuilishlie murther his own brother John Diasius, a most innocent and a most godly man, onely bycause he had embraced ȳ Gospel of Iesu Christ, and wolde not retorne again to Rome?

But it may chaunce, to this they will say: These thinges may somtime happen in the best gouerned common welth, yea and against the Magistrates willes: and besides, there be good lawes made to punyshe suche. I graunt it be so: but by what good lawes (I would know) haue

these

these greate myscheues benne punyshed
emongest them? Petrus Aloisius after
he hadde don that notorious Acte that I
spake of, was alwayes cherished in his
fathers bosome Pope Paule the third,
and made his very derling. Diasius af=
ter he had murthered his owne brother,
was deliuered by the Popes meanes, to
thend he might not be punyshed by good
lawes. John Casus Archiepũs Bene=
uentanus is yet alyue, yea and lyueth at
Rome, euen in the eyes and syght of the
most holye Father. They haue putte to
death infinite numbres of our bretherne,
only bycause they beleued truely and sin=
cerelie in Iesu Christ. But of that great
and foule numbre of harlottes, fornica=
tours, Adulterers, what one haue they
at any time (I say not killed) but eyther
excommunicat, or once attached? Why,
volupteousnesse, adulterie, rybaudrie,
whoredome, murthering of kinn, incest,
and others more abhominable partes,
are not these coumpted synne at Rome?
                    F.b.   Dz

Or yf they be synne, ought Chriſtes vy-
car, Peters ſucceſſour, the moſt holye
Father, ſo lightly and ſlytely beare them
as though they were no ſynne, and that
in the Citie of Rome, and in that principall tower of all holyneſſe

O holy Scribes and Phariſes, which
knew not this kind of holines. O what
holynes, what a Catholike faith is this?
Peter did not this teach at Rome, Paul
did not ſo liue at Rome: they did not prac-
tiſe brothelry which theſe do opēly: they
made not a yearely reuenewe and profite
of harlottes: they ſuffered no common
Adulterours and wicked Murtherers
to go vnpunyſhed. They did not receiue
them into their intire familiaritie, into
their Councell, into their houſ houlde,
nor yet into þ cōpany of Chriſten men.
Theſe menne ought not therfore ſo vn-
reſonablie to triumphe againſt our ly-
uing. It had ben more wyſedom for thē,
eyther firſte to haue proued good their
owne lyfe befoze the worlde, or at leaſte

to

to haue cloked it a litle more conningly.
For we do vse stil the ould and auncient
lawes (and asmuche as men maye do in
the maners vsed at these dayes, when al
thinges are so wholy corrupte) wee dili=
gently and earnestlye put in execution
theecclesiasticall discipline : wee haue not
commen brothell houses of strumpettes,
nor yet flockes of Concubynes, nor
heardes of harlot haunters. Neyther do
we preferr adulterie before matrimony,
neither do we exercise beastly sensualitie.
Neyther do we gather ordinarie rentes
and stipendes of stewes, nor do suffer to
escape vnpunyshed incest and abhomi=
nable naughtines, nor yet such manquel=
lers as the Aloisians, Casias, and Dia=
sias were. For yf these thinges woulde
haue pleased vs, wee neded not to haue
departed from these mennes felowship,
amongest whom suche enormities be in
their chiefe pride and pryce. Nother ne=
ded we for leauing them to ronne into þ
hatred of menne, and into most willfull
                              daungers

daungers. Paule the fourthe not many
monethes since, hadde at Rome in prison
certaine Augustine fryers, manye Byſſhops, and a greate numbre of other deuout men, for Religion sake; hee racked
them and tormented them: to make them
confeſſe, hee lefte no meanes vnaſſayed.
But in thend how many brothels, how
many whoremōgers, how many adulterers, how many inceſtuous perſōs could
he find of all thoſe? Our God be thāked,
although we be not ſ mē we ought a pro
feſſe to be, yet whoſoeuer we be, cōpare vs
w̄ theſe men, a euē oure own life a innocencie wil ſone proue vntrue, a condemn
their malicious ſurmiſes. For we exhorte
the people to all vertue and well doinge,
not onelye by bokes and preachinges, but
also w̄ oure examples and behauiour.
We alſo teache that the Goſpell is not a
boaſting or bragging of knowledg, but

De Apoll
f. 45. ſ̄ it is ſ̄ law of life, a ſ̄ a Chriſtian man
(as Tertulliā ſaith) ought not to ſpeak ho
norably, but ought to liue honorably: nor
that

that they be the hearers of the lawe, but
the doers of the lawe, which are iustified before God.

Besides all these matters wherewith
they charge vs, they are wōt also to add
this one thinge, which they enlarge with
all kinde of spitefulnes: that is, that we
be men of trouble, ỷ wee plucke ỷ sword
and Scepter out of Kinges handes: that
we arme the people, that we ouerthrowe
iudgemente places, destroy the lawes,
make hauocke of possessiōs, seke to make
the people Princes, turne all things vp-
syde downe: and to be short, ỷ we would
haue nothinge in good frame in a common welth. Good lorde, how often haue
they sette on fyre Princes heartes with
these wordes, to thend they might quēche
the light of the Gospell in the very firste
apperinge of it, and might begin to hate
the same or euer they were able to know
it, and to the end that euery magistrate
might thinke he saw his deadly ennemy,
as often as he saw any of vs. Surely it

*Tertul. &
Apolleg
cap. 31.*

shoulde

should excedingly greeue vs to be so ma=
littiouslie accused of moste hainous trea=
son , onlesse we knewe that Christe him=
selfe, the Apostles, and a numbre of good
and Christian men were in time past bla
med and enuied in manner for the same
faultes. For although Christ taught thei
should giue vnto Cesar that which was
Cesars, yet was he charged with sediti=
on in that he was accused to deuise some
conspiracie and to couete the kingdome.
And herebpon they cryed out with open
mouth against him in the place of iudge=
ment, sayeng: Yf thou let this man scape,
thou arte not Cesars friend.

And though ꝑ Apostles did likewise e=
uermore & stedfastly teach, ꝑ Magistrats
ought to be obeyed , ꝑ euery soule ought
to be subiect to the higher powers, not
onely for feare of wrath & punishment,
but euen for conscience sake, yet bear thei
the name to disquiet the people , and to
stirre vp the multitud to rebel. After this
sorte did Haman specially bring the na=
tion

tion of the Iewes into the hatred of the *In the booke of Hester* kinge Assuerus, bicause, saide hee, they were a rebellious & stubborn people, & dispised the ordinaunces and commaun= dementes of princes. Wicked king Achab saide to Elie the Prophet of God, It is *3.Rg.c 18* thou that troublest Israell. Amasias y priest at Bethell laid a conspiracie to the prophete Amos charge before kinge Ie= roboam sayeng, See, Amos hath made *Amos.7* a conspiracie against thee in the middest of the house of Israell . To bee breefe: Tertullian saithe, this was the generall *In Apolo. cap. 7.* accusation of all Christians whiles he li= ued, that they were traytours, they were rebelles, and the enemies of mankinde. Wherefore if now a dayes the truthe be likewise euell spoken of, and beinge the same truth it was then, yf it be now like dispitefully vsed as it was in times past, though it be a greuous and vnkind dea= linge, yet can it not seeme vnto vs a new or an vnwonted matter. Forty yeares agone and vpward, was it an easy thing

for

for them to deuise aginst vs these accus-
sed speaches & other sorer then these, when
in the middest of the darkenesse of that
age firste beganne to springe and to giue
shine, some one glimmeringe beame of
truthe vnknowen at that time and vn-
hearde of, when also Martin Luther &
Hulderike Zwinglius beinge moste excellent menne, euen sent of God to giue
light to the whole world, firste came vnto the knowledge and preachinge of the
Gospell, wheras yet the thinge was but
newe, and the successe thereof vncertain:
and when mens mindes stoode doubtful
and amased, and their eares open to all
slaunderous tales: and when there could
bee imagined against vs no fact so detestable, but the people then woulde soone
beleeue it for the nouelty and strangenes
of the matter. For so did Symmachus,
so did Celsus, so didde Julianus, so did
Porphirius the olde foes to the Gospell
attempt in times past to accuse all Christians of sedition and treason, before
                                        that

eyther Prynce or People were able to know who those Christians were, what thei professed, what thei beleued, or what was their meaning.

But now sithens our very ennemies do see and cannot deny, but we euer in al our wordes and writinges haue diligent= lie put the people in mynde of their dew= tie, to obey their Princes and Magistra= tes, ye though they be wicked: for this doth very trial and experience sufficient= lie teache, and all mennes eyes, whosoe= uer and wheresoeuer they be, do well y= nough see and wytnes for vs, yt was a foule parte of them to charge vs with these thinges: and seing they could fynde no new and late faults, therfore to seke to procure vs enuye only with stale and out worne lyes. We geue our lorde God thanks, whose only cause this is, there hath yet at no tyme been any suche ex= ample in all the Realmes, Dominions and common weales whiche haue recei= ued the Gospil!. For we haue ouerthro=

G.i.   W:ii

wen no kingedome, we haue decayed no
mans power oz right, wee haue disoz=
dered no commō welth. There continue
in thir owne accustomed state and aun=
cient dignitie the kinges of oure coun=
trie of Englande, the kinges of Den=
marke, the kings of Suecia, the Dukes
of Saxonie, the Counties Palatine, the
Marquesies of Brandeburgh, the Lans=
graues of Hessia, the common wealthes
of the Heluetians and Rhetians, and the
free cities, as Argentine, Basil, Frank=
forde, Ulme, August and Norrenberge,
doe all I saye abide in the same authozi=
tie and estate wherein they haue beene
heeretofoze, oz rather in a muche better,
foz that by meanes of the Gospell
they haue their people moze obedient vn=
to them. Lette them go I praye you in=
to those places where at this presente
through Goddes goodnes the Gospell
is taught, where is there moze maiestie
where is there lesse arrogancie and tir=
rannye ? where is the Prince moze ho=
                                    nozed

noured? where be the people lesse vnrulye? where hathe there at anye time the common wealthe or the Churche beene in moze quyet? Perhappes ye will say, from the firste beginninge of this doctrine, the common sorte euerye wheare beganne to rage and to ryse throughout Germany. Alowe it were so, yet Martin Luther the publisher and setter forwarde of this doctrine, didde write marueous vehementlye and sharpely agaiust them, and reclamed them home to peace and obedience.

But whereas it is wont sometime to be obiected, by personnes wantinge skil, touchinge the Heluetians chaunge of state and killinge of Leopoldus the duke of Austria, and restoringe by force their Countrie to libertie, that was donne as appeereth playnelye by all stories, for twooe hundreth and threescore yeares past or aboue, vnder Boniface the eight, when the authoritie of the Byshop of Rome was in greatest iolitie, about two

hundereth

hundreth yeres before Huldericke Zuin-
glius eyther beganne to teache the Goſpell, oȝ yet was boȝne. And euer ſence
that tyme, they haue hadde all thinges
ſtill and quiet, not onelye from foȝreine
ennemies, but alſo from ciuell diſſenſi-
on. And yf it were a ſinne in the Heluetians to deliuer their owne countrie
from foȝeine gouernemente; ſpecialiye
when they were ſo proudelye and tȝan-
nouſlye oppȝeſſed, yet to burthen vs
with other mennes faultes, oȝ them
with the faultes of their foȝefathers, is
againſt all right and reaſone.

But O immoȝtall God, and will the
Byſſhoppe of Rome accuſe vs of trea-
ſon? will hee teache the people to obeye
and folowe their Magiſtrates? oȝ hath
hee anye regarde at all of the Maieſtie
of Pȝinces? whye doothe hee then as
none of the olde Byſſhoppes of Rome
heretofoȝe euer didde, ſuffre hym ſelfe
to bee called of his flaterers, Loȝde of
Loȝdes, as though hee woulde haue all
kinges

Auguſt.
Steuchus.
Antonius
de Roſellis

kynges and Princes, whoe and what
so euer they are, to bee his vnderlinges ?
whye doothe hee vaunte hym selfe to bee
kyng of kynges , and to haue kyngelye
Royaltie ouer his Subiectes? why com=
pelleth he al emperors & princes to swere
to him fealtie and true obedience? Whye
doth he boaste that the Emperours ma= *De Maior*
gestie is a thowsandfould inferiour to *& obedi,*
Solute.
hym ? and for this reason, speciallye by=
cause God hath made two lyghtes in *De maior.*
the heauen , and bycause heauen and *& obed en*
Vnam sactā.
yearthe were created not at two begin=
ninges, but at on. Why hath he and hys
complices(like Anabaptistes and Liber=
tines, to thende they myght ronne on
more licenciouslye and careleslye)shake
of the yoke, and exempted themselues
from being vnder all ciuell power? why
hath he his Legates (asmuche to saye
as most sutle spyes) lieng in wayte in all
kynges Courtes,Councells, and priuey
chambres ? whye doth he,when he lyst,
sette Christian Princes one against an
G.iii.   other

other, and at his owne pleasure trouble the whole worlde with debate and discorde? why dothe hee excommunicate and commaund to be taken as a heathen and a Pagan any Christian prince that renounceth his authoritie? and why promiseth he his Indulgences & his pardōs largely to any that will (what way soeuer it be) kil any of his ennemies? Doth hee maintaine Empires and kingdomes? Or dothe hee once desire that common quiete should be prouided for? You must pardonne vs good Reader, though wee seeme to vtter these thinges more bitterlye and bitingly then it becommeth Diuines to doe. For bothe the shamfulnes of the matter, and the desire of rule in the Bysshoppe of Rome is so exceeding and outragious, that it could not well be vttered with other words, or more mildly. For he is not ashamed to say in open assemblie, that all iurisdiction of al kinges dothe depend vpon himselfe. And to feed his ambitiō & greedines of rule, hath he pulled in peeces the Empire of Rome,

Clement.5. in Concilio. Viennensi. *Lo pag4.*

and

and vexed and rent whole Christendom
asunder: falsely and traiterouslie also did
he release ʒ Romains, ʒ Italians, & him
selfe to, of the othe wherby they and hee
were straightly bound to bee true to the
Emperour of Grecia, and stirred vp the
Emperours subiects to forsake him, and
calling Carolus Martellus out of Frāce
into Italie, made him Emperour: such a
thing as neuer was seene before. He put
Chilpericus the Frenche king, being no
euel prince, beside his realm, only because
he fansied him not, and wrongfullie placed Pipin in his roume. Againe, after he
had cast out king Philip, if he could haue
brought it so to passe, he had determined
& apointed ʒ kingdom of Fraunce to Albertus king of Romaines. He vtterly destroyed the state of ʒ most flourishing cyty
& cōmō weale of Florēce his own natiue
coūtrie, & brought it out of a free & pea-
sable state, to be gouerned at ʒ pleasure
of on mā: he brought to passe by his pro-
curement ʒ whole Sauoy on the one side
was miserably spoyled by Themperour

Zacharias papa.

Clemens papa. 7.

Idē Clemē.

G. iiii.   Charles

Charles the fifth, and on the other ſyde
by the Frenche kinge, ſo as the vnfortu-
nate Duke had ſcant one Citie left him
to hyde his head in. Wee are cloyed with
exaumples in this behalfe, and it ſhoulde
bee very tedious to recken vp all the notorious deedes of the Byſhops of Rome.
Of which ſide were they, I beſeche you,
whiche poyſoned Henry Themperour,
euen in the receauinge of the ſacrament?
whiche poyſoned Victor the Pope, euen
in ÿ receauing of ÿ Chalice? which poyſoned our king John kinge of England
in a drinkinge cuppe? whoſoeuer at leaſt
they were, and of what ſect ſoeuer, I am
ſure they were neither Lutherians, nor
Zwinglians. What is hee at this daye,
whiche alloweth the mightieſt kinges
and Monarches of the worlde to kiſſe
his bleſſed feete? What is hee that commaundeth the Emperour to goe by him
at his horſe bridell, and the Frenche king
to holde his ſtirrop? Who hurled vnder
his table Fraunces Dandalus the duke
of

of Venice kinge of Creta and Cypres, faſt bound with chaines, to feed of bones amonge his dogges: Who ſet the Empe= riall crowne vpon the Emperour Henry the ſixt hys head, not with his hand but with his foote, and with the ſame foote againe caſt the ſame crowne of, ſayinge withall: hee had power to make Empe= rours, and to vnmake them againe at his pleaſure? Who put in armes Henry the ſonne againſt Themperour his fa= ther Henry the fourth, and wrought ſo that the Father was taken priſoner of his owne ſonne, and beinge ſhorne and ſhamfullye handeled, was thruſte into a monaſterie, where with hunger & ſorow he pined away to death? Who ſo ilfauo= redlye and monſtrouſlye put the Empe= rour Frederikes necke vnder his feet, and asthough that were not ſufficient, added further this texte out of the Pſalmes: Thou ſhalt go vpon the Adder and coc= katrice, and ſhalt treade the Lyon and Dragon vnder thy feete? Suche an ex=

G.v.   ample

Margin notes: Sabellicus. Caleſtinus papa. Hildebrand. papa. Innocentius papa. j.

ample of scorninge and contemninge a
Princes maiestie, as neuer before this
was heard tell of in any remembrance,
except I weene, either of Tamerlanes
the kinge of Scithia a wilde and barba
rous creature, or els of Sapor king of ŷ
Persians. All these notwithstandinge
were Popes, all Peters successours, all
most holy fathers, whose seuerall wordes
wee must take to be as good as seuerall
Gospels. Yf we be compted traytours
whiche do honour oure Princes, whiche
giue them all obedience as muche as is
due to them by Godds word, and which
doo praye for them, what kinde of men
then bee these, whiche haue not onely done all the thinges before saide, but
also alowe the same for speciallye well
don? Do they then either this way instruct ŷ people as we do, to reuerēce their
magistrate: or can they with honesty appeache vs as seditious personnes, brea-
kers of the common quiete, and despisers
of princes maiestie?

Truely

Truely we neither putte of the yoke
of obedience from vs, neyther doe wee
disorder realmes, neither doe we sette vp
or pull downe kinges, nor translate go-
uernementes, nor giue oure kinges poy-
sonne to drinke, nor yet holde to them
oure feete to be kissed, nor opprobriously
triumphinge ouer them, leape into their
neckes with oure feete. This rather is
oure profession, this is our doctrine, that
euerye soule of what callinge soeuer
he be, be he Monke, bee he preacher, bee
he prophet, be he Apostle, ought to be sub
iect to kings & magistrates: yea and that
the Byshop of Rome himselfe, onlesse he
will seeme greater then the Euangelists,
then the Prophetes, or the Apostles,
ought bothe to acknowledge and to call
the Emperour his Lorde and maister:
which ye old bishops of Rome, who liued
in times of more grace, euer did. Our co-
mō teachig also is, ye we ought so to obey
princes as mē sent of God, & ye whoso w̄-
standeth thē, withstandeth Gods ordinance,

Chrysost. in
13.cap. ad
Romanos.

Gregorius
papa lxod
in epist.

This

This is oure scholinge, and this is well
to be seene bothe in oure bookes and in
our preachinges, and also in the maners
and modest behauiour of oure people.

But where they saye, we haue gon a-
waye from the vnitie of the catholique
Churche, this is not onelye a matter of
malice, but besides, though it bee moste
vntrue, yet hath it some shew and appa-
rance of trouth. For the common people
and ignoraunt multitude giue not credit
alone to thinges true and of certaintie,
butte euen to suche thinges also, yf anye
chaunce, which may seeme to haue but a
resemblaunce of trouth. Therfore we see
that subtle and craftie persones, when
they had no truth on their side, haue euer
contended and hotely argued vi things
likely to be true, to the intent they which
were not able to espie the very grounde
of the matter, might be caried a waye at
least with some pretense and probabilitie
therof. In times past where the firste
Christians, oure forefathers, in makinge
their

their prayers to God, died tourne them=
selues towardes the Easte, there were
that sayde, they worshipped the sunn,
and reckened it as God. Againe, where
oure forefathers saide, that as touchinge
immortall and euerlasting life, thei liued
by no other meanes but by the flesh and
bloud of that lambe who was without
spott, that is to say, of oure sauiour Je/
sus Christ, ÿ enuious creatures and foes
of Christes Crosse, whose only care was
to bringe Christian religion into slaun=
der by al māner of wayes, made peo=
ple beleeue, that they were wicked per=
sons, that they sacrificed mens fleshe, and
dronke mennes bloud. Also where oure
forefathers saide, that before God there
is neither man nor woman, nor for attei=
ninge to the true righteousnes there is
no distinction at all of personnes, and
that they didde call one an other indiffe
rentlye by the name of Sisters and
Brothers, there wanted not menne
whiche forged false tales vpon the same,
saying,

Tertull in Apol.ca.16

Tertull in Apologen. cap 8.9

Tertull. in
Apologet
fa 9:

ſayenge that the Chꝛiſtians made noe
difference amonge them ſelues, eyther
of age oꝛ of kinde, but like bꝛute beaſtes
without regarde had to do one with an
other. And where foꝛ to pꝛay & heare the
Goſpell, they mette often together in ſe-
cret and byeplaces, becauſe Rebelles
ſomtime were wonte to do the like. Ru-
moꝛs were euery where ſpꝛedd abꝛoade
howe they made pꝛiuie confederacies,
and counſeled together either to kill
the magiſtrates, oꝛ to ſubuert the common wealth. And where in celebꝛatinge
the holye myſteries, after Chꝛiſtes inſtitution, they tooke bꝛeade and wyne,
they were thought of many not to woꝛ-
Auguſtinus.
ſhippe Chꝛiſte, but Bacchus and Ceres,
foꝛſomuche as thoſe vaine Goddes were
wooꝛſhipped of the Heathen in like ſoꝛt,
after a pꝛophane ſuperſtition, with bꝛead
and wyne. Theſe thinges were beleued
of manye, not bicauſe they were true in
deed (foꝛ what coulde be moꝛe vntrue?)
but bicauſe they were lyke to bee true,

and

and through a certain shadow of truth
myghte the more easilye decciue the
simple. On this fashion likewise dooe
these menne slaunder vs as Heretiques,
and saye that wee haue lefte the Church
and felowshippe of Christe: not bicause
they thinke it is true, for they dooe not
muche force of that, but bicause to ig=
norannte folke it myght perhappes som=
waye appeere true. Wee haue in deede
putt oure selues aparte, not as heretikes
are woonte, from the Churche of Christ;
but as all good menne oughte to doo,
from the infection of naughtye persons
and hypocrites.

Neuerthelesse in this poynte they
triumphe marueloullye that they bee
the Churche, that theyre Churche ys
Christes spowse, the piller of truthe,
the arke of Noe, and that without it
there is no hope of saluation. Con=
trarywise, they saye that wee bee ronne=
gates, that we haue torne Christes seat;
that wee are plucked quyte off from the
body

body of Chriſte, and haue forſaken the
catholique faithe. And when they leaue
nothinge vnſpoken that may neuer
ſo falſelie and malitioſlie be ſaide againſt
vs, yet this one thynge are they neuer
hable truely to ſaye, that we haue ſwar-
ued eyther from the worde of God, or
from the Apoſtles of Chriſt, or from the
primatiue Churche. Surelye wee haue
euer iudged the primatiue Churche of
Chriſtes tyme, of the Appoſtles, and of
the holie fathers to be the catholique
Churche: neyther make we doubt to name it Noes arke, Chriſtes ſpouſe, the
piller and vpholder of al trueth: nor yet
to fire therin the whole meane of our e
ſaluation. It is doubtles an odiouſe
mater for one to leaue the ſellowſhipp
whereunto he hath ben accuſtomed, and
ſpecially of thoſe men, who though they
be not, yet at leaſte ſeme and be called
Chriſtians. And to ſay truely, we do not
diſpiſe the Churche of theſe men (howe
ſoeuer it be ordered by thē now a dayes)
partely

partely for the name sake yt selfe, & partely for that the Gospell of Jesu Christ
hath once ben therin truely and purelye
set furth. Neyther had we departed ther-
from, but of very necessitie, and much a-
gainst our wils. But I put case, an Idol
be set vp in the Churche of God, and the
same desolation which Christe prophe-
cied to comme, stoude openly in the holy
place? what yf som theefe or pirat inuade
and possesse Noes arke? These folkes
as often as they tell vs of the Churche,
meane therby themselues alone, and attribute all these titles to their owne selues, boasting as they did in tymes past
whiche cryed The temple of the Lorde,
The temple of the lorde: or as the Pha-
riseis and Scribes dyd, whiche craked
they were Abrahams children. Thus
with a gay and iolie shewe deceiue they
the simple, and seke to choke vs with the
very name of the church. Muche like as
yf a theefe, when he hath gotten into an
other mans house, and by violence ey-

ther

ther hath thruſt out oꝛ ſlayne the ow-
ner,ſhould afterwarde aſſigne the ſame
houſe to hym ſelfe,caſting furthe of poſ-
ſeſſion the right inheritour: Oꝛ yf An-
tichꝛiſt after he hath once entred into the
Temple of God, ſhould afterward ſaye,
This houſe is myne own,ꝗ Chꝛiſt hath
nothinge to do withall. Foꝛ theſe menne
nowe after they haue left nothyng re-
mainig in ẏ churche of God ẏ hath any
liknes of this Church,yet will they ſeeme
the Patrones and the valiaunte mayn-
teners of the Churche, very like as Gra-
chus amongeſt the Romaynes ſtoode in
defence of the treaſury,not withſtanding
with his prodigalitie and fond expences
he had vtterlye waſted the whole ſtocke
of the treaſurie . And yet was there
neuer any thing ſo wicked oꝛ ſo far out
of reaſon,but lightelye yt might be couered ꝗ defended by the name of the church.
Foꝛ the waſpes alſo make honycom-
bes as well as Bees, ꝗ wicked men haue
companyes lyke to the Churche of God,
yet foꝛ all that they be not ſtreight wey
the

the people of God which ar called ý people of God:neither be they al Israelits
asmany as ar com of Israell ý father.
The Arrians notwitstanding thei were
heretiques, yet bragged they that they
alone were Catholiques, calling all the
rest now Ambrosias, now Athanasias,
now Johannites. And Nestorius, as
saith Theodorete, for all he was an Heretique, yet couered he hym selfe τ ο
ορθοδοξιασ προσχηματι, that is to weete,
with a certaine cloke and colour of the
true & right faith. Ebion though he a-
greed in opinion with ý Samaritanes,
yet as saith Epiphanius, he woulde be
called a Christiau. The Mahomptes at
this day,for al ý al histories make plaine
mention,and themselues also cannot denye,but they toke their first begynning
of Agar the bondewoman , yet for the
very name and stockes sake,chuse they
rather to be caled Saracenés,as though
they came of Sara the freewoman and
Abrahams wyfe. So likewise the false

Augustinus in epist. 48. ad vincent.

Prophetes of all ages whiche stode vp
againſt the Prophetes of God, whiche
reſiſted Eſayas, Ieremye, Chriſt, and
the Appoſtles, at no tyme craked of any
thing ſomuche, as they dyd of the name
of the Churche. And for no nother cauſe
did they ſo ſcarcely bere them and cal the
Ronneawayes and Apoſtatas, then for
that they forſoke their fellowſhipp, and
kepte not thordinaunces of the Elders:
wherfore yf we would ſolow the iudge=
mentes of thoſe men only, who then go=
uerned the Churche, and would reſpecte
nothing els neyther God nor his word,
yt muſte nedes bee confeſſed, that the
Apoſtles were rightlie and by iuſt lawe
condemned of the to death, bycauſe they
fell from the Byſhops and preiſtes, that
is you muſt thike, from the Catholique
Churche: and bycauſe they made many
new alterations in Religion contrarie
to the Byſhops and Preiſtes willes, yea
and for all their ſpurninge ſo erneſtlye
againſt it: wherfore like as it is written
that

that Hercules in olde time was forced
in striuing w Anteus that huge giaunt,
to lyfte him quite vp from the earth that
was his Mother ere he could conqueere
him, euen so must our Aduersaries be
heaued from their Mother, that is from
this vaine colour a shadow of ý church,
wherewith they so disguise and defende
themselues, otherwyse they cannot be
brought to yelde vnto the word of God.
And therefore saith Ieremye the Prophete, Make not suche great boaste that
the Temple of the Lorde is with you,
this is but a vaine confidence, for these
are lyes. The Aungell also saith in the
Apocalyps, They say theybe Iewes but
they be ý Synagoge of Sathan. And
Christ sayd to the Pharisies when they
vaunted them selfe of the kynred a bloud
of Abraham: Ye are of your father the
Deuel, for you resemble not your father
Abraham. asmuche to saye, ye are not
the men ye woulde so faine be called, ye
begile the people with vaine titles, and

Iohan.8.

H.iii. abuse

abuſe the name of the Churche, to the
ouerthrowing of the Churche.

So that theſe mens parte had ben
firſt to haue clearely and truely proued
that the Romiſhe churche is the true
and right inſtructed Churche of God, &
that the ſame, as they do order it at this
day, dothe agre with ye primatiue church
of Chriſt, of the Apoſtles, and of the holye Fathers, whiche we doubt not but
was in dede ye true catholique Church.
For our partes yf we could haue iudged
ignoraunce, errour, ſuperſtition, Idolatrie, mennes Inuentions, and the ſame
cōmōlie diſagreinge with ye holy Scrip
tures, eyther pleaſed God, or to be ſufficient for thobtainige euerlaſtyng ſaluation, or yf we could aſſertaine our ſelues
that the worde of God was written but
for a time only, and afterwarde againe
ought to be abrogated and put awaye,
or els that the ſayinges and commaundementes of God ought to be ſubiecte to
mans will, that whatſoeuer God ſayeth
and

and commaundeth, except the Byſhopp
of Rome willeth and commaundeth the
ſame, it muſt be taken as void an vnſpo=
ken. Yf we coulde haue brought our ſel=
ues to beleue theſe thinges , we graunt
there had ben no cauſe at all why wee
ſhould haue lefte theſe mennes cōpanie.
As touching that we haue now don , to
departe from that Churche , whoſe er=
rours were proued & made manifeſt to ꝑ
worlde, which Church alſo had alredy eui
dētly departed from Gods worde , & yet
not to departe ſomuche from it ſelfe, as
from therrours therof, & not to do this
diſorderlye or wickedly, but quietlie and
ſobrelye, we haue don nothing herein a=
gainſt the doctrine eyther of Chriſt or of
his Apoſtles. For neyther is the Churcᵫ
of God ſuche as it may not be duſked wᵗ
ſome ſpot, or aſketh not ſometime repa=
ration: els what nedieth there ſo many aſ=
ſembles and Councelles , without the
which, as ſaith Egidius , the Chriſtian
faith is not hable to ſtand: For loke ſaith
he

In Concil.
Lateranēse
sub Iulio.2.

he, howe often Councelles are diſconti=
nued, ſo often is the Church deſtitute of
Chriſt. Oꝛ yf there be no peryle that har=
me maye come to the church, what nede
is there to reteyne to no purpoſe ꝑ names
of Byſhops, as is now commenlye vſed
amonge them? Foꝛ yf there be no ſhepe
that may ſtrey, whye be they called ſhe=
pardes? yf there be no Citie that may be
betraied, why be they called watchemen?
yf there be nothing that may ronne to
ruyne, why be thei called Pillers? Anone
after the firſt creation of the woꝛlde the
churche of God began to ſpreade abꝛode,
and the ſame was inſtructed wyth the
heauenly woꝛd, whiche God hym ſelfe
pꝛonounced with his owne mouth. It
was alſo furniſhed with diuine ceremo=
nies. It was taught by ꝑ ſpirit of God,
by the Patriarches and Pꝛophetes, and
continued ſo euen till the tyme ꝑ Chriſte
ſhewed himſelfe to vs in the fleſh. This
notwithſtāding, how often o good God,
in the meane whyle, and howe hoꝛribly
was

was the same Churche darkened and de=
cayed? where was that Churche then,
when all flesshe vpon earth had defyled
their owne wape? where was it when
amōgest the nombre of the whole world
there were only eyght persones (& they
neither all chast and good)whom Gods
will was shoulde be saued aliue from
that vniuersall destruction and mortali=
tie? When Ely the Prophete so lamenta=
blie and byterly made mone, that onelye
himselfe was left of all the whole world
whiche dyd truely and dewly worshipp
God? And when Esay said, The siluer of
Goddes people(that is of the Churche)
was become Drosse: and that the same
Citie whych a foretime had ben faithful,
was now become an harlot, and that in
ȳ same was no part found thoroughout
the whol body from the head to the fote?
Or els when Christ him selfe sayde, that
the house of God was made by ȳ Pha=
rifies and Preistes a Denne of theues?
Of a trouth, the Church euen as a cor=

1. Regum. 19

Esai. 1.

Math. 21

H.b. nefield

nefyld except it be ared, manured, tilled ɋ
trimmed, in stede of wheate, it wil bring
furthe thystles , darnell and nettilles .
For this cause did God send euer among
both Prophettes ɋ Apostles, ɋ last of al
his own Son , who might bring home
the people into the right waye , and re=
payre a new, the tottering Church after
she had erred.

But least some manne should say that
the forsaid thinges happened in þ tyme
of the law onely , of shadowes, and of
infancie, when truth laye hid vnder fi=
gures and ceremonies, whē nothing as
yet was brought to perfection , when
the law was not graue in mennes hear=
tes but in stone (and yet is that but a foo=
lishe saying ,) for euen at those dayes
was there the very same God that is
now, the same spirite, the same Chyiste,
the same faith , the same doctrine , the
same hope, the same inheritaunce , the
same league, and the same efficacie and
vertue of Goddes worde, Eusebius also
saith

faith, all the faithfull euen from Adam
vntil Chꝛist, were in very dede Chꝛistias,
though they were not so termed. But
as I said, leaste men should thus speake
still, Paul the apostle found the like faul=
tes and falles euen then in the pꝛime and
chiefe of the Gospel, in chiefe perfection,
and in lighte, so that he was compelled
to wꝛite in this soꝛte to the Galatians,
whom he had wel befoꝛe that instructed:
I feare me (quod he) leaste I haue labou=
red emongest you in vayne, and leaste ye
haue heard ꝑ Gospel in vaine. O my litle
Chⁱldꝛen, of whom I trauaile a new, til
Chꝛist be fashioned againe in you: And
as foꝛ the Churche of the Coꝛinthians,
how fouly it was defiled, is nothing nee=
deful to rehearce. Now tel me, might the
Churches of the Galathians and Co=
rinthians goe amisse, and the churche
of Rome alone may it not fayle ner goe
amysse? Surely Chꝛist pꝛophecyed long
befoꝛe of his churche, that ꝑ time should
come, when dessolation should stande in
the

the holy place. And Paul faith, that Antichrist should once set vp his owne tabernacle and stately seath in the temple of God: and that the time shuld be, whē men should not awaye with holesome doctrin, but be turned back vnto fables & lies, and that wythin the very Church. Peter likewise tellyth, how there should be teachers of lyes in ye church of Christ: Daniell the Prophete speaking of the later times of Antichrist, Truthe sayth he, in that seasone shalbe throwen vnder foote, and troden vppon in the worlde. And Christ sayeth, how the calamitie & confusion of thinges shalbe so exceeding great, that euen the chosen, yf it were possible, shalbe brought into errour: and how all these thinges shal come to passe not amōgest Gentiles and Turkes, but that they should be in the holye place, in the Temple of God, in the churche, and in the companie an felowship of those whiche professe the name of Christ.

Albeit these same warnynges alone maye

may suffice a wyse man to take heede he
do not suffer hym silfe rashelye to be deceiued with the name of the Churche, &
not to staye to make further inquisition therof by Gods worde, yet bysyde
al this, many fathers also, manye learned and godly men, haue often and carefully complained, how all these thinges
haue chaunced in their lyfe time. For eũe
in the middest of that thick myst of darkenes, God would yet ther shoulo be som,
whoe thoughe they gaue not a cleare &
bright light, yet shuld they kyndle, were
it but some sparke, which menne might
espye being in the darkenes.

Hylarius, when thinges as yet were
almoste vncorrupt, and in good case to,
Ye are yll deceyued, saith he, with ỹ loue
of walles, ye do ill worship the Church,
in that ye worship it in houses and buil-
dinges: ye do yll bryng in the name of
peace vnder roofes. Is there anye doubt
but Antichrist will haue his seate vnder
the same: I rather recken hilles, wodes,
pooles,

Contra
Auren-
tium.

pooles, marishes, prisons, & quauemires;
to be places of more safetie : for in these
the Prophetes either abiding of their ac=
corde, or drowned by violence, didde pro=
phecie by the spirite of God.

Gregorie, as one which perceaued and

forsaw in his mind the wrack of al things
wrote thus to John Byshop of Constantinople, who was the firste of all o-
thers that commaunded himselfe to bee
called by this newe name, the vniuersall
Byshop of whole Christes Church. Yf the
Churche saith he, shall depend vpon one
manne, it will at once fall downe to the
grownd. Who is he that seeth not how this
is come to passe longe since: for longe a-
gone hathe the Byshop of Rome wil=
led to haue the whole Churche depende
vpon himselfe alone. Wherefore it is no
meruail, though it be clean fallen downe
longe agone.

Bernard the Abbot aboue foure hundred

yeares past writeth thus : Nothinge is
nowe of sinceritie and purenes emongest
the

the Cleargie, wherfore it resteth that the
man of sin should be reuealed. The same
Bernarde in his worke of the conuersion of Paul, It semeth now saith he, that
persecution hath ceased: no no, persecution seemeth but nowe to beginne, euen
from them whiche haue chiefe præeminence in the Churche. Thy friendes and
neighbours haue drawen necre, & stoode
vp against thee: from the sole of thy foot
to the crowne of thy heade, there is no
part whole. Iniquitie is proceeded from
the Elders, the Iudges and deputies
which pretende to rule thy people. We
cannot saye nowe, Loke how the people
be, so is the priest. For the people be not
so ill as the priest is. Alas, alas o Lorde
God, the selfe same persons be the chiefe
in persecutinge thee, which seeme to loue
the highest place, and beare moste rule
in thy church. The same Bernard. again
vpon the Canticles writeth thus. All they
are thy friendes, yet are they all thy foes,
all thy kinsefolke, yet are they all thy
aduersaries,

aduersaries, being Christs seruants, thei
serue Antichrist, Beholde in my rest, my
bitternes is moste bitter.

In libello de Pronota Pugnarum. Roger Bacon also a man of great fame,
after he had in a vehement Oration tou-
ched to the quicke the wofull state of his
owne time, These so many errours saith
he, require & loke for Antichrist. Gerso cō
plaineth how in his daies al ȳ substãce &
efficacie of sacred diuinitie was brought
into a glorious contention & ostētatiō of
wits, & to very sophistrie. The Friers of
Lions, mē as touchig ȳ maner of their
life, not to be mislikd, wer wōt boldly to
affirm, ȳ the Romish church (frō whence
alone al counsel & ordres was thē sought
was the very same harlot of Babylon, &
towt of Diuels, wherof is prophesied so
plainely in ȳ Apocalyps. I know wel e-
nough ȳ authoritie of ȳ forsaid persōs is
but lightly regarded amōgest these men.
How thē if I cal furth those for witnes-
ses who themselues haue vsed to honor?
what if I say ȳ Adryan the Byschop of
Rome

Rome did franklye confesse, that all these
mischieues brast out first from the highe
throne of the Pope: Pighius acknowle-
geth herein to be a fault, that many abu-
ses are brought in, euen into the verye
Masse, which Masse otherwise he wold
haue seeme to be a reuerend matter. Ger-
son saithe, that through the number of
moste fonde ceremonies, all the vertue of
the holye Ghoste, whiche ought to haue
full operation in vs, & all true Godlines
is vtterlye quenched and deade. Whole
Grecia and Asia, complaine howe the
Byshoppes of Rome with the martes
of their Purgatories & Pardons, haue
both tormented mennes consciences, and
picked their purses.

As touching p tyranny of the Byshops
of Rome and their barbarous Persian-
like pride, to leaue out others whom per-
chaūce thei recke for enemies, bicause thei
freely & liberally find fault with their vi-
ces, the selfe same men whiche haue ledd
their lyfe at Rome in the holye Citie,

J.i.   iii

in the face of the moste holye Father, whoe also were able to see all their secretes, and at no tyme departed from ye Catholike faith: As for example Laurentius Valla, Marsilius Patauinus, Fraunces Petrarke, Hierome Sauanorola, Abbett Ioakim, Baptist of Mantua, and before all these, Bernarde the Abbotte, haue manye a tyme and muche complayned of yt, geuinge the worlde also sometyme to vnderstande, that the Bysshoppe of Rome hymselfe (by youre leaue) is verye Antichriste. Whether they spake yt truelye or falselye, lette that goe: sure I am they spake it plainelye. Neyther canne anye manne alledge that those authors were Luthers or Zwinglius schollers, for they were not onelye certaine yeares, but also certaine ages or euer Luther or Zwinglius names were hearde of. They well sawe that euen in their dayes errours had crept into the Churche, and wished earnestly they might be amended.

Ing

And what maruaile yf the Churché
were then caryed awaye with errours
in that time, specially when neither the
Byſhop of Rome who thē only ruled ÿ
roſte,noʒ almoſte any other, either didde
his dewtie, oʒ once vnderſtoode what
was his duetie. Foʒ it is harde to be be=
leeued, whyles they were ydle and faſt
a ſleepe, that the Diuell alſo all that
whyle either fell a ſleepe, oʒ els continu=
ally lay ydle. Foʒ how they were occupi=
ed in the meane time, and with what
faithfulneſſe they tooke care of Goddes
houſe, though wee holde oure peace,yet
I praye you lette them heare Bernarde
their owne friend.The Byſſhops (ſaith   Bernarde ad
Eugnium.
he) who now haue the charge of Gods
churche,are not teachers but deceauers,
they are not feeders butte begylers,they
are not Prelates butte Pylates. Theſe
wooʒdes ſpake Bernarde of that Byſ=
ſhoppe,who named himſelfe the higheſt
Byſſhoppe of all, and of the other Byſ=
ſhoppes likewyſe whiche then hadde the
                              I.ii.   place

place of gouernement. Bernard was nô
Lutherian, Bernard was no heretike, he
had not forsaken the Catholike churche,
yet neuerthelés he didde not lette tô call
the Bishoppes that then wire, deceiuers,
begilers, and Pylates . Nowe when the
people was openly deceiued, and Christian mennes eyes were craftely bleared,
and when Pilat satte in iudgementplace
and condemned Christ & Christes members to the swoorde and fyer, Oh good
Lord, in what case was Christes church
then? But yet tell me, of so manye and
grosse errours, what one haue these men
at anye time refourmed, or what faulte
haue they once acknowleged & côfessed?

But forsomuche as these men auouché
the vniuersall possession of the catholike
Churche to bee their owne, and call vs
Heretiques, bicaucause wee agree not in
iudgemente with them, let vs knowe I
beseeche you, what propre marke and
badge hathe that Churche of theyrs,
whereby it maye bee knowen to bee the
Churche

Church of God. Iwys it is not so hard
a matter to finde out Goddes Churche,
yf a manne will seeke it earnestlye and
diligentlye. For the Churche of Godde
is sette vpon a highe and glisteringe
place in the toppe of an hill, and buylte
vpon the foundacion of the Apostles
and prophettes: There saith Augustine, *August, de*
lette vs seeke the Churche, there lette vs *Vnitate Eccle.*
trye oure matter. And as he saith againe *cap.3.*
in an other place, The Churche must *Idem.ca.4.*
be shewed out of the holy and canonicall
scriptures: and that whiche can not bee
shewed out of them, is not the Churche.
Yet for all this I wote not howe, whether it be for feare or for conscience, or des-
pearing of victory, these men alway abhor
and flie the woorde of God, euen as the
theefe fleeth the gallowes. And no wonder truely, for lyke as men saye the Can-
tharus by and by perisheth and dyeth, aſ
sone as it is laide in balme, notwithstandinge balme be otherwise a most sweete
smellynge ointment: euen so these men

I.iii.   well

well see their owne matter is dampped
and destroyed in the woozde of God, as
if it were in poyson. Therefore the holy
scriptures whiche oure Saujoure Jesu
Chziste didd not onely vse foz authozitie
in all his speache, butte didde also at last
seale vp the same with his owne bloude:
these menne to the entent they myghte
with lesse busines dziue the people from
the same, as from a thinge daungerous
and deadlye, haue vsed to call theim A
bare letter, vncertaine, vnpzofitable,
domme, killing, and dead: which seemeth
to vs all one, as yf they shoulde say, The
scriptures are to no purpose oz as good
as none. Hereunto they adde also a simi:
litude not very agreeable, howe the scri:
ptures be like to a nose of wax, oz a ship:
mans hose: how they may be fashioned
and plyed al manner of waies, and serue
al mennes turnes. Wotteth not the Byss:
shop of Rome that these thinges are spo:
ken by his owne minions? oz vnderstan:
deth he not, he hath suche champions to
fight

Albertus
Pighius,
in Hierar.

fight for him. Let him harken then how
holilye & how godlye one Hosius wryteth
of this matter, a Byshop in Polonia as
he testifieth of himselfe: a man doubtlesse
wel spoke & not vnlerned, & a very sharp
and stout mainteinour of that syde. One
will maruaile I suppose, howe a good
manne coulde either conceaue so wickedlye, or wryte so dispytefullye of those
woordes whiche hee knewe proceeded
from Goddes mouthe, and speciallye in
suche sorte, as hee woulde not haue it
seeme his owne priuate opinion alone,
butte the common opinion of all that
band. He dissembleth I graunt you in
deede, and hydeth what hee is, and setteth fourth the matter so, as though it
were not hee and his syde, butte the
Zwenkfeldian heretiques that so didd
speake. Wee saythe hee, will bidde a-
waye with the same scriptures, whereof wee see brought not onelye diuerse,
butte also contrarye interpretations:
and wee will heare God speake, rather
                                          then

Hosius de
expresso
verbo Dei.

then wee will resorte to these naked elementes, and appoynt oure saluation to
reste in them. It behoueth not a manne
to bee experte in the lawe and scripture,
butte to bee taught of God. It is butte
loste labour that a manne bestoweth in
the scriptures, for the scripture is a creature, and a certaine bare letter. This is
Hosius sayeng, vttered altogether with
the same spirit and the same mind, wherwith in times past Montane and Mar-
tion were moued, whoe as men reporte,
vsed to saye when with a contempt they
reiected the holye scriptures, that themselues knew many mo and better things
then eyther Christe or the Apostles euer
knewe.

What thenne shall I saye heere,
O ye principall postes of Religion, O
ye Archegouernours of CHRISTES
Churche, is this that youre reuerence
which ye geue to Goddes woorde? The
holye Scriptures whiche S. Paule
saith came by the inspiration of Godde,
whiche

Whiche God dyd commende by so many
miracles , wherin are the moste perfit
printes of Christes owne steppes ,which
all the holy Fathers, Apostles, and Aun=
geles ,whiche Christ hym selfe the sonne
of God , as often as was nedefull dyd al=
leadge for testimonie and proufe:will ye,
as though they were bnworthie for you
to heare ,bid them Auaūt away:that is,
wil ye inioyne God to kepe silence,who
speakith to you mostclearely by his own
mouth in ẏ Scriptures? Or that word,
wherby alone,as Paul saith, we are re=
conciled to God, and whiche the Pro=
phet Dauid saith , ys holye and pure
and shall last foreuer, will ye call that
but a bare and dead lettre?Or wil ye say
that all our labour is lost,whiche is bes=
towed in that thinge which Christ hath
commaūded bs diligently to searche and
to haue euermore before our eyes ? And
wil ye saye that Christ and the Apostls
ment with subtelty to deceiue the people,
when they exhorted them to reade the ho=

J.b₂   lie

lie Scriptures, that therby they might
flow in al wisedom and knowledge: No
maruaile at al, though these men dispise
vs and all our doinges, which set so litle
by God himselfe & his infallible saiengs.
Yet was it but want of witt in them, to
thintent they might hurt vs, to do so extreme iniury to the word of God.

But Hosius will here make exclamation saieng, we do him wrong, and that
these be not his owne wordes, but the
words of the heretique Zwenkfeldius.
But how than, yf Zwenkfeldius make
exclamation on the other syde, and saye
that the same very wordes be not his
but Hosius owne wordes? For tell me
where hath Zwēkfeldius euer written
thē? Or yf he haue wrttē them, & Hosius
haue iudged the same to be wicked, why
hath not Hosius spoken somuch as one
worde to confute them? Howsoeuer the
mater goeth, although Hosius paraduē-
ture wil not allowe of those wordes, yet
he doth not disallow the meaning of the
wordes

wordes. For wel nere in all controuer-
sies,and namely touching the vse of the
holy communion vnder both kindes, although the wordes of Chrst be plaine
and euident , yet doth Hosius disdaine-
fully reiect them,as no better then colde
and dead elementes: and commaundeth
to giue faith to certaine new lessons a-
pointed by the Church,& to I wot not
what reuelations of the holye Ghoste.
And Pighius saieth, men ought not to
beleue,no not ȳ most cleare and manifest
wordes of the scriptures, onles the same
be allowed for good by the interpretatiō
and auctoritie of the churche.

And yet as though this were to litle,
they also burne the holye scriptures , as
in times paste wicked kyng Aza dyd,or
as Antiochus,or Maximinus did , and
are wont to name thē Heretiques boks.
And out of doubt to see to,they woulde
faine do as Herode in oulde time dyd in
Jewrie, that hee myghte with more *Eusebius*
suretye kepe still his dominiō.Who being

an

an Idumean borne, and a straunger to
the stocke and kinred of the Iewes, and
yet coueting much to be take for a Iew,
to thende he might establish to him and
his posteritie þ kyngdom of that coun-
trey which he had gotten of Augustus
Cesar, he commaunded ail the Genea-
logies and Petigrees to be burnte & made
out of the waye, so as there shoulde remaine no recorde, wherby he might be
knowen to them that came after, that he
was an Aliaunt in bloud: wheras euen
from Abrahams time these monumentes
had been safelye kepte amongeste the
Iewes and layde vp in theire thresury,
bicause in them it might easely & moste
assuredly be found of what linage euery
one did descende. So(in good faith)doe
these menne when they woulde haue all
their owne doinges in estimation, as
though they had ben deliuered to vs eue
from the Apostles or from Christe hymselfe, to thende there might be founde no
where any thinge able to conuince such
                                    their

their dreames and lies, either they burne
the holie Scriptures, or els they craftely
conueye the m from the people surely.

Uery rightlye and aptly doth Chry=
sostome wꝛitte against these menne. He=
retiques, saith he, shutt vp the dooꝛes a=
gainst the trueth: foꝛ they know ful wel,
yf the dooꝛe were open , the Churche
shuld be none of theirs . Theophylact al=
so: Gods woꝛde saith he, is the Candle
whereby the theefe is espyed: and Tertul=
lian saith, the holy Scripture manifest=
lye findeth out the fraude and theaste of
Heretiques. Foꝛ why do they hyde, why
do they kepe vnder the Gospell, whiche
Chꝛist would haue pꝛeched alowde from
the house top ? Why whealme they that
light vnder a Bushell, whiche ought to
stande on a Candlestick? why trust they
moꝛe to the blyndenes of the vnskilfull
multitude and to ignoꝛaunce, then to the
goodnes of their cause: thinke they their
slightes are not alredy perceiued, and ẛ
they cā walke now vnespied, as though
they

Chrysost. ꝫi opere imꝑꝼ̃a

they had Giges ryng to go inuisible by,
vpon theyre finger ? No no: all men
see nowe well and well agayne, what
good stuffe is in that Chest of the Bys=
hop of Romes bosome . This thinge
alone of it selfe maye be an argumente
sufficiente , that they worke not vp=
rightly and truely.Worthely ought that
mater seme suspicious which fleeth trial,
and is afrayde of the light: for he that
doth euill,as Christ saith,seekith darke=
nesse,& hateth light.A conscience ỹ kno=
with it selfe clecre,cōmeth willingly into
open shew,that the workes whiche pro=
cede of God may be seen.Neither be they
so very blind,but they se this wel ynogh
howe their owne kyngedome strayght
way is at a pointe,yf the scripture once
haue the vpper hande : and that lyke as
men say,the Idolles of diuells in times
past,of whom menne in doubtfull mat=
ters were then wont to receiue aunswers,
were sodenly striken domme at the sight
of Christ,when he was borne and came
into

into the world: euen so they see that now
al their suttle practises wil sone fal down
hedlong vpon the sight of the Gospell.
For Antichrist is not ouerthrowen but
with the brightnes of Christes cominge.

As for vs, we runne not for succour
to the fyer as these mennes guyse is, but
we runne to the scriptures: neyther doe
we reason with the sworde, but with þ
worde of God: and therewith as sayth
Tertullian, do we feed our fayth: by it do
we styr vp our hope, and strengthen our
confidence. For wee knowe that the
Gospell of IESV CHRIST is the
power of God vnto saluation, and that
therein consisteth eternall lyfe. And as
Paule warneth vs, wee do not heare, no
not an Aungel of God coming from hea
uen, yf he go about to pull vs from any
parte of this doctrine. Yea more then
this, as the holy martyr Iustine spekith
of hym selfe, we would giue no credence
to God him selfe, yf he should teache vs
any other Gospell.

For

For where these menne hyd the holie Scriptures away, as domme and frutles, and procure vs to come to God him selfe rather, who speaketh in the Church and in Councelles: whiche is to saye , to beleue their fansies and opinions. This waye of fynding out the truth is verye vncertaine and exceding daungerous, & in maner a Fantastical & a mad way, and by no meanes allowed of the holye Fathers. Chrysostom saith, there be many oftentymes whiche boast themselues of the holye Ghoste: but truelye who so speake of their owne head, doe falselye boast they haue the spirite of God. For like as, saith he, Christ denied he spake of him selfe when he spake out of the lawe and Prophets, euen so now, yf any thing be preassed vpon vs in the name of the holy Ghoste saue the Gospell, we ought not to beleue it. For as Christ is the fulfilling of the lawe and the Prophetes, so is the holye Ghoste the fulfyllinge of the Gospell . Thus farre goeth Chrysostom.

ſtome.

But here I looke thei wil ſay, though
they haue not the Scriptures, yet maye
chaunce they haue the Auncient Doctours, and the holy Fathers with them.
For this is a high bragge they haue euer
made, how that al antiquity and a continuall conſent of all ages dothe make on
their ſide : and that all our caſes be but
new & yeſter dayes worke, & vntill theſe
fewe laſte yeares neuer heard of. Que-
ſtionleſſe there can nothing be more ſpit-
fully ſpoken againſt the religion of God
thē to acuſe it of noueltie, as a new come
vp matter. For as ther can be no chaũge
in God him ſelfe, no more ought there to
be in his religion.

Yet neuertheleſſe we wote not by what
meanes , but we haue euer ſeene it come
ſo to paſſe from the firſt beginning of al,
that as often as God did giue but ſome
light, and did open his truth vnto men,
though ŷ truth wer not only of greateſt
antiquitie, but alſo from euerlaſting, yet

K.i.   of

of wicked men & of the aduersaries was
it called Newfagled and of late deuised.
That vngracious and bloud thirsti Haman, when he sought to procure the king
Assueruses displeasure against ý Jewes,
this was his accusation to him: Thou
hast here(saith he)a kinde of people that
vseth certaine new lawes of their owne,
but stifnecked & rebellious against al thy
lawes. When Paule also began first to
preach & expoūd ý Gospel at Athenes, he
was called A tidinges bringer of newe
Gods: as muche to saye, as of new religion. for (said the Athenians) maye wee
not knowe of thee what newe doctrine
this is? Celsus likewise when he of set
purpose wrote against Christ, to thende
he might more scornefully scoffe out the
Gospel by the name of noueltye, What
saith he, hath God after so many ages
nowe at last, and so late bethought himselfe? Eusebius also wryteth, that Christian religion from the beginning for ve
ry spite was called Νια καὶ ξένη, that is to
say

say New & strange. After like sorte, these
men condemne all our matters as strange
& newe , but they will haue their owne,
whatsoeuer thei are to be praised as thin
ges of long continuace. Doing much like
to p̃ enchaũters & sorcerers now a daies,
which working w̃ diuels vse, to say, they
haue their bokes and al their holy & hidd
mysteries from Athanasius , Cyprian,
Moses, Abell, Adam, & from the Arch-
aungell Raphael, because p̃ their cõnig
cõming from suche patrones & founders, might be iudged the more high and
holy. After the same fashion these men,
bicause they would haue their owne religion whiche they themselues, and that
not longe since, haue brought forth into
the world to be the easiter and rather ac
cepted of foolishe persons, or of suche as
taste little whereabouts thei or other do
go, thei are wont to say, they had it from
Augustine, Hieronie, Chrysostome , frõ
the Apostles, and from Christe himselfe.
Ful wel knowe thei, p̃ nothinge is more

in the peoples fauour, oz better liketh the
common sozte then these names.

But how if the thinges whiche these
men are so desirous to haue seeme newe,
be found of greatest antiquitie? Contrariwise, howe if all the thinges well nye,
whiche they so greatly set out with the
name of antiquitie, hauing been wel and
thzoughly examined, be at length founde
to be but new, and deuised of verye late?
Southly to say, no man that had a true
and right consideracion, would think the
Iewes lawes and cerimonies to be new
foz all Hammans accusation: foz they
were grauen in very auncient Tables of
most antiquitie. And although many did
take Chzist to haue swarued from Abzaham & the old fathers, & to haue bzought
in a certaine newe religion in his owne
name, yet aunswered hee them directly:
Yf ye beleeued Moyses, ye woulde beleeue mee also, foz my doctrine is not so
new as you make yt. Foz Moses an au-
thoz of greatest antiquitie, and one to
whome

whome ye geue al honor, hath spoken of me. Paule likewise, though the Gospell of Jesus Chriſte be of many counted to be but new, yet hath it (ſaith he) the teſtimonie moſt old, both of the law and prophetes. As for our doctrine whiche wee may rightlier cal Chriſtes catholik doctrine, it is ſo farre of from newe, that God who is aboue all moſt auncient, & the father of our Lorde Jeſus Chriſte, hath left the ſame vnto vs in ý Goſpel, in ý prophets & Apoſtles wooreks, beinge monuments of greateſt age. So that no man can nowe thinke oure doctrine to be newe, onleſſe the ſame thinke either the prophetes faithe, or the Goſpell, or els Chriſte himſelfe to be newe.

And as for their religion, if it be of ſo longe continuance as thei woulde haue men weene it is, why doe they not proue it ſo by the exaumples of the Primatiue Churche, and by the Fathers and Councells of olde tymes? Whye lyeth ſo auncient a cauſe thus longe in the duſte,

deſtitute of an Aduocate ⁊ fyer and
ſworde they haue had alwayes ready at
hande, but as for the olde Councels ⁊ the
fathers ,al Mum, not a word. They did
ſurely againſt all reaſon to beginne firſt
with theſe ſo bloudy and extreme meaus
if thei could haue found other more caſy
and gentle wayes . And yf they truſte ſo
fully to antiquitie, and vſe no diſſimula-
tion, why didde John Clement a coun-
trye manne of owres , but ſewe yeares
paſt , in the preſence of certaine honeſt
menne and of good credite,teare and caſt
into the fyer certaine leaues of Theodorete the moſte auncente father and a
grecke Byſſhoppe, wherein he plainelye
and euidentlye taughte , that the nature
of breade in the Communion was not
chãged, abolished or brought to nothing
And this didde he of purpoſe,bicauſe he
thought ther was no other copy thereof
to be foũd. Why ſaith Albertus Pighius
ꝑ the auncient father Auguſtine had a
wronge opinion of originall ſinne⁊ And
that

Diſtin.7.27.
Quidam.

that he erred and lyed, and vsed false logique as touching the case of matrimonie,
concluded after a vow made which Augustin affirmeth to be perfect matrimony in dede, and cannot be vndone again.
Also when they did of late put in printe
the auncient father Origenes worke v-
pon the Gospell of John. why left they
quyte out þ whole sixth Capitre, wherin it is likely, yea rather of verye suerty,
that the sayd Origene had written many thinges concerning the Sacrament
of the holye Communion, contrarie to
these mennes myndes, and woulde put
furthe that booke mangled rather then
ful and perfit, for feare it should reproue
them & their parteners of their errour.
Call ye thys trusting to antiquitie, whē
ye rente in peces, kepe back, mayme
and burne the aunciēt fathers workes?
    It is a worlde to see, how wel fauou-
redlye and howe towardlye, touchinge
Religion, these men agree with the Fathers, of whom they vse to vaunte that
                                    they

Augusti. de bono nidu. c. p. 10.27. 4. Nuptiarum bonum.

Liber hodie extat & circumfer- tur mutilas.

they be their own good. The old Councel Eliberine made a decree, that nothing
that is honored of the people, shoulde be
painted in the Churches. The olde father Epiphanius saith, it is an horrible
wickednes, and a sinne not to be suffered
for any man, to set vp any picture in the
Churches of the Christians, yea though
it were the picture of Christe himselfe.
Yet these menne store all their temples
and eche corner of them with paynted
and carued ymages, as though without
them, religion were nothinge worth.

The olde fathers Origene and Chry-
soltome exhorte the people to reade the
scriptures, to buy them bokes, to reason
at home betwixte themselues of diuine
matters: wiues with their husbāds, and
parentes with their children: These men
condeinne the scriptures as dead elemēts
and asmuche as euer thei maye barre the
people from them. The Auncient fathers
Cyprian, Epiphanius & Hierome say, it
is better for one whoe perchaunce hathe
made

Origen.in Leuit. ca.16. Chrysost.in Matthæ.1.Hom.2. Idem in Iohan.36.

Cypri.epist. 11.lib.1. Epipha.cōtra Apostolicas. hæresiōs.

made a bowe to leade a sole lyfe, and af=
terwarde lyueth vnchastely, and cannot
quenche the flames of luste, to marye a
wyfe, and to lyue honestlye in wedlocke.
And the ould Father Augustine iudgeth
the selfe same mariage to be good and
perfit, and ought not to be broke again:
These menne yf a man haue once bound
hym selfe by a bowe, though afterward
he burne, kepe queanes, and defile hym
selfe with neuer so sinfull and desperate
a lyfe, yet they suffer not that persone to
marye a wyfe: or yf he chaunce to mary,
they alow it not for mariage. And they
comonlye, teache it is muche better and
more godlye to kepe a Concubine and
and harlot, then to liue in that kynde of
mariage.

The ould Father Augustine complai=
ned of the multitude of vayne ceremo=
nies, wherewt he euē thē sawe mēs min=
des and consciences ouercharged: These
men as though God regarded nothyng
els but their ceremonies, haue so out of

Hieronym.
ad Deracteriꝗ
dem.

Ad Iano=
arium.

B.b.	measure

measure increased them, ỹ there is now almoste none other thinge left in theire Churches and places of prayer

Augusti. At opere mõ achorum

Again, that olde father Augustin denieth it to be leefull for a Monke to spende his tyme slouthfully and ydleye, and vnder a pretensed and counterfeite holines to liue all vpon others. And who so thus lyueth, an olde father Apollonius like= neth hym to a theefe. These men haue (I wote not whither to name them) droues or heardes of monkes) who for all they do nothig, nor yet once intend beare any shew of holines, yet lyue they not onelye vppon others, but also ryot lauyshly of other folkes labours.

Cõcil. Rom. 847.ɔ.

The olde Councell at Rome decreed, that no man should come to the seruice sayd by a Priest well knowen to keepe a Concubine. These menne let to searme Concubines to their preistes, and yet cõ= streigne men by force against their will to heare their cursed paltrie seruice.

Canõ.8.

The oulde Canons of the Appostles commaunde

commaunde , that Byſhop to be remo=
ued from his Office , whiche will both
ſupplie the place of a ciuill Magiſtrate,
and alſo of an eccleſiaſtical perſō :Theſe
menne for all that , both do and will needes ſerue both places. Nay rather ẏ one
Office which they ought chiefly to exe=
cute, they once touch not,and yet no bo=
dy commaundeth them to be diſplaced.

The olde Councell Gangrenſe com=
maundeth,that none ſhould make ſuche
difference betwen an vnmaried Prieſt &
a maried preiſt,as he ought to think the
one more holye then the other for ſingle
lyfe ſake. Theſe menne put ſuche a diffe=
rence betwene them,that they ſtreight
waye thinke al their holie ſeruice to be de
filed, yf it be done by a good and honeſt
man that hath a wyfe.

The aūcient Emperour Juſtinian commaunded,that in the holy adminiſtratiō
all thinges ſhould be pronounced with a
cleare, lowde,and tretable voyce,that ẏ
people might receiue ſome fruite therby.

In Nouel
Cōſtitu. tit.
c.146.

Theſe

These menn least the people shoulde vnderstande them, mumble vp all their seruice, not onlye with a drowned and hollowe voice, but also in a strange and Barbarous tonge.

Concil.Cart.
3.cap.47.

The ould Councell at Carthage commaunded nothing to be read in Christes congregation, but the canonicall Scriptures: These menne read suche thinges in their Churches as themselues knowe for a trouthe to be starke lyes, and fonde fables.

But yf there be any that thinke, that these aboue rehersed auctorities be but weake and slender, bycause they were decreed by Emperours, and certein petie Byshopps, and not by so full and perfit Councelles, taking pleasure rather in ye auctoritie and name of ye Pope: let suche a one know, that Pope Iulius doth euidently forbid, that a priest in ministring the Communion, shoulde dippe ye bread in the Cuppe. These menne contrarie to Pope Iulius decree, diuide ye bread, and dip

De Cōs.dist.
2.Cum enim
nemo.

dip it in the wyne.

Pope Clement saith, it is not lawfull for a Byshop to deale with both swordes: for yf thou wilt haue both saith he, thou shalt deceiue both thy selfe, and those that obey the. Now a dayes the Pope chalengeth to hym selfe both swordes, and vseth both, wherefore it ought to seeme lesse maruaile, yf ȳ haue folowed whiche Clement saith, that is, that he hath deceiued both his own selfe, & those which haue giuen eare vnto him.

Pope Leo saith, vpon one daye it is lawfull to say but one masse in one Churche: These men say daily in one Church comonly tenne Masses, twentie, thirty, yea often tymes moe. So ȳ the poore gaser on, can scant tell which waye he were best to turne hym.

Pope Gelasius sayth, it is a wicked deed and sibb to sacriledge in any man to diuide the Communiõ, and when he receiued one kinde, to absteine from the other. These menne contrarie to Goddes
worde

worde and contrarie to Pope Gelasius
commaunde that one kinde onely of the
holy Communió be giuen to the people,
& by so doing, they make their preistes gil
ty of sacriledge.

But yf they will saye that all these
thinges are worne now out of vre, and
nye dead, and pertaine nothing to these
present tymes, yet to thend all folke may
vnderstande what faith is to be geuen
to these men, and vpon what hope they
call togithers their generall Councelles,
let vs see in few wordes what good heed
they take to the selfe same things, which
they them selues these very last yeres (&
the remembraunce thereof ys yet new &
freshe) in their owne generall Councell
that they had by order called, decreed and
commaunded to be deuoutely kepte. In
the last Councell at Trident, scant four=
tene yeares paste, it was ordeined by the
common consent of all degrees, that one
man shoulde not haue two benefices at
one time. What is become now of that
ordinaunce

ordinaūce ꞓ is ꝑ same to so sone worne
out of mynde and cleane consumed? For
these men ye se giue to one man not two
benefices onely, but sundry Abbaies ma=
ny times, sometime also two Bishopry=
kes, sometime thꝛee, sometime foure, and
that not onely to an vnlearned man, but
often times euē to a man of warre.

In the sayde Councell a decree was
made, that all Byshops should pꝛeach ꝑ
Gospell. These menne neyther pꝛeache
noꝛ once go vp into the Pulpet, neyther
thinke they it any parte of their Office.
What great pompe ꝗ crake then ys this
they make of antiquitie ? Why bꝛagge
they so of the names of the auncient Fa=
thers, and of the new and olde Councel=
les? Whye will they seme to trust to their
auctoꝛitie, whome when they lyst, they
despise at their owne pleasure?

But I haue a special fansy to cōmon
a woꝛde oꝛ two rather with the Popes
good holinesse, and to saye these thinges
to his owne face. Tell vs I pꝛaye you,
                                          good

good holy Father, seyng ye do crake so
muche of all antiquitie, and boast your
selfe that all menne are bounde to you
alone, which of all the Fathers haue at
any time called you by the name of the
highest Prelate, the vniuersall Byshop,
or the head of the Churche? Whiche of
them euer said, that both ð swordes were
commited to you? whiche of them euer
said, that you haue auctoritie and a right
to call Councelles? whiche of them euer
saide, that the whole worlde is but your
diocesse? which of them, that al Bishops
haue receiued of your fulnes? whiche of
them, that al power ys gyuen to you as
well in heauen as in yearth? whiche of
them, that neyther kynges nor the whole
Clergie, nor yet all people togyther, are
able to be iudges ouer you? whiche of
them, ð kynges & Emperours byChri-
stes commaundement and will, do receiue
aucthoritie at your hand? which of them
with so precyse and mathematicall limi-
tacion hath siruded and determined you
to

(marginal notes, left side:)
De Maior. & obedientia. Vnam San-ctam

Demand w.

Concilium. Lateranense Sub Iulio. 2
1 istinct. 9. Innocentij.

to be feuenty & feuen times greater then
the mightieſt kinges? Whiche of them,
that more ample authoritie is geuen to
you, then to ý reſidew of ý Patriarkes?
Which of thē, ý you are ý Lord God? or
that you are not a meere naturall man,
but a certaine ſubſtaunce made and gro=
wen together of God and man? Whiche
of them, that you are the onelye heade=
ſpringe of all lawe? Whiche of them,
that you haue power ouer purgatories?
Which of them that you are able to com=
maunde the Aungels of God as you liſt
your ſelfe? Which of them that euer ſaid
that you are Lorde of Lordes, and
the kinge of kinges? Wee canne alfo
go further with you in like ſorte. What
one amongeſt the whole numbre of the
olde Byſſhops and fathers, euer taught
you either to ſay priuate Maſſe whyles
the people ſtared on, or to lyſte vp the
ſacrament ouer your heade, in whyche
point conſiſteth nowe all your religion?
or els to mangle Chriſtes ſacraments, &

L.i.   to

De Maior et obedien Solid.

Extrv. Ioan. 22. Cū inter. In gloſa in ed tione imperſſa pariſiis, et Lugdim.

Antonius de Roſellis.

to bereaue the people of the one parte,
contrarye to Christes institution and
plaine expressed wordes. But that wee
may once come to an ende: What one is
there of all the Fathers, whiche hathe
taught you to distribute Christes bloud
and the holy martyrs merites, and to sell
openly as marchandizes your pardons,
and all the roomes and lodginges of pur
gatorie? These men are wont to speake
muche of a certaine secreat doctrine of
theires, and manifolde and sundrye rea-
dings. Then let them bring furthe som-
what now if thei can, that it may apeare
thei haue at least reade or do knowe som-
what. They haue often stoutly noysed in
all corners where they went, how all the
partes of their religiō be very old, & haue
been approued not only by ye multitude,
but also by the consēt & continual obser-
uation of al nations and times: let them
therfore once in their life shew this their
antiquitie: let them make appeere at eye,
that the thinges wherof they make such

a dog

a doore, haue taken so longe and large en=
creafe : let them declare that all Chrifti=
ftian nations haue agreed by confent to
this their religion.

Nay nay, they tourne their backes,
as we haue faid alreadye, and flee from
their owne decrees, and haue cut of and
aboliſhed againe within a ſhoꝛte ſpace,
the ſame thinges which but a few years
befoꝛe themſelues had eſtabliſhed, foꝛ e=
uermoꝛe foꝛſoothe to continewe. Howe
ſhoulde one then truſt them in the fa=
thers, in ꝑ olde Councels, ⁊ in the woꝛds
ſpokē by God? They haue not good Loꝛd
they haue not(J ſay)thoſe thinges which
they boaſt they haue: they haue not ꝑ an=
tiquitie, they haue not that vniuerſalitie,
they haue not that confent of all places,
noꝛ of all times. And though thei haue a
deſire rathet to diſſemble, yet thei them=
ſelues are not ignoꝛaūt herof : ye ⁊ ſom=
tune alſo they let not to cōfeſſe it openly.
And foꝛ this cauſe they ſay, that the oꝛdi=
naūces of the old Councels and fathers

L.ii.   be

be such as may now and then be altered,
and that sundry and diuers Decrees serue
for sundry & diuers times of the church.
Thus lurke they vnder the name of the
Church, and begile seely creatures with
their vaine glosinge. Yt is to be meruai-
led, that either men be so blynde as they
canne not see this, or if they see it, to bee
so pacient, as they canne so lightly and
quietly beare it.

But where as they haue commaunded that those Decrees shoulde be voyde
as thinges now waxen to olde, & y haue
loste their grace, perhappes they haue
prouided in their steede certaine other
better thinges, and more profitable for
the people. For it is a common sayenge
with them, that if Christe himselfe or
the Apostles were aliue againe, they
coulde not better nor godlyer gouerne
Goddes Churche, then it is at this presente gouerned by them. They haue
put in their steede in deede, butte it is
chaffe in steede of wheate, as Hieremie
saith,

faithe , and suche thinges as accordinge
to Esayes wordes, God neuer required at
their handes.They haue stopped vp saith
he, al the vaines of cleere springing wa=
ter , and haue digged vp for the people
deceiuable and puddelike pyttes full of
myre and filth , whiche neither haue nor
are able to hold pure water. They haue
plucked away from the people the holie
Communion , the worde of God, from=
whence all comforte shoulde bee taken,
the true worshippinge of God also , and
the right vse of sacramentes and prayer,
and haue geuen vs of their owne to play
withall in the meane whyle, salt, water,
oyle boxes, spittle, palmes, bulles, iubi=
lies, pardons, crosses, sensinges , and an
endclesse rabble of ceremonies (and as a
man might teacm with Plautus) prettie
games to make sporte withall. In these
things haue they set al their religiō, tea=
chinge ý people that by these God may
be duely pacified, spirits be driuen away
and mens consciences well quieted . For

these

these to, be the orient colours and preci-
ous sauours of Christian religion: these
thinges doth God looke vpon,& accep-
teth them thankfully:these must come in
place to be honored and put quite away,
the institutiōs of Christ and of his Apo-
stls.And like as in times past when wicked kinge Ieroboam had take from the
people ý right seruing of God,& brought
them to worship golden calues,least per-
chaũce they might afterwards chaunge
their minde and slippe away,getting
them again to Ierusalem to the Temple
of God there, hee exhorted them with a
long tale to be stedfast, saying thus vnto
them: O Israell, these Calues be thy
Gods. In this sorte commaunded your
God you should worshippe him. For it
shoulde be wearisome and troublous for
you to take vpō you a iorney so farre of,
and yearly to go vp to Ierusalem, there
to serue and honour your God. Euen after the same sorte euery whit, when these
men had once made the lawe of God of
noue

none effect through their owne traditi=
ons, fearing that the people should after=
warde open their eyes and fall an other
way, and shoulde somwhence els seeke a
surer meane of their saluation , Iesu,
how ofte haue thei cried out: This is the
same worshippinge that pleaseth God ,
and whiche hee straitly requireth of vs,
and wherwith he wil be tourned from
his wrath , that by these thinges is con=
serued the vnitie of the Church , by these
al sinnes clensed and consciences quieted:
and who so departeth from these, hath
left vnto himselfe no hope of euerlasting
saluation. For it were wearisome and
troublous (saye they) for the people to
resorte to Christ, to the Apostles , and to
ye aunctent fathers, and to obserue conti=
nually what their wil and commaunde=
ment should be. This ye may se, is to w=
draw the people of God fro ye weake cle=
ments of the worlde , fro ye leauen of the
Scribes & Pharisies, and from the tra=
ditions of me. It were reaso no doubt ye

L.iiii.   Christe

Chriftes commaundementes and the A-
poftls were remoued, that thefe their de-
uifes might come in place. O iufte caufe
I promife you, why that auncient and
fo longe alowed doctrine fhould be now
abolifhed, and a newe forme of religion
be brought into the Churche of God.

And yet whatfoeuer it be , thefe menne
crye ftil that nothing ought to be changed, that mens mindes are well fatiffied
herewithal, that the Churche of Rome
ý church which cannot erre, hath decreed
thefe thinges. For Siluefter Prierias
faith ý the Romifh churche is the fquyer
a rule of truth, and that ý holy fcripture
hath receiued from thence bothe authoritie and credite. The doctrine faith he, of
the Romifh church , is the rule of mofte
infallible faith, from the whiche the holy fcripture taketh his force . And Indulgences and pardons (faith he) are not
made knowē to vs by ý authoritie of the
fcriptures, but they are knowē to vs by
the authoritie of the Romyfhe Church,
                                        an

and of the Byſhops of Rome, whiche is greater. Pighius alſo letteth not to ſay, that without the licence of the Romyſhe Church, we ought not to beleue the very plaine ſcriptures: much like as yf any of thoſe that cānot ſpeake pure ⁊ cleane Latin, and yet can bable out quickely ⁊ redily a litle ſome ſuch law Latin as ſeruith the Courte, would needes hold that all others ought alſo to ſpeake after the ſame way which Mametrectus ⁊ Catholicō ſpake many yeare ago, ⁊ which them ſelues doe yet vſe in pleadyng in Courte, for ſo may it be vnderſtand ſufficiently what is ſaid, and mennes deſires be ſatiſfyed, and that it is a fondenes now in the later end to trouble y worlde with a new kind of ſpeaking, and to cal againe the old fyneſſe and eloquence that Cicero and Ceſar vſed in their dayes in the Latin tonge. Somuch ar theſe men beholden to the follie and darknes of the former tymes. Manye thynges as one writeth, are had in eſtimation often tymes,

L.b.

mes, bycause they haue ben once dedicate to the temples of the Heathen goddes: euen so see wee at this daye many thinges alowed and highlye sett vp of these menne, not bycause they iudge them so much worth, but only bycause they haue ben receyued into a custome, and after a sorte dedicate to the Temple of God.

Our Churche saye they, cannot erre: they speake that (I thinke) as the Lacedemonians longe synce vsid to say, that yt was not possible to fynde any Adulterer in all their common welth: wheras in dede they were rather all Adulterers, and had no certeintie in their mariages, but had their wyues common amongest them all. Or as the Canonistes at this day, for theire bellies sake vse to saye of the Pope, that forsomuche as he is Lord of all benefices, though he sell for money Byshopzickes, monasteries, preiste hod, spirituall promotions, and partith with nothing freely, yet bicause he counteth al his owne he cannot committ Simony, though

Summa
Angelica
di 110ue
papa.

though he woulde neuer so saine . But
how stronglye and agreablye to reason
these things be spoken, we are not as yet
able to perceue, except perchaunce these me
haue plucked of the wynges from the
truth , as the Romaines in olde tyme did
proine and pinion their goddesse Uic=
torie, after they had once gotte her home,
to thende that with the same wynges
she shoulde neuer more be able to flee
awaye from them againe . But what yf
Ieremye tell them , as is afore rehersed,
that these be lyes? what yf ý same Pro=
phete saye in an other place,that the selfe
same menne who ought to be kepers of
the vineyarde, haue brought to naught
and destroyed the Lordes vynearde ?
How yf Christ saye,that the same perso=
nes who chiefely ought to haue a care
ouer the Temple,haue made of ý Lords
Temple a denne of Theues ? Yf it
be so that the Churche of Rome cannot
erre,it must nedes folowe,that the good
lucke therof is farre greater then al these
mennes policie, For suche is their lyfe,

their

Theodoritus de Schismate.

Plutarchus.

their doctrine and their diligence, that
foz all them the Churche may not onely
erre, but also btterly be ſpoyled and pe-
ryſhe. No doubt, yf that Churche maye
erre whiche hath departed from Godds
worde, from Chriſtes commaundementes, from the Apoſtls ozdinaunces, from
the primatiue Churches cramples, from
the old Fathers and Councelles ozders,
and from their own Decrees, and which
wil be bound w̄ in the compaſſe of none
neither oulde noz new, noz their owne,
noz other folkes, noz mannes lawe, noz
Goddes law, then yt is out of all queſtion, that the Romyſhe Churche hath
not onely had power to erre, but that it
hath ſhamefully and moſt wickedly erred in very deed.

But ſay they, ye haue ben once of our
felowſhip, but now ye are become foʒſa-
kers of your profeſſion, and haue departed from bs. It is trew we haue departed from them, and foʒ ſo doing we both
giue thankes to almightie God, ⁊ great-
lye

lye reioyce on our owne behalfe. But yet
foz all this, from the pzimatiue Church,
from the Apostles, and from Chzist wee
haue not departed, true it is. We were
bzought vp with these menne in darke=
nes, and in ẏ lack of knowledge of God,
as Moses was taught vp in the lear=
ning and the bosome of the Egyptians.
We haue ben of youre company saith
Certullian, J confesse it, and no mat=
uaile at all, foz saith he, menne be made
and not boꝛne Chꝛistians. But where=
foꝛe J pꝛay you haue they them selfe, the
citizens and dwellers of Rome remo=
ued, and come downe from those seauen
hilles, wherbpon Rome sometime stood,
to dwel rather in the plaine called Mars
his field? They wil say peraduenture, by
cause the conductes of water, wher with
out menne cannot commodiouslye liue,
haue now failed and ar dꝛied vp in those
hilles. Well then, lett them giue vs lyke
leaue in seekingthe water of eternal lyfe,
that they giue them selfes in seekyng the,
water

water of the well, for the water berely
fayled amongeſt them. The elders of the
Iewes ſayth Ieremye, ſent their litle
ones to the waterings, and they finding
no water, beyng in a miſerable caſe and
vtterly marred for thurſt, brought home
againe their veſſells emptie. The nedye
& poore folke ſaith Eſaye, ſought about
for water, but no wheare founde they
any, their tonge was euē withered with
thirſt. Euen ſo theſe menne haue broken
in peeces al the pypes and cōduites, they
haue ſtopped vp al the ſprings, & choked
vp the fountaine of liuyng water with
durte and myre. And as Caligula many
yeres paſt locked faſt vp al the ſtorehou-
ſes of corne in Rome, & thereby brought
a generall derth and famyne amongeſt
the people, euē ſo theſe men by damming
vp all the fountaines of Goddes word,
haue brought the people into a peeriful
thirſt. They haue brought into ẏ world
as ſaith the Prophete Amos, a hungre
and a thurſt, not the hunger of breade,

no

nor the thurst of water, but of hearing
the worde of God. With greate distresse
went they scattering about, seeking some
sparke of heauenly light to refresh their
consciences withall, but that light was
alredy thoroughly quenched out, so that
they could finde none. This was a ruefull state. This was a lamentable forme
of Goddes Churche. It was a miserie
to liue therin without the Gospel, without light, and without all comfort.

Wherfore though our departing wer
a trouble to them, yet ought they to consider withall, how iust cause wee had of
our departure. For yf they wil saye, it is
in no wise lawfull for one to leaue the felowship wherin he hath bē brought vp,
they maye al well in our names or vpon
our heades condemne both the Prophetes, the Apostles, and Christ him selfe.
For whye complayne they not also of
this, that Lot went quitte his way out
of Sodome, Abraham out of Calde, the
Israelites out of Egypte, Christ frō the
Jewes,

Iewes, and Paule from the Pharisees?
For except it be possible there maye be a
lawful cause of departing, we see no reasone whye Lot, Abraham, the Israelites, Christ and Paule may not be accused of sectes and seditiō, aswel as others.
And yf these men will needes condemne
vs for Heretiques, bycause we do not all
thinges at their commaundement, whom
(in gods name)or what kynde of menne
ought they them selues to be taken for,
whiche despise the commaundement of
Christ, & of the Apostles? If we be scis-
matiques bycause we haue lefte them,
by what name shall they be called themselues which haue forsaken the Grekes,
frō whom they first receiued their faith,
forsaken the primatiue Church, forsaken
Christ hymselfe and the Apostls, euen as
Children should forsake their parentes?
For though those Grekes, who at this
daye professe religion and Christes name, haue many thinges corrupted amōgest them, yet houlde they still a greate
numbre

number of thofe thinges whiche they re=
ceiued from the Apoſtles . They haue
neyther priuate Maſſes , nor mangled
Sacramentes , nor Purgatories , nor
Pardons. And as for the titles of hygh
Byſhops, & thoſe glorious names , they
eſtime them ſo , as whoſoeuer he were
that woulde take vpon hym the ſame, &
woulde be called eyther Vniuerſall byſ=
ſhop, or the Hed of the vniuerſal church,
they make no doubt to call ſuche a one,
both a paſſing proude man, a man that
worketh deſpite againſt all ẏ other Byſ=
ſhoppes his bretherne, and a plaine He=
tetique .

Now then ſynce it is manifeſt and
out of all peraduenture, that theſe men
are fallen from ẏ Grekes, of whom they
receiued the Goſpell, of whome they re=
ceiued the faith, the true Religion and ẏ
Church, what is ẏ mater why they will
not now be called home again to ẏ ſame
men, as it were to their originals & firſt
founders : And whye be they afraide to

M.i.   take

take a paterne of the Apostles and olde
fathers tymes, as though they all had
ben voyde of vnderstanding? Do these
menne, wene ye, see more or set more by
the Church of God, then they dede who
firste deliuered vs these thinges?

We truely haue renounced that church
wherin we could neyther haue þ worde
of God sincerely taught, nor the Sacraments rightlye administred, nor the name of God dewly called vppon, whyche
Churche also themselues confesse to be
faulty in many poinctes: And wherein
was nothing able to stay any wise mã,
or one þ hath consideration of his owne
sauetie. To conclud, wee haue forsaken
the Church as it is now, not as it was
in olde time, and haue so gon from it, as
Daniell went out of the Lyons denne,
and þ three Children out of the furnesse:
and to say trouth, we haue ben cast out
by these menn (beyng cursed of them, as
they vse to saye, with boke, bel, and can-
dell) rather then haue gon awaye from
them

them of our felues.

And wee are come to that Churche
wherein they themfelues cannot denye
(if thei wil fay truely and as thei thinke
in their owne confcience) but all thinges
be gouerned purely and reuerently, and
afmuch as we poffibly could, very neere
to the order vfed in the olde time.

Let them compare our Churches and
theirs togither, and they fhall fee that
themfelues haue mofte fhamefully gon
from the Apoftles, and we mofte iuftely
haue gon from them. For we folowinge
the eraumple of Chrift, of the Apoftles,
and the holy fathers, giue the people the
holye Communion whole and perfite:
But thefe men contrary to all ý fathers,
to all the Apoftles, and contrarye to
Chrift himfelf, do feuer the facraments,
and plucke away the one parte from the
people, and that with mofte notorious
facriledge, as Gelafius termeth yt.

Wee haue broughte againe the
Lords fupper vnto Chriftes inftitution,
M.ii.   and

and will haue it to be a Communion in
very deede, common and indifferent to
a great number, accordinge to the name.
But these men haue chaunged al things
contrarie to Christes institution, & haue
made a priuate Masse of the holy Com=
munion: and so it commeth to passe, that
we giue the Lordes supper vnto the peo
ple, and they giue them a baine pagent
to gase on.

We affirme togither with the aunci=
ent fathers, that the body of Christe is
not eaten but of the good and faithfull,
and of those that are endued with the
spirit of Christe. Their doctrine is, that
Christes very bodie effectually, & as they
speake, really and substantially, may not
only be eaten of the wicked and vnfaith=
sul nien, but also (which is monstrous to
be spoken) of myse and dogges.

Wee vse to praye in Churches after
that fashion, as accordinge to Paules
lesson, the people maye knowe what wee
pray, and may answere Amen, with a ge
nerall

1. Corinth. 14.

neral confent. Thefe men like foundinge
mettall, pelle out in the churches vnkno=
wen and ftraunge wordes wout vnder=
ftanding, without knowledge, and wout
deuotiõ, yea I doe it of purpofe, bicaufe ý
people fhould vnderftand nothing at all.

But not to tarey about rehearfing all
poyntes wherein we and thei differ, for
they haue wel nye no end, we tourne the
fcriptures into al tongues, they fcant fuf=
fer them to be had abroad in any tongues
we allure ý people to reade and to heare
Gods word, thei driue the people frõ it.
We defire to haue our caufe knowen to
al ý world, they flee to come to any trial.
We leaue vnto knowlege, they vnto ig=
noraunce: We truft vnto light, thei vnto
darkenes: We reuerence as it becometh
vs, the writings of ý Apoftles and Pro=
phetes, & they burne them. Finally, wee
in Gods caufe defire to ftand to Goddes
onely iudgement, they wil ftand only to
their owne. Wherfore if they wil waye
all thefe thinges with a quiet mind, and
M.iii.   fully

fullye bente to heare and to learne, they
wil not only alow this determinatiō of
oures who haue forsaken errours, and
folowed Christe and his Apostles, butte
themselues also will forsake their owne
selues, and ioyne of their owne accorde
to oure side.

But peraduenture they will saye, it
was treason to attempt these matters
without a sacred generall Councell: for
in that consisteth the whole force of
the Churche: there C H R I S T hath promised he will euer bee a present assistant.
Yet they themselues without tarrienge
for anye generall Councell, haue broken
the commaundementes of Godde, and
the decrees of the Apostles: and as wee
sayde a little aboue, they haue spoyled
and disanulled almoste all, not onelye
ordinaunces, but euen the doctrine of
the primatiue Churche. And where they
saye it is not lausull to make a chaunge
without a Councell, what was he that
made vs these lawes, or from whence
                                    hadde

hadde they this Iniunction?

Kinge Agesilaus, truelye, didde butte fondelye, whoe when hee hadde a determinate aunswere made him of the opinion and will of myghtye Jupiter, woulde afterwarde bringe the whole matter befoze Apollo, to knowe whether hee alowed thereof as his father Jupiter didde oz no: But yet shoulde wee dooe muche moze fondelye, when wee maye heare Godde him selfe plainelye speake to vs in the moste holye scriptures, and maye vnderstande by them his will and meaninge, yf wee woulde afterwarde (as thoughe this were of none effecte) bringe oure whole cause to be tryed by a Councell, which were nothinge els but to alke whether menne would allowe as God did, & whether me would confirme Gods commaundement by their authozity. Why J beseech you, except a Councell wil & comaund, shal not truth be truth, oz God be God? Yf Christ had ment to do so from ð beginning, as

Plutar. chus.

M.iiii.   that

that he would preache oz teache nothing
without the Byſſhops conſent, but refer
all his doctrine ouer to Annas and Cai=
phas, where ſhould nowe haue been the
chziſtian faith:oz who at any time ſhould
haue hearde the Goſpell taught: Peter
verily, whome the Pope hath oftener in
his mouth and moze reuerently vſeth to
ſpeake of, then he dothe of Jeſu Chziſt,
did boldly ſtand againſt the holy Coun=
cel, ſaieng, It is better to obey God, then
men. And after Paule had once intirely
embzaced the Goſpel, and had receiued it
not ſrõ men, noz by man, but by the only
will of God, he did not take aduiſe ther=
in of fleſhe and bloud, noz bzought ý caſe
befoze his kinſemen ⁊ bzethzen, but went
furth with into Arabia to pzeache Gods
diuine myſteries, by Goddes onelye au=
thozitie

Yet truely wee doe not deſpiſe Coun=
celles, aſſemblies, ⁊ conferences of Byſ=
ſhops and learned men:neyther haue we
done ý wee haue done altogether wout
Byſſhops

Byſhops oꝛ without a Councell. The matter hath ben treated in open Parliament, with long conſultation, and befoꝛe a notable Synode and Conuocation.

But touchyng this Councell whiche is now ſõmoned by ꝑ Pope Pius, wherin men ſo lightly are condemned whiche haue ben neither called, hearde, noꝛ ſeene, yt is caſie to geſſe what we maye looke foꝛ, oꝛ hope of yt. In times paſte when Nazianzene ſawe in his daies how men in ſuche aſſemblies were ſo blynde and wilfull, that they were caried with affections, and laboured moꝛe to get the victoꝛy then ꝑ trueth, he pꝛonounced openly, that he neuer had ſene a good ende of any Councell: what woulde he ſay now yf he were a liue at this daye, and vnder ſtode the heauing and ſhoving of theſe men? foꝛ at that time, though the matter were laboured on all ſydes, yet the controuerſies were wel heard, and open erꝛours were put cleane awaye by the generall voice of all partes: But theſe men

M.v.   will

wil neyther haue the cafe to be freely dif=
puted, no2 yet how many errours foeuer
there be, fuffer they any to be chaunged.
Fo2 it is a comon cuftome of theirs, of=
ten and fhamelefly to boaft that their
Churche cannot erre, that in it there is
no faulte, and that they mufte giue place
to vs in nothynge. O2 yf there be anye
faulte, yet muft it be tried by Byfhopes
and Abbottes, only bycaufe they be y di=
recters & Rulers of matters, and they be
the Church of God. Ariftotle faith, that
a Citie cannot confift of Baftardes: but
whether the Churche of God may con=
fifte of thefe men, let their owne felues
confider. Fo2 doubtles neither be the Ab=
bottes legitimat Abbottes, no2 the By=
fhopes naturall right Byfhoppes. But
graunt they be the Churche: let them be
heard fpeak in Councelies: let the alone
haue auctoritie to gyue confent: yet in
olde tyme when the Churche of God(yf
ye will compare it with their Churche)
was very well gouerned, both Elders
and

and Deacons as faith Cyprian, and cer=
teine alſo of the common people were cal=
led ther vnto, and made acquainted with
eccleſiaſticall matters.

But I put caſe theſe Abbottes and
Byſhopes haue no knowledge: what yf
they vnderſtande nothing what Religiõ
is, nor how we ought to thinke of God?
I put caſe the pronouncyng and mini=
ſtringe of the lawe be decayed in preiſts,
and good counſell faile in the Elders,
and as the Prophete Micheas faith, the
night be vnto them in ſtede of a viſion,
and darkenes in ſted of prophecſieng. Or
as Eſaias faith, what yf al ÿ watcheme
of ÿ city are become blinde? what yf ÿ ſalt
haue loſt his propre ſtrengh and ſaueri=
nes, and as Chriſte faith, be good for no
vſe, ſcant woorthe the caſtyng on the
doungehyl?

Wel yet then, they wil bring al mat=
ters before the Pope, who cannot erre.
To this I ſay, firſte it is a madnes to
thynke that the holy Ghoſte taketh his
flight

flight from a generall Councell to run
to Rome, to thende yf he doubt or sticke
in any matter, and cannot expound it of
him selfe, he maye take counsell of some
other spirite, I wote not what, that is
better learned then him selfe. For yf this
be true, what neded so many Byshopps,
with so great charges and so farre ior-
neyes, haue assembled their Conuocatiõ
at this present at Trident? Yt hadde ben
more wisedom and better, at least it had
ben a moche nearer way and handsom-
mer to haue brought all thinges rather
before ý Pope, and to haue come streghe
furth, and haue asked counsell at his diuine breast. Secõdly, it is also an vnlau-
full dealing to tosse our matter from so
many Byshoppes and Abbottes, and to
bryng it at laste to the trial of one onely
man, specially of hym who him selfe ys
appeached by vs of hainous and foule
enormities, and hath not yet put in hys
aunswere: who hath also afore hand cõ-
dempned vs without iudgement by or-
dec

ter pronounced, and or euer we were cal=
led to be iudged.

How saye ye, do wee deuise these ta=
les? Is not this the course of the Coun=
celles in these dayes? are not all thynges
remoued from the whole holy Councell
and brought before the Pope alone? that
as though nothing had ben don to pur=
pose by the iudgementes and consentes
of suche a numbre, he alone maye adde,
alter, diminishe, disanull, alow, tempt
and qualifie what soeuer he lyst? whose
wordes be these then? and whye haue
the Byshoppes and Abbottes in the last
Councell at Trident but of late conclu=
ded with sayng thus in the ende, Sauing
alwyes the auctoritie of the sea Apo=
stolique in all thynges? Or whye doth
Pope Pascall write so proudelie of him
selfe as though saith he, there were any
general Councell able to prescribe a law
to the Church of Rome, wheras al cou=
celles both haue ben made and haue rece=
ued their force & strength by the Church

De Electione
& Electi
pot. flatrura,
Sign. fc.48c.

of

of Romes auctoritie : and in ordinaun=
ces made by Councelles ,is euer plainely
excepted the auctoritie of the Byshop of
Rome. Yf they will haue these thynges
alowed for good, why be Councels cal=
led : but yf they commaunde them to be
voyd, why are they left in their bokes as
thinges alowable:

But be it so; Let the Byshop of Rome
alone be aboue all Couceiles, ý is to say,
lette some one parte be greater then the
whole, let hym be of greater power, let
hym be of more wysedome then all his,
and in spite of Hieromes head, let ý auc=
thoritie of one Citie be greater then the
aucthoritie of the whole worlde .Howe
then if the Pope haue sene none of these
things, & haue neuer read either ý scrip=
tures or ý olde fathers, or yet his owne
coucelles: How if he fauour ý Arrias, as
once Pope Liberius did: or haue a wic=
ked and a detestable opinion of the lyfe
to come, and of the immortalitie of the
soule, as Pope John had but few yeres
syncé

Hieron. ad
Euagrium.

synce ? o2 to encreale nowe his owne di=
gnitie,do co2rupt other Councelles, as
Pope Zolimus co2rupted the Councell
holden at Nice in times palt,and do say
that thole thinges were deuiled and ap=
poincted by the holy Fathers,which ne=
uer once came into their thought,and to
haue the ful sway of aucto2itie,do wrelt
the Scriptures,as Camotenlis laith,is
an vlual cultome with the Popes?How
yf he haue renounced the faith in Ch2ilt,
and become an Apoltata,as Liranus
sayth many Popes haue bene? And yet
fo2 all this,shall the holye Gholte with
turning of a yand,knock at his b2ealt,#
tue wherer he will o2 no,yea # wholy a=
gainlt hys will,kindle hym a lyght so as
he maye not erre?shall he ltreght waye
be the head sp2ing of al right,and shal al
trealure of wisdome and vnderltanding
be founde in hym ,as it were laide vp in
lto2e? O2 yf thele thinges be not in hym,
can he giue a right and apte iudgement
of so weightie matters? O2 yf he be not
able

able to iudge, wold he haue that al those
matters should be brought befoze hym
alone?

What will ye say, yf the Popes Ad=
uocates, Abbottes and Byshops dissem=
ble not the matter, but shew them selues
open enemies to the Gospell, & though
they see, yet they will not see, but wrye
the Scriptures and wyttingly & know=
ingly corrupt and counterfeite the word
of God, and fouly and wickedlye applye
to the Pope al the same thinges whiche
euidently and propzely be spoken of the
person of Christ only, noz by no meanes
can be applied to any other? And what
though they saye, the Pope is all and
aboue all? Oz, that he can do asmuch as
Christ can: and that one iudgemet place
and one Councel house serue foz ye Pope
and foz Christ both together? Oz that
the Pope is the same light which should
come into the worlde? whiche wozdes
Christ spake of hym selfe alone: and that
who so is an euil doer, hateth and flieth
from

Hostien. cap.
Quanto

Albas Pano.
de elect. ra
Venerabil's

Correlius
Episcopus
in Con il
Tridetino

from that light ? Oz that all the other
Byſſhoppes haue receaued of the Popes
fulnes? Shoztly, what though thei make
Decrees expzeſſye agaiſt Gods wozde,
and that not in huckermucker oz couert-
ly, but openly & in the face of the wozlde:
muſte it needes yet be Goſpell ſtraighte
whatſoeuer theſe men ſay? ſhall theſe be
Gods holy army ? oz will Chziſte bee at
hande amonge them there: ſhall the holy
ghoſt flow in their tongues, oz can they
with truth ſay, We and the holy Ghoſte
haue thought ſo? In dede Peter Aſotus
and his companion Hoſius ſticke not to
affirme, that the ſame Councell wherein
our ſauiour Ieſu Chziſte was condemned to dye, had both the ſpirit of pzophe-
ſieng, and the holy Ghoſt, and the ſpirite
of truth in it : and that it was neither a
falſe noz a trifflinge ſaieng, when thoſe
Byſhoppes ſayde, We haue a lawe, and
by our law he ought to dye, and ÿ their ſo
ſayenge did light vpon the very trouthe
of iudgement: foz ſo be Hoſius wozdes,

Duraniðus.

Hoſius cõt.
Brentium,
lib.t.

                              N.i.   And

and that the same plainelye was a iuste
decree, wherebp they pronounced that
Chrilt was worthy to die. This me thinketh is ſtraunge, that theſe men are not
able to ſpeake for themſelues and defend
their owne cauſe, but thei muſt alſo take
parte with Annas and Caiphas. For yf
they will call that a lawfull and a good
Councell, wherein the Sonne of God
was moſte ſhamfully condemned to dye,
what Councell will they then alowe for
falſe and naught? And (yet as all their
Councels, to ſay truth, commonly be)ne-
ceſſitie compelled them to pronouce theſe
thinges of the Councell holden by Annas and Caiphas.

But wil theſe men (J ſay)refourme vs
the churche, beinge themſelues both the
perſons guilty and the Judges to? Will
they abate their own ambitiō and pride?
Wil they ouerthrow their owne matter,
and giue ſentence againſt them ſelues,
that they muſt leaue of to be vnlearned
Byſhoppes, ſlowbellies, heapers together

ther of benefices, takers vpon them as
princes and men of warre? Will the Abbottes the Popes deere darlinges iudge
that monke for a theefe, which laboureth
not for his liuing? and that it is against
all lawe, to suffer suche a one to liue and
to be found either in citie or in countrie,
or yet of other mennes charges? Or els
that a monke ought to lye on the groūd,
to liue hardly with hearbes and peason,
to study earnestly, to argue, to praye, to
worke with hande, and fully to bend him
selfe to come to ῥ ministery of ῥ churche?
In faith, assone will the Pharisies and
Scribes repaire againe the Temple of
God, and restore it vnto vs a house of
prayer, in steede of a theeuish denne.
Ther haue ben, I know, certain of their
own selues which haue foūd fault, wῒ ma
ny errours in ῥ church, as Pope Adrian,
Eneas siluius, Cardinal Poole, Pighius
& others, as is afore saide, they held after-
wardes their Counceel at Trident in ῥ self
same place where it is now appointed.
                    N.ii.   There

There assembled many Byshoppes and
Abbottes and others whom it behoued.
For that matter they were alone by
themselues, whatsoeuer they did no body
gainesaid it: for they had quite shut out
and barred oure syde from all manner of
assemblies, and there they sat sixe yeares
feedinge folkes with a meruelous expec-
tation of their doings. The first sixe mo-
neths, as though it were greatly nedeful,
they made many determinations of the
holy Trinitie, of the father, of ý Son,
and of the holy Ghost, which were godly thinges in deede, but not so necessarye
for that time. Let vs see in all that while
of so many, so manifest, so often confessed by them ý so euident errours, what
one errour haue they amended ? from
what kinde of idolatrie haue they reclai-
med the people ? What superstition haue
they taken away ? What peece of their
tyranny and pompe haue they diminis-
shed ? as though all the worlde may not
nowe see, that this is a Conspiracie and
not

not a Councell, and that these Byſhopes
whom the Pope hath now called to ge=
ther, be wholy ſworne & become bounde
to beare him their faithfull allegiaunce,
and wil do no manner of thing, but that
they perceiue pleaſeth him, and helpeth
to aduaunce his power, and as hee will
haue it : Or that they reckon not of the
number of mennes voyces, rather then
haue weight and conſideracion of the
ſame: Or that myght doth not often
times ouercome the right.

And therefore we knowe that diuers
times many good men and Catholique
Byſhops did tarry at home, and would
not come when ſuch Councels were cal=
led, wherein men ſo apparauntly labou=
red to ſerue factions and to take partes,
bicauſe they knewe they ſhould but loſe
their trauaile and dooe no good, ſeeinge
where vnto their enemies mindes were
ſo wholye bent. Athanaſius denyed to
come when hee was called by the Em=
perour to his Councell at Ceſarea, per=

P.iii.   ceiuinge

ceiuinge plaine he shoulde butte come a=
monge his ennemies whiche deadly ha=
ted hym . The same Athanasius when
he came afterwarde to the Councell at
Sirmium, and foresaw what would be
the ende by reasone of the outrage and
malyce of his ennimies, hce packed vp
his carriage, and went away immediate
ly. John Chrysostome, although ẏ Em=
perour Constantius commaunded hym
by four sundry lettres to come to the Ar=
rians Councel, yet kept he hym selfe at
home still. When Maximus the Byshop
of Hierusalem sate in the Councell at
Palestine, the olde Father Paphnutius
toke him by the hande and ledde hym
out at the doores sayenge : It is not
leeful for vs to conferre of these matters
with wicked menne . The Bysshopes
of the Easte woulde not comme to the
Syrmian Councell, after they knewe
Athanasius had gotten hymselfe thence
againe . Cyrill called menne backe by
letters from the Councell of them, which
were

Tripa tita
Hist.lib.10
cap.13.

Euseb lib.2
cap.17.

Zpzomes
nue lib.3.
cap 4.

were named Patropaſſians. Paulinus
Byſſhoppe of Tryer, and manye others
moe, refuſed to comme to the Councell
at Millaine, whenne they vnderſtoode
what a ſtyrre and rule Auxentius kepte
there : for they ſawe yt was in vaine
to go thither, where not reaſone but faction ſhoulde preuayle, and where folke
côtended not for ẙ truth and right iudgement of the matter, butte for partialitie
and fauour.

And yet for all thoſe fathers hadde
ſuche malitious and ſtiffe necked ennemies, yet if they hadde come, they ſhould
haue hadde free ſpeache at leaſt in the
Councelles. Butte nowe ſithens none
of vs maye bee ſuffered ſo muche as to
ſitte, or once to bee ſeene in theſe mennes
meetinges, muche leſſe ſuffered to ſpeake
freelye oure minde, and ſeinge the Popes
Legates, Patriarches, Archebyſhops,
Byſſhoppes, and Abbottes, all beinge
conſpyred togeather, all linked together,

N.iiii.   m.

in one kinde of fault, and all bounde by
one othe, sit alone by themselues, & haue
power alone to giue their consent: and at
last when they haue all done, as though
thei had done nothing, bringe all their o-
pinions to be iudged at the wil & plasure
of ý Pope, being but one man, to thend
he may pronoúce his own sétéce of himselfe, who ought rather to haue aunswered to his complaint, sitheus also ý same
auncient & Christian libertie which of al
right shoulde speciallý bee in Christian
Councelles, is now vtterly taken away
from the Councel: for thèse causes I say
wise and good men ought not to maruaile at this day, though we doe the like
now, that thei see was don in times past
in like case of so many Fathers and Catholike Byshops, which as though we
chuse rather to sit at home and leaue our
whole cause to Gode, then to iorney
thither, whereas wee neyther shall haue
place, nor bee able to dooe anye good:
whereas wee can obtaine no audience,

whereas

whereas Princes Embassadours be but
vsed as mockyng stockes, and whereas
also all wee be condemned alredy before
trial, as though ý matter were a forhãd
dispatched and agreed vpon

Neuerthelesse we can beare pacientlye
& quyetely our owne priuate wronges:
but wherfore do they shut out Christian
kynges, and good Princes from their
Conuocation? why do they so vncour=
teouslỹ, or with such spite leaue thẽ out,
& as though they were not either Chri=
sten menne, or els could not iudge, will
not haue them made acquaynted with
the cause of Christian Religion, nor vn=
derstand ý state of their own Churches?
Or yf the sayd kynges & Princes hap=
pen to entermedly in suche matters, and
take vpon them to do that they may do,
that they be commaunded to doe, and
ought of duty to do, & the same thinges
that we know both Dauid and Salo=
mon and other good Princes haue don,
that is, yf they whiles the Pope and his

R.v.　　　Prelates

Prelates flugge and fleepe, or els mische-
vouflye withſtande them, doe bridle the
Preiſtes ſenſualitie, and driue them to
do their dewty, and kepe them ſtill to yt:
yf they do ouerthrow Idols, yf they take
away ſuperſtition, and ſet vp again the
true woꝛſhiping of God, whye do they
by and by make an out crye vpon them,
that ſuche Princes trouble all, and preſſe
by violence into an other bodyes office,
and do therby wickedly and malepartly.
What ſcripture hath at any time foꝛbid-
den a Chꝛiſtiā Prince to be made priucy
to ſuch cauſes? Who but themſelues a-
lone made euer any ſuche lawe?

They will ſaye to this, I geſſe, Ciuell Princes haue learned to gouerne a
common welth, and to oꝛdꝛe matters of
warre, but they vnderſtande not the ſe-
cret myſteries of Religion. Yf that be ſo,
what is the Pope I pꝛaye you, at this
day, other thē a Monarche oꝛ a Prince?
oꝛ what be the Cardinals, who muſt be
no nother now a days but Princes and
kynges

kyngs sonnes : What els be ÿ Patriar=
ches,and for the moſt part the Archebyſ=
ſhops,the Byſhops,ÿ Abbots:what be
they els at this preſent in ÿ Popes king=
dome,but worldely Princes,but Dukes
and Earles, gorgiouſly accompanied w̄
bandes of men whither ſoeuer they go:
Oftentimes alſo gaylye arayed wyth
cheynes ꞇ collers of golde.They haue at
times to,certeine ornamētes by them ſel=
fes,as Croſſes,pillers,hattes,miters and
Palles, which pompe the auncient Byſ=
ſhops Chryſoſtom,Auguſtine and Am=
broſe neuer had. Setting theſe thinges
aſide,what teache they: what ſay they:
what doe they : how lyue they : I ſaye
not,as maye become a Byſhopp,but as
may become euen a Chriſtian man . Is
it ſo great a mater to haue a baine title,
and by chaunging a garment onely to
haue the name of a Byſhop:

Surely to haue the principall ſtaye ꞇ
effecte of all maters commited wholy to
theſe mennes handes,who neyther know

no2 will know thefe thinges, no2 yet fet
a iote by any poinct of Religion, faue y
which concernes their belly and Ryot, z
to haue them alone fit as Judges, and to
be fet vp as ouerfeers in y watch to wer
being no better then blynd fpyes: of the
other fide, to haue a Chriftian Prince of
good vnderftanding and of a right iudg=
gement, to ftande ftill like a blocke o2 a
ftake, not to be fuffred: nother to giue his
voice, no2 to fhewe his iudgement, but
onely to wayt what thefe men fhall will
and commaund, as one whiche had ney=
ther eares no2 eyes no2 wytt, no2 hearte,
and whatfoeuer they giue in charge, to
alowe it without exception, blindly ful=
filling their commaundementes, be they
neuer fo blafphemous and wicked, yea
although they commaunde him quite to
deftroye all Religion, z to crucifie again
Chrift him felfe. This furely befides that
it is p2oud and fpitefull, ys alfo beyond
all right and reafon and not to be endu=
red of Chriftiā and wyfe P2inces. Why

F

I praye you, may Cayphas and Annas
vnderstand these matters, and may not
Dauid and Ezechias do the same? Is it
lawfull for a Cardinall being a man of
warre and delightius in bloud, to haue
place in a Councell, & is it not lawful for
a Christian Emperour or a kynge? wee
truely graunt no further libertie to our
Magistrates, then that we know hath
both ben giuen thẽ by the word of God,
and also confirmed by the exãples of the
very best gouerned cõmon welthes. For
besids that a Christian Prince hath the
charge of both Tables cõmited to him
by God, to thende he maye vnderstande
that not temporall matters only, but al=
so Religious & ecclesiasticall causes per=
taine to his Office. Besides also that
God by his Prophettes often and ear=
nestly cõmaundeth the king to cut down
the groues, to breake downe the Ima=
ges and aultres of Idoles, and to write
out the boke of y law for him selfe : and
besides that the prophet Esaias saith, a
king

kyng ought to be a patrone and nurse
of the Churche : I saye besides all these
thinges, we se by histories and by exam=
ples of the best times, that good Princes
euer tooke thadministration of ecclesia=
stical matters to partain to their ducty.
Moses a Ciuile Magistrat & chief guide
of the people, both receiued from God, &
deliuered to ý People al the order for re=
ligion and Sacrifices , and gaue Aaron
the Byshop a vehemét and soare rebuke
for making the golden calfe, and for suf=
fering the corruption of Religion . Io=
sua also, though he were no nother then
a Ciuil Magistrat, yet assone as he was
chosen by God, and set as a Ruler ouer
the people, he receiued comaundements,
specially touching Religion and the ser=
uice of God . Kynge Dauid, when the
whole religió was altogethers brought
out of frame by wycked kyng Saul,
brought home againe the Arke of God,
that is to say, he restored Religió again,
and was not onely amongest them him
selfe

Exod.32.

Iosua.ca.1.

1.Paral.13.

selfe as a counseller and furtherer of
the worke, but he appoincted also hym=
nes and Psalmes, put in order the com=
panies, and was the only doer in setting
furth that whole solemne shewe, and in
effect ruled the preistes. Kyng Salomō
builte vnto the Lord the Temple, which
his father Dauid had but purposed in
his minde to do: & after the finishing ther
of, he made a goodly oration to the peo=
ple, concerning Religion and the seruice
of God, he afterward displaced Abiathar
the Preist, and set Sadock in his place.
After this, when the Teple of God was
in shameful wyse polluted thorough the
naughtines and negligēce of the preists,
Kyng Ezechias commaunded the same
to be clensed from the ruble and filthe, ŷ
preistes to light vp candelles, to burne
Incense, and to do their diuine seruice,
according to the olde allowed custome.
The same kyng also commaunded the
brasen Serpent, whiche then the people
wickedly worshipped, to be taken down
                                        and

2.Paral.5.

1.Regū.na.2.

2.Paral.29.

4.Regū.18.

and beatē to poudcr. kyng Jehosaphat ouerthrew and vtterly made awaye the hil aultres and Groues, wherby he saw Goddes honoure hindered , and the people holden backe with a priuate superstition from the ordinarie Tēple whiche was at Jerusalem, wherto they should by ordre haue resorted yearely from euery part of the Realme. kynge Josias W great diligence put the Preilts and Byshops in mynde of their ducty: kyng Joyas bridled the Ryot and arrogancie of the preiltes. Jehu put to death the wicked Prophetes.

And to rehearse nomōre exampls out of the old law, let vs rather cōsider since the birthe of Christ, howe the Churche hath ben gouerned in the Gospels time. The Christian Emperours in old time, appoincted the Councelles of the Byshops. Constantiue called the Councell at Nice, Theodotius the first, called the Councell at Constātinople. Theodotius the second, the councel at Ephesus, Martian

2. Parill. 17.

4. Regum. 23.

4. Regum. 12.

4. Regum. 10.

tian the Councell at Chalcedone: and
when Rufine the heretike had alleadged
for authoritie, a Councell whiche as hee
thought, shoulde make for him: Hierom
his aduerrsarie to confute him, Tell vs
(quod hee) what Emperour commaun=
ded that Councell to be called? The same
Hierome againe in his Epitaphe vpon
Paula, maketh mention of the Empe=
rours letters, whiche gaue commaunde=
ment to call the Byshoppes of Italie
and Grecia to Rome to a Councel. Con=
tinuallye for the space of fiue hundreth
yeares, Themperoure alone appointed
theccelesiasticall assemblies, and called the
Councelles of the Byshops togither.

We nowe therefore marvail the more
at the vnreasonable dealinge of the Byf=
shoppe of Rome, who knowinge what
was the Emperoures right when the
Churche was well ordered, knowinge
also that it is nowe a common right to
all princes, for so muche as Kinges are
now fully possessed in the seuerall partes

of

of the whole Empire, dothe so without
consideration assigne that office alone
to himselfe, and taketh it sufficient in
summoning a general Councell, to make
a man that is prince of the whole world
no otherwise partaker thereof then hee
woulde make his owne seruaunte. And
although the modestie and mildenes of
the Emperour Ferdinando be so greate
that hee canne beare this wronge, bycause peraduenture hee vnderstandeth
not well the Popes packinge, yet ought
not the Pope of his holines to offer him
that wronge, nor to claime as his owne
an other mans right.

But hereto some will replye: the Emperour in deede called Councelles at that
tyme ye speake of, bycause the Byshop
of Rome was not yet growen so greate
as hee is nowe, but yet the Emperour
didde not then sitte togeather with the
Byshoppes in Councell, or once bare
any stroke with his authoritie in their
consultation. I aunswere nay, that it

is

is not so, for as witnesseth Theodorete,
Themperour Constantine sate not only
togetther with them in the Councell at
Nice, butte gaue also aduice to the Bys=
shoppes howe it was best to trye out the
matter by the Apostles and Prophettes
wrytinges, as apeereth by these his own
woordes. In disputation (saithe hee) of
matters of diuinitie, wee haue sette be=
fore vs to followe the doctrine of the
holye Ghoste. For the Euangelistes
and the Apostles woorkes, and the Pro=
phertes sayinges shewe vs sufficientlye
what opinion wee ought to haue of the
will of God. The Emperour Theo=   *Socrat.lib.5.*
dotius (as sayeth Socrates) didde not   *cap.5.*
onely sitte amongest the Byshoppes, but
also ordered the whole arguinge of the
cause, and tare in peeces the Heretiques
bookes, and allowed for good the iudge=
mente of the Catholiques. In the Coun=
cell at Chalcidone a Ciuile magistrate
condemned for heretikes by the sentence
of hys owne mouthe, the Byshoppes   *[illegible marginal note]*

D.ii.   Dioscoras,

Dioſcozus, Juuenall, and Thalaſius,
and gaue iudgement to put them down
from that promotion in the Curche. In
the third Councell at Conſtantinople,

Actione. 2. Conſtantine a ciuile Magiſtrate, dyd
not only ſit amongeſt the Byſhops, but
dyd alſo ſubſcribe with them: For ſaith
he, we haue both read and ſubſcribed. In
the ſecond Councell called Arauſicanum,
the Princes Embaſſadours being noble
menne bozne, not only ſpake their minde
touching Religion, but ſet to their handes alſo, aſwel as the Byſhops. For thus
is it written in the later end of that Coū-
cel, Petrus, Marcellinus, Felix and Liberius, being moſt noble menne, and the
famous Lieutenauntes and Capitaines
of Fraunce, & alſo Peeres of the Realm,
haue giuen their conſent, and ſet to their
handes. Further, Spagrius, Opſio,
Pantagattus, Deodatus, Cariattho and
Marcellus, menne of very great honour
haue ſubſcribed. Yf it be ſo then, that
Lieutenauntes, chyeſe Capitaines and
Peeres

Peeres haue had authoritie to subscribe
in Councell , haue not Emperours and
Kinges the like authoritie?

Truely there hadde been no neede to
handle so plaine a matter as this is, with
so many wordes and so at length, if wee
hadde not to doe with those menne who
for a desire they haue to striue and to
winne the masterp, vse of course to denp
all thinges be thei neuer so cleere, yea the
very same which they presentlp see and
beholde with their owne eyes. The Em=
perour Justinian made a law to correct
the behauiour of p Cleargie, and to cutt
shorte the insolencie of the priestes. And
albeit hee were a Christian and a Catho
lique prince, yet putte hee downe from
their Papall Throne, twooe Popes,
Syluerius and Uigilius, not withstan=
dinge they were Peters successours, and
Christes vicars.

Lette vs see then, suche men as haue
authoritie ouer the Byshoppes, suche
menne as receaue from God commaun=

dementes concerning Religion, suche as
brynge home againe the Arke of God,
make holy hymnes, ouer see the preistes,
builde the Temple, make Orations touching diuine seruice, clense the Temples,
destroye the hil Auitres, burne the Idolles groues, teache the preistes their dewtie, write them out Preceptes how they
should lyue, kill the wicked Prophetes,
displace the high Preistes, call togyther
the Councelles of Byshops, sit togither
with the Byshoppes, instructing them
what they ought to doe, condemne and
punysh an Hereticall Byshop, be made
acquaynted with matters of Religion,
whiche subscribe and giue sentence, and
do al these things, not by an other mans
Commissio, but in their own name, and
that both vprightly and godly. Shall
we say it perteineth not to suche men to
haue to do with Religion? or shall wee
saye, a Christian Magistrate whyche
dealith amongest others in these maters
doth either naughtelie, or presumpteouslye,

fye, oz wickedlye: The moste aunci=
ente and Chzistian Emperoures and
kinges that euer were, didde busy them=
selus with these matters, and yet were
they neuer foz this cause noted eyther
of wickednesse oz of pzesumption. And
what is hee that canne finde oute eyther
moze catholique pzinces oz moze notable
eraumples:

Wherefoze yf it were lawfull foz
them to dooe thus beinge but Ciuile
Magistrates, and hauinge the chiefe
rule of common weales, what offence
haue oure Pzinces at thys daye made,
whiche maye not haue leaue to dooe
the lyke, beinge in the like degree: Oz
what especiall gifte of learninge oz of
iudgemente, oz of holynes, haue these
menne nowe, that contrarye to the cu=
stome of all the auncciente and Catho=
lique Bysshoppes, who vsed to conferre
with pzinces and peeres concerninge re=
ligió, thei do now thus reiect and cast of

O.iiii.   Chzistian

Chaiſtian Princes from knowing of the
cauſe, and from their meetinges.

Well thus doinge, they wiſelye and
warelye prowide for them ſelues and for
their kingedome, whiche otherwiſe they
ſee is like ſhortly to come to naught. For
if ſo be, they whom God hath placed in
greateſt dignitie, didde ſee and perceiue
theſe mennes practiſes, howe Chriſtes
commaundementes be deſpiſed by them,
how the light of the Goſpell is darkened
and quenched out by them, & how themſelues alſo be ſubtilly begiled and mocked
and vnwares be deluded by them, & the
way to ƥ kingedom of heaue ſtopped vp
before them, no doubt they would neuer
ſo quietlye ſuffer them ſelues neyther to
be diſdaigned after ſuche a prowde ſorte,
nor ſo diſpitefully to be ſcorned and abu-
ſed by them. But nowe through their
own lacke of vnderſtanding, & through
their owne blyndeneſſe, theſe menne
haue them faſt yoked and in their daunger.

Wee

We truely for our parts, as we haue
sayd, haue don nothing in altering Re=
ligion, either vpon rashenes or arrogan=
cie, nor nothing but with good leasure
and great consideration. Neyther had
we euer intended to do it, except both the
manifeste and most assured will of God
opened to vs in his holy scriptures, and
the regarde of our owne saluation had
euen constreyned vs therevnto. For
though wee haue departed from that
Churche which these menne call catho=
lique, and by that meanes gett vs enuy
amongest them that want skill to iudge,
yet is this ynough for vs, and it ought
to be ynough for euery wise and good
man, and one that maketh accoumpte of
euerlasting lyfe, that we haue gon from
that Church whiche had power to erre,
whiche Christ, who cannot erre, tolde so
long before it should erre, and which we
our selues did euidently see with our eyes
to haue gon both from ye holy Fathers
and from the Apostles, and from Christ

O.v.   his

his own selfe & from the primitiue & ca=
tholique churche: and wee are come as
nere as we possibly could to the Church
of the Apostles and of the old catholique
Byshops and Fathers, whiche Churche
we knowe hath hetherunto ben sounde
and persite, and as Tertullian termeth
it, a pure virgine spotted as yet with no
Idolatrie, nor with any foule or shame=
full faulte: and haue directed according
to their customes and ordinaunces not
onely our doctrine, but also the Sacra=
ments & the sourine of common prayer.

And as we knowe both Christe hym
selfe and all good men here tofore haue
don, we haue called home againe to the
originall and first foundation that Reli=
gion which hath ben sowly sorsowed &
vtterly corrupted by these men. For wee
thought it mete thence to take ẏ paterne
of reforminge Religion, from whence
the ground of Religion was first taken,
Bycause this one reasone, as saythe the
most auncient Father Tertullian, hath
great

great force againste all Heresies. Looke what soeuer was first, that is trew: and what soeuer is latter, that is corrupt. Irenēus oftentimes appealed to ye oldest Churchs, which had ben nerest to Christes time, and which it was hard to beleue had erred. But whye at this daye is not the same respect and consideratiō had? Whye returne wee not to the paterne of the ould Churches? whye maye not we heare at this time amongst vs ye same saiing which was opēly pronounced in times past in the Councel at Nice by so many Byshopes and Catholique Fathers, and nobody once speakyng againste it. ἐδει ἀρχαῖα κρατεῖτω: that is to saye, hould still the old customes. When Eldras went about to repayre the ruynes of the Temple of God, he sent not to Ephesus, although the moste beautifull and gorgious Temple of Diana was there, and when he purposed to restore ye Sacrifices and ceremonies of God, he sent not to Rome, although peraduenture

ture, he had hearde in that place were the
solemne Sacrifices called, Hecatombæ,
and other called Solitaurilia, lectisternia,
and Supplicatiõs, and Numa Pompi-
lius ceremoniall bokes, he thought it y-
noughe for hym to set before his eyes, &
to folow the paterne of the old Temple
which Salomon at the beginning builded, accordyng as God had appoincted
hym, and also those olde custromes and
Ceremonies whiche God hymselfe had
written out by special words for Moses.

The Prophet Aggeus, after the Tẽ-
ple was repaired againe by Eldras, and
the people mighte thinke they had a very iuste cause to reioyce on their own behalfe, for so great a benefit receiued of almightie God, yet made he them al burst
out in teares, bycause that they whyche
were yet aliue, and had sene the former
building of the Temple before the Ba-
bylonians destroyed it, called to mynde
how far of it was yet from that beautie
and excellencie whiche it had in the olde
                                    tymes

times paſt befoze. Foz thē in deed would
they haue thought ẙ Temple wozthely
repaired, yf it had aunſwered to the
auncient paterne, and to the maieſtie of
the firſt Temple. Paul bycauſe he wold
amende the abuſe of the Lozdes ſupper
which ẙ Cozinthians euen then begonne
to cozrupte, he ſett befoze them Chziſtes
inſtitution to folow, ſayng: J haue deliuered vnto you ẙ which J firſte receiued of the Lozd. And when Chziſt dyd
confute the errour of the Phariſees, Ye
muſt, ſaith he, retozne to the firſt beginning, foz frō the beginning yt was not
thus. And whẽ he founde great faulte
with ẙ pzeiſts foz their vncleanes of lyfe
and couetouſnes, and woulde clenſe the
Temple from al euil abuſes, This houſe
ſaith he, at ẙ firſt beginning was a houſe
of pzaier, wherin all the people myght
deuoutely and ſincerely pzaye together,
and ſo were your partes to bſe it nowe
alſo at this daye. Foz it was not builded
to thende it ſhould be a denne of theues.
Likwiſe

Likewise al the good and commendable
Princes mentioned of in the Scriptures,
were praised, specially by those wordes
that they had walked in the wayes of
their Father Dauid. That is bycause
they had retorned to the first and originall foundation, and had restored Religion euen to the perfection wherin Dauid left it. And therfore whē we likewise
sawe all thinges were quite trodden vnder foote of these men, and that nothing
remained in the Temple of God but pi-
teful spoyles and decayes, we reckened it
the wisest and the safest waye to sett before our eyes those Churches which we
knew for a suerty that they neuer had
erred, nor neuer had priuate Masse, nor
prayers in straynge and Barbarous
language, nor this corrupting of Sacramentes and other toyes.

And forsomuche as our desire was to
haue the Temple of the Lord restored a
new, we would seke no other foundatiō,
then the same which we knew was long
agone

agone layde by the Apostles, that is to
wyte, our sauiour Iesu Christ. And for-
somuch as we heard God hym selfe speaking vnto vs in his word, and sawe also
the notable Examples of the oulde and
primatiue Churche: againe how vncertaine a mater it was to wait for a generall Councell, and that the successe therof
woulde be muche more vncertaine, but
specially for somuche as we were moste
ascerteined of Goddes will, and counted
it a wickednes to be to careful and ouer-
cumbred about the iudgementes of mortall menne, we could no longer stand ta-
kyng aduise with flesshe and bloud, but
rather thought good to do ÿ same thing
that both might rightlye be don, & hath
also many a time ben don aswel of good
men as of many catholique Byshopes:
that is .to remedie our own Churches
by a Prouinciall Synode . For thus
know we the ould fathers vsed to putt
in experience before they came to the publique vniuersal Councel. There remaine

geb

yet at this daye Canons written in Coū-
celles of free Cities, as of Carthage vnder Cypꝛian, as of Ancyra, of Neocesaria
and of Gangra, also whiche is in Pa-
phlagonia as some thinke, befoꝛe that ye
name of the generall Councel at Nice
was euer heard of. After this fashion in
olde time did they spedely meet with, and
cut shoꝛt those Heretiques ye Pelagians &
the Donatistes at home with priuate
disputation, without any general Councell. Thus also when the Emperour
Constantius euidētly and earnestly toke
part with Auxentius the Byshop of the
Arrians faction, Ambꝛose the Byshopp
of the Chꝛistians appealed not vnto a
generall Councel, where he saue no good
could be don, by reason of ye Emperours
might and great labour, but appealed to
his owne Cleargie and people, that is to
say, to a Pꝛouinciall Synode. And thus
it was decreed in the Councell at Nice,
that the Byshops should assemble twise
euery yeare. And in the Councel at Carthage

thage it was decreed, that the Byſſhops
ſhoulde meete togeather in eche of their
prouinces, at leaſt once in the year, which
was done as ſaith the Councel at Chal=
cedone, of purpoſe, that if any errours
and abuſes had happened to ſpringe vp
any where, they might immediatelye at
the firſt enterie be deſtroyed where they
firſte begonne. So likewiſe when Se=
cundus and Palladius reiected the Coū=
cell at Aquila, bicauſe it was not a gene=
rall and a common Councell, Ambroſe
Byſſhoppe of Millaine made aunſwere,
that no man ought to take it for a newe
or ſtraunge matter that the Byſſhops of
the weſte parte of the worlde didde call
togeather Synodes, and make priuate
aſſemblies in their Prouinces, for that it
was a thing before then vſed by the weſt
Byſſhoppes no fewe times, and by the
Byſſhoppes of Grecia vſed oftentymes
and comonly to be done. And ſo Charles
the great being Emperour, held a prouin
ciall Councell in Germanie, for puttinge

P.i.   away

awaye Images, contrary to the seconde
Councell at Nice. Neither pardy euen
amongest vs is this so very a straunge
and newe a trade : for we haue hadde ere
nowe in Englande prouinciall Synods,
and gouerned oure Churches by home
made lawes . What shoulde one saye
more ? of a truthe euen those greatest
Councelles, and where moste assemblie
of people euer was (wherof these menne
vse to make suche an exceedinge recke=
ninge) compare them with all the Chur=
ches whiche throughout the worlde ac=
knowledge and professe the name of
Christe, and what els I praye you can
they seeme to bee, butte certaine priuate
Councelles of Byshoppes, and prouin=
ciall Synodes ? for admitte peraduen=
ture, Italie, Fraunce, Spaine, Eng=
lande, Germanie, Denmarke, and Scot=
lande meete togithers , yf there want
Asia, Grecia, Armenia, Persia, Media,
Mesopotamia, Egypt, Ethiopia, India,
and Mauritania , in all whiche places
there

there bee bothe manye Chriſtian menne
and alſo Byſſhoppes, howe canne anye
man, beinge in his right mynde, thinke
ſuche a Councel to bee a generall Coun=
cell? or where ſo manye partes of the
worlde doe lacke, howe canne they true=
lye ſaye, they haue the conſente of the
whole worlde? Or what manner of
Councell, weene you, was the ſame laſt
at Trident? Or howe might it bee tear=
med a generall Councell, when out of all
Chriſtian kyngedomes and Nations,
there came vnto it butte onelye fourtye
Byſſhoppes, and of thoſe ſome ſo cun=
ninge, that they might be thought meete
to bee ſente home againe to learne their
Grammar, and ſo well learned, that thei
had neuer ſtudied Diuinitie?

What ſo euer it bee, the truthe of
the Goſpell of I E S V S C H R I S T De=
pendeth not vpon Councelles, nor as
S. Pawle ſaithe, vpon mortall crea=
tures iudgementes. And if they whiche
ought to be carefull for Gods Churche,

P.ii.   will

will not be wyse but slacke their duety,
and harden their heartes againſt Godde
and his Chriſte, goinge on ſtill to per-
uert the right wayes of the Lorde, God
will ſtirre vp the very ſtones, and make
childryn and babes cunninge, whereby
there may euer be ſome to confute theſe
mennes lyes. For God is able (not onely
without Councelles, butt alſo will the
Councelles nill the Councelles) to maintaine and auaunce his owne kingedom.
Full manye bee the thoughtes of mans
heart (ſaith Salomon.) but the counſell of the Lorde abydeth ſtedfaſt. There
is no wiſedome, there is no knowledge,
there is no counſell againſt the Lorde.
Thinges endure not, ſaithe Hilarius,
that be ſet vp with mennes workeman-
ſhip. By an other manner of meanes
muſt the Churche of God be builded and
preſerued, for that Churche is grounded
vpon the foundation of the Apoſtles
and Prophets, and is holden faſt together by one corner ſtone, which is Chriſt
Jeſu.

Jeſu.

But merueilous notable and to very
good purpoſe foꝛ theſe dayes bee Hieromes woꝛdes: Whoſoeuer (ſayth hee)
the Diuell hathe deceiued and enticed to
fall a ſleepe as it were with the ſweete
& deathly enchautments of p̄ marmaids
the Sirenes, thoſe perſones doth Gods
woꝛde awake vp, ſayinge vnto them:
Ariſe thou that ſleepeſt, lifte vp thy ſelfe,
and Chꝛiſt ſhall giue the light. Therfoꝛe
at the comminge of Chꝛiſte, of Goddes
woꝛde, of the eccleſiaſticall doctrine, and
of the full deſtruction of Niniue, and of
that moſte bewtifull harlot, then ſhall
the people whiche heretofoꝛe hadde been
caſt in a traunce vnder their maiſters,
bee rayſed vp, and ſhall make haſte to go
to the Mountaines of the Scripture,
and there ſhall they finde hilles, Moſes,
verely and Joſua the ſonne of Nun: o-
ther hilles alſo which ar the Prophetes:
and hilles of the newe teſtament, whiche
are the Apoſtles and the Euangeliſtes:

P.iii.   And

*Hieron in
Naum
cap.3.*

And when the people shall flee for suc=
cour to suche hilles, and shall bee exerci=
sed in the reading of those kind of moun=
taynes , though they finde not one to
teache them (for the haruest shall bee
greate, butte the labourers fewe) yet
shall the good desire of the people bee
well accepted, in that they haue gotten
them to suche hilles , and the neglygence
of their maisters shall bee openly repro=
ued . These bee Hieromes sayenges,
and that so playne, as there needeth no
Interpretour . For they agree so iuste
with the thinges wee nowe see wyth
oure eyes haue already come to passe, y
wee maye verelye thinke hee mente to
foretell, as it were by the spirite of pro=
phesie, and to painete before oure face
the vniuersall state of oure tyme , the
fall of the moste gorgeous harlotte Ba=
bylon , the repairinge againe of Goddes
Churche , the blyndenesse and slewthe
of the Byshoppes , and the good will
and forwardenesse of the people . For
who

who is so blinde that hee seeth not these
menne bee the maisters, by whome the
people, as sayth Hieroine, hathe been
ledde into errour, and lulled a sleepe?
Or who seeth not Rome, that is their
Niniue, whiche sometime was painted
with fairest colours, but now her vizer being pulled of, is both better seen and lesse
sette by? Or who seeth not that good
menne beinge a waked as it were out
of their deade sleepe, at the lighte of the
Gospell, and at the voyce of God, haue
resorted to the hilles of the Scriptures,
waiting not at all for the Councelles of
suche maisters?

Butte by your fauoure, some will
saye, These thinges ought not to haue
been attempted without the Byschoppe
of Romes commaundement, forsomuche
as hee onely is the knotte and bande of
Christian societie: he onely is that priest
of Leuies order, whom God signified in
the Deuteronomy, from whom counsell

P.iii.   in

in matters of weight and true iudgemēt
ought to be fetched, and who so obeyeth
not his iudgement, the same man ought
to bee killed in the sight of his brethren:
and that no mortall creature hathe au=
thoritie to bee iudge ouer him whatso=
euer hee dooe: that Chriſte reigneth in
heauen and hee in earthe: that hee alone
canne dooe as muche as Chriſt, or God
hym ſelfe canne dooe, bicauſe Chriſt and
hee haue but one Councell houſe: That
without him is no faythe, no hope, no
churche, and who ſo goeth from him,
quite caſteth awaye and renounceth his
owne ſaluation. Suche talke haue the
Canoniſtes, the Popes paraſites ſurely,
but with ſmall diſcretion or ſobrenesse:
for they coulde ſcant ſaye more, at leaſte
they coulde not ſpeake more highlye of
Chriſte him ſelfe.

As for vs truely, we haue fallen from
the Byſhoppe of Rome vpon no maner
of worldlye reſpect or commoditie, and
woulde to Chriſte hee ſo behaued him=
ſelfe

felfe, as this falling away neded not: but
fo the cafe ftoode, that onles we left him,
wee could not come to Chuft. Neyther
will he now make any other league w̄
vs, then fuche a one as Nahas the kyng
of the Ammonites would haue made in
tymes paft with thē of the citie of Ja=
bes, whiche was to put out the right eye
of eche one of the Inhabitantes. Euen fo
will the Pope pluck from vs the holye
Scripture, the Gofpell of our faluation,
and all the confidence which we haue in
Chuft Jefu. And vpon other condition
can he not agree vpon peace with vs.

For wheras fom vfe to make fo great
a vaunte, that the Pope is onely Peters
Succeffour, as though therby he carried
the holy Ghoft in his bofome & cannot
erre, this is but a matter of nothing and
a very trieflyng tale. Gods grace is pro=
mifed to a good mynde, and to one that
fearith God, not vnto Sees and Suc=
ceffiōs. Riches faith Jerome, may make
a Byfhop to be of moze might then the

1. Regum.11.

rest : but all the Byshoppes whosoeuer they be, are the Successours of the Apostles. Yf so be, the place and consecrating onely be sufficient (why then) Manasses succeded Dauid, and Caiphas succeded Aaron. And it hath ben often seene, that an Idoll hath stand in the Temple of God. In old tyme Archidamus the Lacedemonian boasted muche of hym selfe, how he came of the bloud of Hercules, but one Nicostratus in thys wise abated his prydes: Nay, quod he, ȝ semest not to descende from Hercules, for Hercules destroied yll men, but thou makest good men euill. And when the Pharises bragged of their linage how they wereof ȝ kynred and bloud of Abraham, Ye saith Christ, seeke to kyll me, a manne whiche haue toulde you the trouth as I heard it from God: thus Abraham neuer did. Ye are of your Father the dyuel, and wil nedes obey his will.

Yet notwithstandyng, bycause wee will graunt somewhat to succession, tell vs,

vs , hath the Pope alone succeded Pe=
ter ? and wherin I praye you, in what
Religion=in what Office=in what peece
of his lyfe hath he succeded hym = What
one thing(tel me)had Peter euer like vn=
to the Pope = or the pope lyke vnto Pe=
ter = excepte paraduenture they will
saye thus : that Peter when he was at
Rome , neuer taught the Gospell, neuer
fedde ŷ flock,toke away the keyes of the
kingedom of heauē, hyd the treasures of
his Lorde,satte him downe onely in his
Castle in S. Jo'n Laterane,& poincted
out with his finger at the places of Pur=
gatorie, and kyndes of punyshementes,
cōmittyng some poore soules to be tor=
mented,and other some againe sodenlye
releasing thence at his owne pleasure,ta=
king money for so doing: or that he gaue
order to say priuate Masses in euery cor=
net: or that he mumbled vp the holy ser=
uice with a lowe voice and in an vn=
knowen language,or that he hāged vp ŷ
Sacrament in euery Temple and on eue=
rie Aulter , and caryed ŷ same about be=
fore

fore hym whether soeuer he went, vpon
an ambling Iennett, with lightes and
belles: or that he confecrated with hys
holy breath, oyle, war, wulle, belles, cha-
lices, churches & aultres: or that he solde
Iubilees, graces, liberties, aduouſons,
preuentions, firſt fruits, Palles, the wea
ring of Palles, bulles, Indulgences and
pardons: or that he called hym ſelf by the
name of the head of the Churche, The
higheſt Byſhop, Byſhop of Byſhopps,
alone Moſt holy: or that by vſurping he
tooke vpon hym ſelfe the right and aucthoritie ouer other folkes Churches: or
that he exempted him ſelfe frō the power
of anye ciuille gouernement: or that he
mainteined warrs, ſet Princes together
at variaunce: or that he ſytting in his
Chaire with his triple Crowne full of
labelles, with ſumptuous & Perſianlike
gorgiouſnes, with his Royall ſcepter,
with his Diademe of goulde and glitte-
ring with ſtones, was caried about not
vpon Paalfrate, but vpon the ſhoulders

of

of noble menne. These things no doubt
did Peter at Rome in times past, and left
them in charge to his Successours as
you would say, from hand to hande: for
these thinges be now a dayes donne at
Rome by the Popes, and be so done, as
though nothing els ought to be don.

Or contrariewise paraduenture they
had rather saye thus, that the Pope doth
now all the same thinges whyche wee
knowe Peter did many a daye a goe:
that is, that he rounneth vp and downe
into euerye Countrepe to Preache the
Gospell, not onelye openlye abroad,
but also priuatelye from house to house:
that hee is diligente, and applyeth that
busines in seasone and out of seasone, in
dewe tyme, out of dew time: that he doth
the part of an Euangelist, that he fulfil-
leth the worke and ministerie of Christ,
that he is þ watcheman of the house of
Israel: receaueth answeares and wordes at Goddes mouth: and euen as he
receiueth them, so deliuereth them ouer
to

to the people : That he is the salte of the
earth: That he ys the light of the world,
that he doth not feed his owne selfe but
his flock, that he doth not entangle him
selfe with the worldlie cares of this lyfe,
that he doth not vse a souerauntye ouer
the Lordes people, that he seeketh not to
haue other menne minister to hym, but
him selfe rather to minister vnto others,
that he taketh al Bishops as his felows
and equals: that he is subiect to Princes
as to personnes sent from God, that he
giueth to Cesar that whiche is Cesars:
and that he as the old Bishops of Rome
dyd (without any question) calleth the
Emperour his Lord: Onles therfore the
Popes do the like now a dayes, and Peter did the thinges a foresayd, there is no
cause at all why they should glorye so of
Peters name and of his succession.

Muche lesse cause haue they to complaine of our departing, and to call vs
againe to be felowes and frendes with
them, and to beleue as they beleue. Men
say

saye that one Cobilon a Lacedemonian,
when he was sent Embassadour to the
kyng of the Persians to treate of a le=
gue, and founde by chaunce them of the
court playng at dyce, he returned streight
waye home againe, leauing his message
vndone. And whē he was asked why he
did slacke to doe the thinges whiche he
had receiued by publique commission
to do, he made aunswere, he thought it
should be a great reproche to his common
welthe, to make a legue with Dicers.
But yf we should content our selues to
retorne to the Pope and his popysshe er=
rours, and to make a couenaunte not on=
ly with dicers, but also with men farre
more vngracious and wicked then a ny
dycers be: Besides that this should be a
great blot to our good name, it shoulde
also be a very daungerous matter both
to kindle Goddes wrath against vs, and
to clogge and condemne our owne sou=
les foreuer. For of very trouthe we haue
departed from hym whome we saw had
blinded

blinded the whole worlde this many an
hundred yeare. From hym who to farre
presumpteouslye was wont to saye,he
coulde not erre, and whatsoeuer he dyd
no mortal man had power to condemne
hym,neyther kynges nor Emperours,
nor the whole Clergie, nor yet all the
people in the worlde togyther, no and
though he should carrie away with him
to Hell a thousande soules . From hym
who toke vpon him power to comaund
not only menne but euen Goddes Aungels,to go,to returne, to leade soules into Purgatorie, and to bring them back
againe when he lyste him selfe : whome
Gregory said,with out all doubt is the
very foreronner and standerd bearer
of Antichrist,and hath vtterly forsaken
the catholique faith: From whome also
those ringeleaders of others,who now
with might and maine resist ý Gospel,&
the trouth whiche they knowe to be the
truth,haue of this departed euery one of
their owne accorde and good will , and
woulde

woulde euen now alſo gladly depart frō
hym, yf the note of inconſtancie & ſhame
and their owne eſtimacion amonge the
people were not a let vnto them. In con=
cluſion, wee haue departed from hym to
whom we wer not bound, and who had
nothyng to laye foz hym ſelfe, but onely
I know not what vertue oz power of
the place where he dweleth, and a conti=
nuaunce of ſucceſſion.

And as foz vs, we of all others moſte
iuſtely haue left him. Foz our Kynges,
yea euen they whiche with greateſt re=
uerence dyd folow and obey the auctho=
ritie and faith of the Byſhops of Rome,
haue long ſynce founde and felte well y=
nough the yoke & tyrannye of the Po=
pes kingdome. Foz ẏ Byſhops of Rome
toke the Crowne of from the head of
our Kynge Henrye the ſecond, and com=
pelled him to put a ſide all maieſtie, and
lyke a meere priuate man to come vnto
their Legate with great ſubmiſſion and
humilitie, ſo as all his ſubiectes might

laugh him to scorne. More thē this, they caused Byshops and Monkes and some parte of the nobilitie to be in the feelde against our kynge John, and sett all the people at libertie from their othe wherby they ought allegeaunce to their king: and at last, wickedly and most abhominable they bereaued the kyng not onely of his kyngdome, but also of his lyfe. Besides this, they excommunicated and cursed kyng Henry theight, the most famous Prince, & stirred vp against him sometime the Emperour, sometime the Frenche kyng, & as muche as in them was, putte in aduenture our Realme to haue ben a very praye and spoyle. Yet were they but foules and mad, to thinke that eyther so mighty a Prince could be feared with bugges and rattles : or els $\bar{y}$ so noble and great a kyngdome myght so easily, euen at one morsel be deuoured and swalowed vp.

And yet as though all this were to litle, they would nedes make all the Realme

alme tributarie to them , & exacted theee
yearely most vniust and wrongfull ta=
xes. So deere cost vs the freendeshyp of
the Citie of Rome . Wherefore yf they
haue gotten these thinges of vs by ex=
tortion thorough their fraude and suttle
sleightes,we see no reason why we may
not plucke awaye the same from them
againe by lawfull wayes & iust means.
And yf our kynges in that darknes and
blindenes of former tymes gaue them
these thinges of their owne accorde and
liberalitie for Religion sake , being mo=
ued with a certaine opinion of their fai=
ned holines , now when ignoraunce &
errour is spied out,may the kinges their
successours take them awaye againe ,
seing they haue the same auctoritie , the
kinges their aunchestours had before.
for the gyft is voide,except it be alowed
by the Will of the giuer:and that cannot
seme a perfit will, which is dymmed and
hindered by errour.
    Thus ye see good Christian Reader,
            D.it.   how

howe it is no new thing , though at this
day the religion of Christ be entertained
with dispites and checkes, being but la=
tely restored and as it were comming vp
againe a new , for somuche as the lyke
hath chaunced both to Christ hym selfe
and to his Apostles: yet neuerthelesse for
feare ye maye suffer your selfe to be led
amysse and seduced with those exclama=
tions of our Aduersaries, we haue decla=
red at large vnto you $\tilde{y}$ very whole ma=
ner of our Religion , what our opinion
is of God the Father, of his onely sonne
Jesus Christ , of the holy Ghost , of the
Church, of the Sacramentes, of the mi=
nistery, of $\tilde{y}$ Scriptures, of ceremonies,
and of euery parte of Christian beleue.
Wee haue sayde that wee abandon and
detest as plagues and poysons all those
olde Heresies, whiche eyther the sacred
Scriptures or the auncient Councelles
haue vtterly condemned : that wee call
home againe asmuche as euer wee can,
the right Discipline of $\tilde{y}$ Church, which
our

our Aduersaries haue quite bzought in=
to a poore weake case: That we pun=
nithe all licentiousnes of lyfe and vnru=
lynes of maners by the olde and long
continued laws,and with asmuch sharp=
penes as is conuenient and lyeth in our
power: That we mainteine still the state
of kingdomes,in the same condition and
plight wherin we haue found the, with=
out any diminithing oz alteration, refer=
uinge vnto our Princes their maiestie
and worldly preeminence safe and with=
out empayzing,to our possible power:
That we haue so gotté our selues away
from that Church which they had made
a denne of Theeues , and wherein no=
thing was in good frame oz once like to
the Churche of God , and whiche them
selfes cófessed had erred many weies,cué
as Lott in times paste gat hym out of
Sodom,oz Abzaham out of Caldie,not
vpó a desire of contention,but by ý war=
ninge of God him selfe : And ý we haue
searched out of ý holy Bible whiche we
are sure cannot deceiue,one sure forme
Q.iii.   of

of Religion, and haue retorned againe
vnto the Primatiue Churche of the aun=
cient fathers and Apostles, that is to
say, to the first ground and beginning of
thinges, as vnto the very foundations
& head springes of Christes church. And
in very troth we haue not tarried for in
this matter the auctoritie or consent of
the Trident Councell, wherein we sawe
nothing don vprightly nor by good or=
dre: where also euery body was sworne
to the maintenaunce of one man: where
our Princes Embassadours were con=
temned: where not one of oure diuines
could be heard, and where partes taking
and ambition was openly and earnest=
lye procured and wrought, but as the
holy Fathers in former time, and as our
predecessours haue commonly don, wee
haue restored our Churches by a Pro=
uinciall Conuocation, and haue cleane
shaken of as our deutie was, the yoke
and tyrannye of the Byshop of Rome, to
whome we were not bounde, who also
had

had no manner of thyng lyke neyther to
Chrilt nor to Peter, nor to an Apoltle,
nor yet like to any Byſhopp at all . Fi=
nally, we ſaye that wee agree amongeſt
our ſelues,touching the whole iudgemēt
and chiefe ſubſtaunce of Chriſtian Reli=
gion, and with one mouth and with
one ſpirite do wooſhipp God and the
Father of our Loꝛd Jeſu Chꝛiſt.

Wherefoꝛe O Chꝛiſtian and godlye
Reader, foꝛſomuche as thow ſeſt the
reaſons and cauſes both whye wee haue
reſtoꝛed Religion , and whye wee haue
foꝛſaken theſe men,thou oughteſt not to
maruaile,though wee haue choſen to o=
beye our Maiſter Chꝛiſte rather then
menne.Paule hath giuen vs warning
how we ſhoulde not ſuffer our ſelues to
be carried away with ſuche ſundꝛy lear=
ninges,and to fly their companies,in eſ=
peciall whiche woulde ſowe debate and
variaunces,cleane contrarie to the Doc=
trine whiche they had receiued of Chꝛiſt
and the Apoſtls.Longe ſynce haue theſe
mennes

mennes craftes and treacheries decaied
and banished and fled away at the sight
and light of þ Gospell, euen as the owle
doth at the sunne rysing. And albeit their
trumperye be builte vp and reared as
highe as the Skye, yet euen in a momēt
and as yt were of the owne selue fallyth
yt downe againe to the ground, and cōmeth to naught. For you must not think
þ al these things haue com to passe rashly oꝛ at aduēture: It hath ben gods pleasure þ against al mennes willes wel nye,
the Gospell of Iesu Chꝛiste shoulde be
spꝛead abꝛoad thoꝛough out the whole
woꝛlde, at these dayes. And therfoꝛe men
folowing godds biddings, haue of their
owne free will resoꝛted vnto the Doctrine of Iesus Chꝛist. And foꝛ our parts
truely wee haue sought hereby neyther
gloꝛie noꝛ welthe, noꝛ pleasure noꝛ ease.
Foꝛ there is plentie of all these thinges
with our aduersaryes. And when wee
wer of their side, we enioyed such woꝛld-
lye commodyties muche moꝛe liberallie
and

and bountefullye, then wee doe nowe. Neyther doe wee eschew concorde and peace, but to haue peace with man, wee will not be at warre with God. The name of peace is a sweete and pleasaunte thinge, saith Hilarius: But yet beware, sayth he, peace is one thinge, and boundage is an other. For yf it shoulde so be as they seeke to haue it, that Christe shoulde be commaunded to keepe silence, that the truth of the Gospell shoulb be betraied, that horrible errours should be cloked, that Christian mennes eyes shold be bleared, & that they might be suffred to conspire openlye against God: this were not a peace, but a moste vngodlye couenaunt of seruitude. There is a peace saith Nazianzene, that is vnprofitable: againe there is a discorde saith he, that is profitable. For we muste conditionallye desire peace, so farre as is lawfull before God, & so farre as we may conuenietly. For otherwise Christ him self broughte not peace into the worlde, but a sworde.

Q.v.   Wherfore

Wherefore yf the Pope will haue vs reconciled to hym, his dewty is first to be reconciled to God: for from thence saith Cyprian, spring schysmes and sectes, bycause menne seeke not the head, and haue not their recourse to the Fountaine of ye Scriptures, and kepe not the Rules gyuen by the heauenly teacher: for saith he, that is not peace but warre: neyther is he ioyned vnto the Churche which is seuered from the Gospel. As for these men they vse to make a marchaundize of the name of peace. For that peace whiche they so faine would haue, is onely a rest of idle bellies. They and we might easily be brought to atonement touchyng all these matters, were it not that ambitió, glutony and excesse did let it: Hence commeth their whyenyng, their hearte is on their Halfepennye. Out of doubt their claymours and styrres be to none other ende, but to maynteine more shamefully and naughtely yll gotten thinges.

Nowe a dayes the Pardoners complaine

plaine of vs, the Dataries, the Popes Collectours, the Bawdes, and others which take Gayne to be godlynesse, and serue not Iesu Christe but their owne bellyes. Many a day ago and in the old worlde, a wonderfull great aduantage grew hereby to these kinde of people, but now they recken all is losse vnto them that Christ gaigneth. The Pope hym selfe maketh greate complaynte at this present, that Charitie in people is waxen coulde. And why so trow ye? Forsooth because his profittes decaye more and more. And for this cause doth he hale vs into hatred all that euer he maye, laieng lode vpon vs with dispitetfull raylings and condemning vs for Heretiques, to thende they that vnderstande not the matter, maye thinke there be no woorse menne vpon earth then we be. Notwith standing we in the meane season are ne- uer the more ashamed for all this: ney- ther ought we to be ashamed of þ Gos pell: for wee sett more by the glorie of

God

God then wee doe by the estimation of menne. Wee are sure all is true that we teach, and we may not either go against our owne conscience, or beare any witnes against God. For yf we denye any part of the Gospel of Jesu Christ before menne, he on the other side wil denye vs before his father. And yf there be anye that will still be offended and cannot endure Christes doctrine, suche saye wee, be blynd & leaders of ý blynde: the truth neuertheles must be preached and preferred aboue all : and wee muste with patience wayte for Goddes iudgement.

Lett these folke in the meane tyme take good heed what they do, and let them be well aduised of their owne Saluation, and cease to hate and persecute the Gospell of the sonne of God, for feare least they feele hym once a redresser and reuenger of his owne cause. God will not suffer him selfe to be mad a mocking stock. The world espyeth a good whyle a gon what there ys a doyng abroade. This

flame.

flame the more it is kept downe, somuch the more with greater force and strength doth it break out and flye abroade. Their vnfaithfulnes shall not diſapoincte goddes faithfull promyſe. And yf they shall refuse to laye away this their hardenes of heart and to receiue the Goſpel of Chriſt, then shall Publicanes and ſynners go before them into the Kingedome of Heauen.

GOD and the Father of oure Lorde IESVS CHRIST open the eyes of them all, that they maye be able to ſee that bleſſed hope whereunto they haue ben called, ſo as wee maye altogither in one, glorifie hym alone, who is the trew God, and alſo that ſame Jeſus Chriſt whome he ſent downe to vs from Heauen: vnto whome with the Father and the holy Ghoſt be giuen all honour and glorie euerlaſtinglye. So be it.

The ende of the Apologie
of the Churche of
Englande,

The manner how the Churche of Englande is administred & gouerned.

The Churche of Englãd is diuided in to two Prouinces, { Canterbury, and Yorke.

The Prouince of Canterbury hath Tharchebyshop of the same, who is Primate of all Englande and Metropolitane.

The Byshop of London.

The Byshop of { Winchester.
Elye.
Chichester
Hereforde.
Salysburie.
Worcetor.
Lincolne.
Couentrie and Lichefield.
Bathe and Welles.
Norwiche.
Exeter.
Rochester.
Peterborough.
S. Danies.
S. Assaph.

The

The Byshop of
{ Landaffe.
Bangor.
Oxforde.
Glocester, and
Bristowe.

The Prouince of Yorke hathe

Tharchebyshop of the same, who is also Primate of England and Metropolitane.

The Byshop of
{ Durham.
Carliell, and
Chester.

Amongest vs heere in Englande no man is called or preferred to bee a Byshop, except he haue first receiued the orders of Priesthoode, and be well hable to instruct the people in ẙ holy scriptures.

Euery one of the Archebyshops and Byshops haue their seuerall Cathedrall churches. Wherein ẙ deanes beare chiefe rule, being men specially chosen both for their learning and godlines, as neere as maye bee.

these

These Cathedrall Churches haue also other dignities and Canôries, wherevnto bee assigned no ydle or vnprofitable persones, but suche as eyther bee Preachers, or professours of the Sciences of good learninge.

In the saide Cathedrall Churches, vpon Sondayes and festiuall dayes, the Canons make ordinarilye special Sermons, wherevnto duely resorte the head Officers of the Cities and the Citizens: and vpon the workendayes thryse in the weeke, one of the Canons doth read and expound some peece of holy Scripture.

Also the saide Archebyshops and Byshops haue vnder them their Archedeacons, some two, some foure, some sixe, accordinge to the largenes of the dioces, the whiche Archedeacons keepe yearly twoo visitations, wherein they make diligent inquisition, and searche both of the doctrine and behauiour as well of the ministers as of the people. They punishe

R.i.   nishe

nisse thoffendors: and if any errours in religion and heresies fortune to springe, thei bring those and other weighty matters before the Byshops themselues.

There is nothing read in oure Churches but the canonical scriptures, which is done in suche ordre, as that the Psalter is read ouer euery moneth, the new Testament foure times in the yeare, and the olde Testament once euery yeare. And if the Curate be iudged of ꝑ Byshop to be sufficiently seene in the holy scripturs, he dothe withal make some exposition and exhortacion vnto godlines.

And for somuch as our Churches and Uniuersities haue ben wōderfully marred, and so fouly brought out of al fashion in time of papistrie, as there can not be had learned pastors for euery paryssh, there bee prescribed vnto the Curates of meaner vnderstandinge, certaine Homelies deuised by learned men, whiche doe comprehende the principall poinctes of Christian

Chriſtian doctrine: as of Originall ſin, of Iuſtification, of Faith, of Charitie, & ſuche like, for to bee read by them vnto the people.

As for Common prayer, The leſſons taken out of the Scriptures, thadminiſtringe of the ſacramentes, and the reſidue of ſeruice done in the Churches, are euery whitt done in the vulgare tongue whiche all may vnderſtande.

Touchinge the vniuerſities.

Moreouer, this Realme of England hathe twoo Vniuerſities, ⎰ Cambridge and ⎱ Oxforde.

And the manner is not to liue in theſe within houſes that be Innes or a receipt for common geaſtes, as is the cuſtome of ſome vniuerſities, but they liue in colledges vnder moſte graue and ſeuere diſcipline, euen ſuche as the famous learned man Eraſmus of Roterodame, beinge heere amongeſt vs about fourtie yeares

B.ii.   paſt

paſt, was bolde to preferre before ẙ verꝑ rules of the Monkes.

In Cambridge bee xiiii Colledges, theſe by name that folowe.

Trinitie Colledge founded by kinge Henrie the eight.
The kinges Colledge.
S. Johns Colledge.
Chriſtes Colledge.
The Quenes Colledge.
Jheſus Colledge.
Bennet Colledge.
Pembroke Colledge, or Pembroke halle.
Peter Colledge, or Peter houſe.
Gunwell and Caius colledge, or halle.
One other Trinitie colledge, or Trinitie halle.
Clare colledge, or Clare halle.
S. Katherins colledge, or Katherin halle.
Magdalene colledge.

In Oxford likwiſe there be Colledges ſome greater ſome ſmaler, to the number of foure and twentye, the names whereof be as followeth.

The

The Cathedrall Churche of Chriſte, wherein also is a great company of ſtudentes.
Magdalene colledge.
Newe colledge.
Marten colledge.
All ſowles colledge.
Corpus Chriſti colledge.
Lincolne colledge.
Auriell colledge.
The Quenes colledge.
Baylie colledge, or Ballioll colledge.
S. Johns colledge.
Trinitie colledge.
Exceter colledge.
Braſennoſe colledge.
Thuniuerſitie colledge.
Gloceſtor colledge.
Brodegate halle.
Hearte halle.
Magdalene halle.
Alborne halle.
S. Marie halle.
Whyte halle.
Newe Inne.
Edmonde halle.

R.iii.   And

And besides these Colledges that be in the Vniuersities, this Realme hath also certein collegiate churches, as Westmynster, Windesour, Eaton, and Wynchester. The two last whereof do bring vp and fynde a greate number of yong Scholers, the whiche after they be once parfect in the rules of Grammer and of versifieng, and well entred in the principles of the Greeke tong and of Rhetorike, are sent from thence vnto the vniuersities: as thus. Out of Eaton colledge they be sent vnto the Kynges colledge at Cambrydge, & out of Wynchester, vnto the New colledge at Oxford.

The Colledges of both the Vniuersities be not only very fayre and goodly builte thorough thexceding liberalitie of ye kynges in olde time & of late dayes, of Byshopps and of noble men, but they be also endowed with marueylous large liuinges and reuenewes.

In Trinitie colledge at Cambrydge, and

and in Chrilles colledge at Orford, beth
whiche were founded by kyng Henry
theight of most famous memorie, are at
the least founde foure hundreth Shol=
lers : and the like number wel neere is to
be seene in certen other Colledges, as in
the kynges Colledge & S. Johns Col=
ledge at Cambrydge: in Magdalene col=
ledge and New colledge of Orford : be=
sides the rest which we now passe ouer.

Euery one of the Colleges haue their
Professours of the tonges and of the li=
beral Sciences (as they cal them) which
do trade vp youth priuatly within their
Halles, to thend they may afterward be
able to go furth thence into the common
scholes as to open disputatiō, as it were
into plain battail, there to try themselfe.

In the cōmon Scholes of both the
Uniuersities, there are found at the kin
ges charge, and that very largely, fyue
Professours & Readers, that is to saye,
                         R.iiii.   The

The Reader of Diuinitie.
The Reader of the Ciuill lawe.
The Reader of Physike.
The Reader of the Hebrewe tongue. and
The Reader of the Greeke tongue.

And for the other Profestours, as of
Phylosophie, of Logique, of Rethorike,
and of the Mathematicalles, the Uniuersities themselues doe allowe stipendes vnto them. And these Profestours
haue the ruling of the Disputaciōs and
other schole exercises whiche be dayly v-
sed in the common Scholes: Amongest
whome, they that by the same Disputa-
tions & exercises are thought to be come
to any ripenes in knowledge, are wont
according to ∮ vse in other vniuersities,
solemnly to take degrees, euery one in ∮
same science and facultie which he pro-
fesseth.

Wee thought good to annexe these
thinges, to thende wee might confute &
confounde

confounde thofe that fpread abroad rumours, how ý with bs nothinge is don in order ẓ as ought to be don:ý there is no Religiõ at al, no Eccleſiaſtical Diſcipline obſerued, no regard had of the ſaluacion of mennes ſoules, but that all is don quite out of ordre and ſeditiouſlye, ý all antiquitie is deſpiſed, that libertie is giuen to all ſenſualitie and lewde luſtes of folkes,that the liuings of the Church be conuerted to prophane and worldlye bſes,wheras in bery trouth we ſeke nothing els but that, that God aboue all moſte good,may haue ſtill his honoure truely and purely reſerued bnto hym, that the rule and waye to euerlaſtinge Saluacion maye be taken from out of his bery word,and not from mens fantaſies, that the Sacramentes maye be miniſtred not like a Maſkary or a ſtage playe,but religiouſly and reuerently according to the rule preſcribed bnto bs by Chriſt,and after the example of the holy fathers whiche floriſhed in the prima-

R.b₂   tiue

true Churche: that that most holye and godly fourme of discipline, whiche was commonly vsed amongest them, may be called home againe : that the goodes of ẙ Churche may not be lauched out amõgest worldlinges & ydel persõs, but may be bestowed vpon the godlye Ministers and Pastours which take paine both in Preaching and teaching: that there may from tyme to tyme arise vp out of the Vniuersities learned & good ministers & others meete to serue ẙ cõmon welth: And finally, that all vncleane and wicked lyfe may be vtterly abandoned and banyshed, as vnworthy for the name of any Christian. And albeit we are not as yet able to obteine this ẙ we haue said, fully & perfitlie , (for this same Stable, as one may rightly call it , of ẙ Romish Augias, cannot so soone be thorouglye cleansed and ridd from the long growen filth and mucke) neuerthelesse this is it whereunto we haue regarde: hether doe wee tende : to this marke do wee direct

oure

our paine and trauaile, and that hither=
to (thorough God his gracious fauour)
not without good successe and plen=
teous encrease: whiche thing may easily
appeere to euery body, yf either we be cō=
pared with our own selues in what ma=
ner of case wee haue ben but few yeares
synce, or els be compared with our false
accusers, or rather our malicious slaun=
derours.

The Lorde defende his Churche, go=
uerne it with his holy Spirite, ⁊ blesse
the same with all prosperous felicitie.

Amen.

Imprinted at London in Paules
churche yard, at the signe
of the Brasen serpent, by
Reginalde Wolfe.

Anno Domini, M. D. LXIIII.

Faultes escaped in the printinge.

Leafe.	Faultes.	Correction.
B.4.	suche one for heretikes,	such ones
F.5.p.2.	Peter did not this	did not thus
F.7.p.2.	yet beare they	yet bare they,
F.8.	they were a rebellious	they be a rebel.
G.3.p.2.	pardons largely	pardōs so largely.
K.5.p.2.	intend beare	intende to beare.
N.1.	haue thought for	thought good for